WEIGHING THE ODDS IN HOLD'EM POKER

KING YAO

Pi Yee Press

WEIGHING THE ODDS IN HOLD'EM POKER

by
King Yao
Pi Yee Press

ISBN 0-935926-25-9

Printed in the United States of America in 2005

2 3 4 5 6 7 8 9 10

ABOUT THE AUTHOR

My earliest memory of playing poker was at age 10, with my classmates. We played for baseball cards before the first class started. Often half of my baseball cards were stolen from my cubbyhole during the school day. I didn't mind since I knew I would win them back the next morning and have many more to add for the thieves to steal.

In high school the poker games were in the cafeteria, for dimes and quarters. In college the poker games were played late at night with too much beer.

After college, I found the perfect job for me. A trading job at Susquehanna Partners, which actually uses poker as part of its training program. Successfully trading derivatives on the exchange floor called for a combination of understanding math, assessing risk, and reading the opponents (brokers, other traders and customers). The traders often played poker after a full day of trading. It soon became clear to me that the same skill set was required in poker and in trading derivatives. I was doing well at both. After eight years, I had accumulated a wide range of trading experiences. I had been a market maker in index equity options, currency options and commodity options. I was also involved with Susquehanna's proprietary hedge fund in mortgage derivatives. Looking back, my trading career was varied and interesting. I was able to go in-depth into many different fields. It was a good training ground for making money gambling.

In 2000 I quit my job and started playing poker full time. I was lucky to be in solid financial position and have the full support of my incredible wife. The daily 45-minute drive from my home to the nearest poker room soon became too much for me; and I found myself playing more online. Lately other gambling endeavors have captured my attention and are taking up my time. I was still interested in writing a book on Hold'em and putting my ideas down on paper. After meeting Stanford Wong at the Sharp Sports Betting Super Bowl Seminar hosted by Pi Yee Press in January, 2004, I decided he was the right publisher to approach with my book idea. The book consumed my life for the next nine months. I learned a lot writing the book, as it forced me to explain my thoughts and decision-making. I'm a better poker player now than I was before I started writing the book.

I am keeping a weblog of my poker and other gambling activities at http://WeighingTheOdds.blogspot.com.

CONTENTS

LIST OF TABLES

ACKNOWLEDGMENTS

There are many people I want to thank for inspiring me and helping me write this book. Thanks to many good poker authors. Their thoughts and work has made great contributions to poker and inspired me for this book. I have learned from their work and will continue to do so. These authors include Jim Brier, Doyle Brunson, Mike Caro, Bob Ciaffone, Roy Cooke, John Feeney, Abdul Jalib, Mason Malmuth, Alan Schoonmaker and David Sklansky.

Thanks to all the people I played poker with early in my poker life. These people include Matt Barasch, Maria Cardoni-Fulkerson, Chris Ferrence, Terry Franks, Marc Holubow, Igor Kaminsky, George Manahan, Cris "Manny" Mansfield, Kirk Schirra, Glenn Schroeder, Aaron Skalka, Shoogie, Michael Stern, Larry Vann, Michael Williams and many others.

Thanks to all the people at Susquehanna Partners and the great working environment there. Poker was an integral part of the training program and encouraged throughout the firm. Trading skills and gambling skills are closely related. The people at Susquehanna Partners were not afraid to use poker as a teaching tool for trading. I learned how to trade many different financial products as well as how to play poker. Thanks to Jay Berkow, Eric Brooks, Arthur Dantchik, Jim Doughan, John Hatolovsky, Chip Loutrel, Paul Mandel, Brian Mason, Matt Mgrdichian, Tim Murtha, Paul Onderdonk, Christie O'Shaughnessy, Steve Peter, Tom Peters, Bill Phipps, Larry "Senior" Pines, Rep Porter, Dean Potashner, Tim Reynolds, Don Rossini, Ian Schaad, Nick Shangloo, Mike Steiner, Tim Strazzini, Jeff Yass, David Yuen and others.

Thanks to all the people who helped me directly with this book. These people provided comments, suggestions, constructive criticism and helpful thoughts. They were not afraid to tell me what they did not like about what I had written. They helped me understand what I needed to improve and work on. These people include Magnus Almroth, David Clinch, Dunbar, William Funchion, Kai Lin, Jerry Martino, Jan Pajak, Lisa Peskay and Jan Suchanek.

Thanks to Rep Porter for his comments and suggestions on the River chapter. Thanks to John Feeney for his comments and suggestions on the two shorthanded chapters. Thanks to Matthew Chan and Brian Wheel. Both read every chapter in the book and provided continuing suggestions, advice, questions and comments.

Thanks to Anna Halbert for a great copyediting job. Thanks to Joanne LaFord of JOW Graphics for a wonderful cover.

Thanks to Stanford Wong for deciding to publish the book with so little information about me. I think it was another good gamble by Stanford.

Thanks to my family. Thanks to my parents who never pushed me in their own direction but allowed me to find my own path. They encouraged me to be creative in the fields I was interested in. Thanks to my sister Su-lin Ong and her family for being supportive of my odd career choice. Thanks to everyone in my extended family, including grandparents, uncles, aunts, cousins and nephews.

Thanks to my wife, Shirley Woo. She was incredibly supportive from the beginning. When I quit my job to play poker, she understood. There is no better wife or friend.

CHAPTER 1
INTRODUCTION

The Purpose of this Book

The purpose of this book is to give you, the reader, the tools to succeed at Hold'em. The idea is to show you how to think through the various situations that you can encounter at a poker table.

Many questions in poker are best answered with "it depends." There are many moving parts and different aspects to Limit Hold'em. The best strategy in any particular situation depends on the cards, how other players play, the size of the pot, the relative position of each player and other issues. A strategy may be correct against one type of player but incorrect against another, or in a certain position but not in another. A strategy may be correct with a certain pot size but not with another. This book discusses the concept of expected value and how it pertains to Hold'em. Strategies such as semi-bluffing, check-raising, raising for free cards and others are shown to be correct or incorrect in different situations. Numerous examples illustrate these concepts.

The book discusses mathematical concepts. You should be able to understand the concepts without necessarily understanding the mathematics behind them. These concepts are presented in such a way that if you want to examine the mathematics, you can do so; but if you would rather not muddle through the math, you can still understand the ideas.

Understanding of the mathematical aspects alone is not enough to turn you into a winner in Hold'em. In order to use the concepts correctly, you need to understand how your opponents play and how they respond to different actions. This ability is less of a science and more of an art. Any formula is only as good as its plugged-in variables. As the saying goes, "garbage in, garbage out."

Who This Book is For

This book is for you if you want to think analytically and learn to become a better Limit Hold'em player. This could mean you are fairly new to the game but understand its rules and mechanics, or that you are an experienced player and want to add to your game. It could also mean you are a sharp player and you already employ many of the concepts in this book, but you want to examine them more closely. If you are a relative beginner who is willing to think analytically, you will get more out of this book than if you are an experienced player who is not willing to think analytically. The key is not how experienced a player you are, but how much you are willing to think about the game.

The Organization

The first section of the book discusses the foundations of Limit Hold'em. You must understand this section before moving on to the other sections. All the subsequent chapters build on and refer to ideas presented in the foundation section. Once you have a good understanding of these foundation topics, the other chapters can be read in any order. The foundation chapters are:

- Player Types: Different types of players, and how to identify them and play against them.
- Expected Value: The concept of expected value and how to apply it in Hold'em.
- Outs: How to identify and count Outs and Non-outs.
- Pot Odds: An accurate and practical method of figuring out pot odds at the poker table.
- Position: The advantages and disadvantages of different positions.

The second section of the book explains in detail five strategies used in Limit Hold'em, and addresses when to use and when to avoid these strategies, and how to defend against them.

- Raising for Free Cards: When to raise for a free card and when not to. Counter-strategies against a player who is raising for a free card.
- Bluffing: What to think about when deciding whether to bluff. How to induce a bluff.
- Semi-Bluffing: What semi-bluffing means and why it is a valuable strategy.
- Slowplaying and Check-Raising: Deceptive strategies and how to use them.

The third section covers hand development, and goes through issues in Limit Hold'em from the first two cards through the showdown.

- Starting Hands: Which cards to play in which positions, and why.
- The Flop: Issues regarding the first three cards on the board. Raising for free cards and check-raising come into play.
- The Turn: The bet size doubles, and the hand gets more interesting. Raising and semi-bluffing are important tools here.
- The River: The final round of the hand. Bluffing and value betting come into play.
- Reading Hands: Figuring out other players' hole cards based on how they play, their actions and the hand situation.

The final section discusses shorthanded play, online poker and other topics.

- Shorthanded Play Overview: An introduction to shorthanded play.
- Common Mistakes in Shorthanded Play: Shorthanded Hold'em is different from a full game. Many players make mistakes in shorthanded games due to not adjusting correctly.
- Online Poker: Issues involved in playing poker on the Internet.
- Extra Topics: Additional topics in Limit Hold'em.

If a topic seems confusing or complicated, take time to think about the issues. When there are mathematical results presented, it may be easier at first to accept the results at face value in order to understand the concept. Once you are comfortable with the information, you can examine the mathematics more closely if you desire. The results and the computation are usually listed separately so that you can see the results without having to follow the calculations. Think critically about whether you agree or disagree, and why.

The Evolution of the Hold'em Player

The series of steps a Hold'em player takes to learn the game resembles the process of human evolution. You must master the previous steps in order to develop to the next step, and avoid getting stuck along the evolutionary path and failing to adapt. You must learn the use of necessary tools, adapt to your environment, and move onto the next stage.

The basic stages in the evolution of the Hold'em player are

- Stage 1: Hold'em Habilis
- Stage 2: Hold'em Erectus
- Stage 3: Hold'em Sapiens
- Stage 4: Hold'em Brain.

Stage 1: Hold'em Habilis

At this stage the poker player has learned the mechanics of the game and the rules. Hold'em Habilis plays many hands as if the winning hand can be any two cards. Although most poker players think they know more than just the rules and the basics of the game, the majority will never develop past this stage. These players will lose in the long run; they are the fish.

Stage 2: Hold'em Erectus

To develop to this stage: the player has to realize that, although any two cards can win any given hand, certain starting hands are more profitable. Hold'em Erectus learns through experience after repeatedly getting K8 beaten by AK. Although many players move up to this stage, most do not develop further. They may know that AQ is a better starting hand than QT, but their understanding is lacking since they play both hands indiscriminately. In order to develop further, the player must learn to be more selective about the cards played and when to play them.

Stage 3: Hold'em Sapiens

The player has learned the advantages and disadvantages of different positions. Hold'em Sapiens plays aggressively when having the best of it, and treads carefully when having the worst of it. Hold'em Sapiens understands how to treat each opponent differently, and adjusts to differences in opponents by avoiding confrontations with the better players while taking advantage of the weaker ones. Many players never get to this point. Instead they develop into Hold'em Neanderthal, a species that cannot adapt to different surroundings, a species headed toward extinction. The Hold'em Sapiens is constantly thinking of ways to get better, learning more about the game and developing toward the Hold'em Brain.

Stage 4: Hold'em Brain

The player understands how others view him or her. The Hold'em Brain is constantly adjusting and adapting to the environment and other players, and understands that Hold'em is a dynamic game. The player takes advantage of all knowledge of the differences in situations, the odds, relative positions and player styles. The player understands that winning pots is not as important as winning money. The Hold'em Brain is sharp.

Speeding up the process

Developing your Hold'em Brain through this evolutionary process would take a long time in a vacuum. Fortunately there are many ways to speed up this process. Reading this book is one of those ways. Instead of inventing the wheel yourself, you can see how the wheel is constructed. You can learn, and maybe use, that knowledge to make a better wheel. Just as important as reading this book is developing your analytical thought process. Think through the hands you have played and what would happen if you had played them differently. Analyze the hands in which you were involved to see if you could have saved or gained a bet. Share your thoughts with knowledgeable poker friends. Get involved in reading and posting on Internet poker forums to get ideas and comments from good players. Keep reading and rereading the good books, and continue to think. Following these steps is a difficult process. Most players veer off the evolutionary path and head toward extinction as lifelong poker losers. In Hold'em there are no easy steps to becoming a winner. Hard work and thinking about the game will get you on the path to success.

Terminology, Acronyms and Conventions Used in This Book

Following is a guide to the terminology, acronyms and conventions used in this book. A glossary is provided in the appendices.

- A, K, Q, J, T: Ace, king, queen, jack and ten are denoted with their first letter. Cards 2 through 9 are denoted with their number.
- A's, K's, 5's: The plural of any card is shown with an apostrophe followed by an "s." For example, a pair of sixes is written as "a pair of 6's."
- Overcard: When your two hole cards are both higher than any card on the board, you have two *overcards*.
- Overpair: When you have a pocket pair with a higher rank than any card on the board, you have an *overpair*.
- Split Pair: A *split pair* is a pair using one of your hole cards and one card on the board.
- Top Pair: A split pair using the highest card on the board is a *top pair*.
- Out: An *out* is a particular card that, if you catch it, will improve your hand to the best hand. You can have multiple outs.
- Open-raise: If you raise in the pre-Flop round after all players before you have folded, you are said to *open-raise*.
- AKo: The "o" after the two cards denotes that the two cards are of different suits. AKo is ace-king offsuit.
- AKs: The "s" after the two cards denotes that the two cards are of the same suit.
- A♣K♠: A picture of a suit after a card denotes the suit of that card. A♣K♠ means the ace of clubs and the king of spades.
- J-T-9 rainbow: In a *rainbow* hand, the cards have too few cards of any one suit to make a flush possible.
- K-J-x: An "x" is a small card that is not important to the discussion. In K-J-x, the "x" card is any card except A, K, Q, J, T or 9, because any of those cards would be relevant.

Poker players come in both sexes. So read "he" to mean "he or she," and read "she" to mean "he or she."

Different Limits

This book discusses low-limit, middle-limit and high-limit games. Dollar amounts for these games as of the publication date:

- Low-limit games: $5-$10 or lower
- Middle-limit games: $10-$20 through $40-$80
- High-limit games: $50-$100 and higher.

Inflation will change the dollar amounts; but you should generally be able to figure out which are the low-limit, middle-limit and high-limit games.

In low-limit games many players see the Flop and many hands require a showdown. The pot is usually large in terms of big bets (a big bet is the betting increment for the Turn and the River). Bluffing is a tough act to pull off.

In middle-limit games the pots are not as big and the hands often get down to heads-up relatively quickly. The players are sharper and more aggressive, and think more about the game. Professional players are often present.

High-limit games are often shorthanded. Fewer players can afford to play the high limits, so the players who do want to play often have to settle for playing with less than a full table.

In general as the limit goes higher:

- the number of sharp players increases
- the average pot size gets lower (in terms of big bets)
- raising, check-raising, semi-bluffing and bluffing increase
- the number of players contesting a pot decreases.

A game in any category may not follow those guidelines. Sometimes a low-limit game plays tighter than a middle-limit game. Sometimes a middle-limit game is more aggressive than a high-limit game. When you are playing, identify the nature of the table by the play of the other players. This variability is part of the beauty and the complexity of Limit Texas Hold'em.

CHAPTER 2
PLAYER TYPES

Knowing how other players play is one of the keys to achieving success at Limit Hold'em. When good players know their opponents well, they know how their opponents act and think. They are able to take advantage of their opponents' weaknesses and steer clear of their strengths. They pay attention to how the other players play, and how often they bet, call or raise in different situations. This chapter focuses on general characteristics and stereotypes of players, how players can change from one stereotype into another, how to adjust when playing against familiar players, and how to size up an unknown player as quickly as possible.

You can profile different characters and stereotypes at the poker table, and assign most players to one of these stereotypes or to a mix of two stereotypes. Identifying the stereotype a player currently matches is crucial because it affects how you should play. A player who plays like one character may slowly morph into another character. Personality can also change due to mood, either from winning and having a good time or from losing and feeling frustrated. Or it could be that you pegged the player incorrectly. Maybe the play you observed was a short-term reflection of a good or bad run of cards, and the player's personality is really closer to a different stereotype. Even the tightest and most conservative players would raise on every hand if they kept getting big pocket pairs. It could also be that the person plays solidly when first seated at the table, but reverts to a typical style after awhile.

If you are sociable, it can be advantageous to talk with the players next to you to expedite learning about their personalities and characteristics. A player's appearance alone may get you part of the way; but appearances can be deceiving. Drawing others into discussion about life, work and hands played may help you get to know them more quickly, and speed up your profiling attempts.

You will be better off if you know how your opponents play. Understanding how they play is more useful when pots become heads-up and in shorthanded games, and less useful in low-limit "no fold'em Hold'em" games. Pots become heads-up on the Flop in shorthanded games more often than in full games. In low-limit games: players are generally looser; thus pots are relatively larger, and more players are involved from Flop to River. With many players involved in the pot, it becomes tougher to use any one player's tendencies to your advantage.

Players can be divided into two major categories: predictable and unpredictable. Each category has its share of bad and good players. Although predictable players are generally passive and unpredictable players tend to be more aggressive, players can be predictable or unpredictable regardless of whether they play loose or tight.

Predictable Players

Predictable players are easier to play against than unpredictable players. When they act, typically the strength of a hand is clear from their actions. When some players bet or raise, they have a strong hand. When they have a strong hand, they never raise on the Flop but wait to raise on the Turn when the bet size doubles. Conversely other players who raise on the Flop never have a made hand, but are raising for a free card. A good sharp player has a better idea of the strength of a predictable player's hands based on her actions, while a poor player might not pick up on it. Different players are predictable in different ways. Here are the stereotypes:

Average players

Average players do not do anything extreme. They like to play, but are neither overly aggressive nor too passive. Average players bet with a good hand, raise with a great hand, call with a mediocre hand, and fold with a poor hand. They find reasons to stay in the hand rather than fold. The average player in any particular limit is different from the average player in another limit. In general the average player of a higher limit game is a better player, plays tighter, is more aggressive, and has a few tricks up the sleeve. Although the average player of the $20-$40 games plays too many hands, it will be fewer hands than the average player of the $5-$10 games plays. Average players bluff, but not often. When they raise, it is usually with a premium hand.

Calling stations

Calling stations are passive and loose. They hate to fold, prefer to check or call rather than bet or raise, and bet only with a good hand. When a calling station raises, you had better run for your life because the hand is a monster. The calling station plays many hands, and has no problem limping while in early position, calling a professional player's early-position raise, or calling a bet with a pair of 8's while there are three overcards on the board. If you play aggressively without a made hand, a calling station will call you down with a middle pair or a bottom pair. Do not bluff, because calling stations will fold only with an exceptionally bad hand. They think poker is mostly a game of luck, and are taking shots at getting lucky. A calling station is an easy opponent to beat.

Rocks

Rocks are not sharp players; but they use a strategy that wins at most limits. Rocks and calling stations have similarities. Like calling stations, rocks bet only with good hands and raise only with strong hands. You must be careful when rocks bet or raise, and be wary when they show aggression. That is where the similarities end. Calling stations play a lot of hands, while rocks play few hands. A rock might sit there for hours folding his starting hands. Rocks do not mind folding blinds, thus becoming prime victims for theft of the blinds. When a rock does play a hand, watch out. He is patient, and may be the best player at the table. Rocks can have an edge in a game, but not as much edge as better players. Rocks can be long-term winners in low-limit games and some middle-limit games, but need to expand their skills in order to win in higher limit games.

Solid players

Solid players have an idea of correct play. They know that patience is needed to win at this game; but they are not overly tight. Solid players play more hands than rocks do, and are usually aggressive. A solid player who raises from early position is likely to have a quality hand. If a solid player open-raises from late position, the hand is harder to predict because she understands it's okay to loosen up in that position and it's okay to steal the blinds. You should normally avoid playing against solid players who are raising. They may not bluff or semi-bluff enough due to not wanting to take chances. Some players play like a solid player but morph into a different type of player after a while at the table. Solid players are good players.

Unpredictable Players

Unpredictable players are not necessarily good or bad players. When they act, it is tougher to pinpoint their hand than it would be with a predictable player's hand. Unpredictable players use strategies such as bluffing and semi-bluffing often, sometimes too often. Though good players can be somewhat unpredictable, there is only so far they can take this. If they are too unpredictable, they will be playing too many hands and giving up too much edge in the quest to be unpredictable. Instead good players choose spots to be unpredictable—spots where playing unpredictably might give them the greatest edge. Players who play unpredictably all the time invariably play too many hands and give up too much edge for their trickiness.

Loose, aggressive players

Loose, aggressive players like to play a lot of hands. Unlike calling stations, who also play a lot of hands, loose, aggressive players like to bet and raise. The betting and raising come when warranted by the cards, but also when not warranted. Loose, aggressive players like to bet and raise with draws, and use the free-card raise often, even when holding merely overcards. Loose, aggressive players who raise for the free card often follow with semi-bluffs and bluffs. It might be necessary to slowplay against these players by calling instead of scaring them off with a raise or a reraise. Let them do the betting for you if a raise by you would cause them to fold a worse hand. Loose, aggressive players frequently try to steal the blinds, even from middle position. They bluff more often than the average player and love fancy concepts such as semi-bluffing, raising for free cards and check-raising; but they overuse these concepts. Their habit of playing many hands and being aggressive with them may make it hard for you to predict their cards. A loose, aggressive player who has the best hand may run over opponents, since other players are more willing to call people who bet and raise too much. Loose, aggressive players are usually not good players; however they can get in streaks where they might seem like the best players around.

Maniacs

A maniac is Mr. Hyde to a loose, aggressive player's Dr. Jekyll. A maniac is out of control and raises on almost every hand. Maniacs raise and bluff often and usually lose their money quickly. Maniacs may not play like maniacs all the time. Sometimes players who are having a bad day turn into maniacs when they are on full tilt. This can happen after they have been dealt a couple of bad beats, which could lead them to play aggressively in order to try get even. A maniac is a horrible player, and is great to have as an opponent.

Professional and tight, aggressive players

Professional players are sharp, and are constantly thinking about the game and their opponents. They are the best players, the ones you least like to see at your table. They play poker for an income, and are unlikely to be playing for the gamble, the entertainment or the competition. Professional players are selective about their hands, and play aggressively when they have solid hands. They are tight, but aggressive. They try to extract the most from their opponents when they have the best of it, and try to get away cheaply when they have the worst of it. They have thought about and studied the game through reading, talking to other players, and thinking about the play of hands on their own. Professional players have a wide range of characteristics in their style. Some are more aggressive than others, and some bluff more than others. There are players who consider themselves to be professionals but who really are not. Loose, aggressive players are most likely to think they are professional players when they are not. They try to duplicate professional players' play by playing aggressively; but they miss out on the fact that they also need to play tight and be selective with their starting hands.

Profiling Players

In order to identify how players play, you should get a sense of their pattern of play. Players tend to be consistent with their styles. If you observe how they play, you have a better idea of what you are up against in future hands. Think of yourself as a detective trying to solve a mystery. A few things to watch for and what they might mean:

Do they like to bet or raise, or do they like to call?

Players who like to bet or raise are aggressive. They are unpredictable because they are willing to bet or raise with a variety of hands. Players who like to call or check are more predictable because when they bet or raise, you can be more confident they have a strong hand.

Do they play straightforwardly, or are they tricky?

Players who are predictable tend to play in a straightforward manner. When they bet, they have a quality hand. When they check, they have a mediocre or poor hand. Tricky players like to check-raise, slow-play, semi-bluff, bluff and raise for free cards, disguising their play in one round but showing the true strength of their hand in another. If a player raises in one round and then folds to a bet in the next round, his raise may have been tricky.

Do they like to raise with a draw, or raise only with a made hand?

Players who like to raise with draws are more unpredictable. They could be raising with made hands as well. When they do raise, it is less clear what type of hand they have. Players who raise only with made hands are more predictable. If you do not have a better made hand yourself, you will have to improve your hand to win.

Do they have a good understanding of the game of Hold'em?

When evaluating the answers to all of the previous questions, consider also whether your opponents have a decent understanding of the game. If they do not, then they may be acting based on their misconceptions. A player who has a straight when there is a possible flush on board may disregard the possibility of her opponents holding a flush, and may think of the strength of her own hand in isolation. These players are unpredictable because they have a poor understanding of the game. Their actions might be misinterpreted by an experienced player.

Sharp players play differently against different players

Sharp players play differently against different players; and they are likely to play differently against other players than they do against you. They may bet for value against weak calling stations, but not against you. They may call down aggressive semi-bluffers, but may not call when you are raising. They may semi-bluff against tight players, but not if they think you are likely to call. When observing how other players play, note if they play differently against different players, and not just how they play in general. It is a mistake to assume sharp players would make the same play against you as they would against an opponent who plays differently from you.

Pre-Flop tight players may not play tight on every round

The typical view of players who play tight pre-Flop is that they can be bluffed out of a pot in later rounds with a well-timed bluff raise or semi-bluff. Although this stereotype may be useful when you do not know the players well, it shows the importance of observing and judging individual players. People who play tight pre-Flop enter a pot with higher-quality hands than other players, and therefore typically have more reason to continue with their hands than if they played more starting hands. On a percentage basis a tight pre-Flop player might fold less often once already in the pot than a looser player. The looser player on average has a weaker starting hand, which is easier to fold when the Flop does not fit. Many players find it tough to fold good starting hands after a bad Flop. Players who play tight pre-Flop get married to these premium pre-Flop hands and keep playing too far into the hand. Observe your opponent's play and learn to identify things that others may miss.

Winning or Losing Can Make a Player Change Styles

There are players who play solidly when they first sit down, and continue to play solidly if they are winning. But some players change their styles drastically if they start to lose, particularly if they take a bad beat. These players will start to play more aggressively, which means they semi-bluff and bluff more. If they continue to lose and get their bluffs called, or worse, take more bad beats, then they could wind up opening up their game and turn into maniacs. This is a situation where knowing how specific individuals normally play is useful.

If you base your impression of a player on what you saw in a previous session, your perception may be off. If you see someone playing like a maniac, you might assume he always plays like a maniac. But next time he might be winning and playing solidly, and thus playing differently.

Distinctions Among Loose Players

There are different kinds of loose players. Identify how these players are loose to take advantage of their weakness. The distinctions are discussed here.

Always loose

A player who is loose on every card, chasing with unwarranted hands and often drawing dead, is a most desirable opponent. The player who is always loose sees a lot of Flops, and doesn't mind cold-calling pre-Flop raises from any position. On the Flop and afterwards, this player is overly optimistic and continues to call with a weak hand even if the board is dangerous, such as 7♠7♥ after the Flop is A♣Q♣9♥.

Loose pre-Flop

This player sees a lot of Flops, but plays decently afterwards.

There are many players who are willing to limp in and call raises in the pre-Flop round, and take their chances to see the Flop. Their philosophy is that they need to see the Flop in order to truly determine the strength of their hand; and they willingly pay the price. Although some continue to play loose after the Flop, there are others who are willing to fold if the Flop does not fit their hand. If you are playing against this type of loose player, you should be confident raising her pre-Flop. You must back that up with another bet on the Flop if it is down to you and her. If your opponent is more likely than other loose players to fold, betting on the Flop is important even if it completely misses your hand. In shorthanded games you want this player as one of your opponents because the hands are often heads-up going into the Flop. Getting her to fold on the Flop means you have won the pot. If there is another player in the hand, then the value of having this type of player in the hand is reduced.

Typical example of this type of player

You open-raise in middle position with a pair of K's. A loose pre-Flop player sits immediately to your left and calls. The two of you see the Flop heads-up.

Your hand: KK
Flop: Q-7-2 rainbow

You bet, and your opponent folds. This is an indication that he was calling your raise with a hand like A9o, A5s, KJ or JTs. These are hands that seem like decent starting hands; but relative to the hand of a tight player raising in middle position, they are no longer strong enough to play.

Loose post-Flop

This player sees an average number of Flops, but plays loose afterwards.

A player who is selective with her starting hands can play loosely on the Flop and afterwards. She may have read poker books with advice on tight pre-Flop strategy. The pre-Flop strategy is often the easiest to memorize, as there are fewer variables. But after the pre-Flop round there are more variables, and memorizing exact strategies becomes more difficult. Thus a player who plays correctly pre-Flop may play too loose post-Flop because there is no chart for her to memorize. The major problem is not folding a decent starting hand if the Flop does not fit. A hand that these players often play incorrectly: two high cards after the Flop does not give them a pair or any draws. They go too far with these cards in the face of strength shown by other players. These players mutter about how a QT beat their AJ. They complain about getting bad beats and about how unlucky they are. AJ is a better starting hand than QT; but once the Flop comes, their relative strength can switch.

Playing Against Different Types of Loose Players

Here is an example of approaching a hand against different types of loose players. Suppose you open-raise on the button with K♠J♠, and only the big blind calls.

Your hand: K♠J♠
Flop: Q♥ 8♦ 6♣

You did not catch a pair on the Flop. With this hand-Flop combination you prefer to be playing against an opponent who plays loose pre-Flop but correctly afterwards. That player is willing to fold to a bet without a pair or a draw with a hand like A♣5♦, which is better than your K♠J♠. The opponent who is always loose might call with A♣5♦. When you miss the Flop, you prefer the opponent to fold an A. Either opponent will call (or check-raise) with a pair. The players who are always loose call with A-high. The players who are not loose all the time fold A-high. Against an always-loose player who calls with A-high, your K-high cannot win unless you improve. But against someone willing to fold A-high: your K-high has a better chance of winning a showdown if neither of you improve. You are less likely to be beaten by an A-high hand, and you can beat a busted straight draw such as JT or J9.

On the other hand if you hit a pair on the Flop, you prefer your opponent to be always loose and thus more likely to pay you off.

Now change the Flop so that you hit top pair.

Your hand: K♠J♠
Flop: J♥ 8♦ 6♣

You do not want an opponent with A♣5♦ to fold. If someone with that hand calls, you get a bad beat once in a while; but your opponent pays a price for that opportunity.

Understanding your opponent is crucial in games where the pots become heads-up often after the Flop. In games where more players are likely to see the Flop, such as looser or lower-limit games, understanding your opponent is less useful because it is not wise to focus on only one player. But in all games knowing how your opponents play is better than not knowing.

Getting Into Your Opponent's Head

Here are the different levels of thinking, with each level built on top of the previous:

1. What do you have?
2. What does your opponent have?
3. What does your opponent think you have?
4. What does your opponent think you think she has?

Sometimes you don't need to go too far up the ladder in the levels of thinking. It depends on the level your opponent is on. If your opponent plays only to the strength of his own cards, then go to step 2: Try to figure out what he has. If your opponent tries to think about your hand, then think about what he thinks you have, and proceed accordingly.

Example hand against a player who thinks on level 2

You have A♦Q♣ and raise in middle position. An average player on the button calls and everyone else folds.

Your hand: A♦Q♣
Flop: A♠2♣2♦

You have a split pair of A's with a good kicker. You bet and your opponent calls.

Turn: 4♥

You should have already tried to figure out what your opponent has. Since she called a raise before the Flop and called the bet on the Flop, it looks as though she has an A or a small to medium pair. An opponent who did not reraise pre-Flop is most unlikely to have AK or AQ, and also unlikely to have a big pair, because most players would reraise with those premium hands. Your opponent called on the Flop and thus has a playable hand, possibly something like A♥9♥ or 6♣6♠.

If you bet again, your opponent will probably call; but a check-raise might extract more from her. When you check, she may think you are checking because you have a big pocket pair and are worried about the A on board. If she has A9 and can think on level 2, she now thinks she has the best hand with pair of A's, though with a mediocre kicker. She is happy to bet into you when she thinks you have KK or QQ. When she does bet, you can check-raise. Most players have a difficult time laying down a hand with top pair after they get check-raised. You are likely to get her to call both the check-raise and another bet on the River.

Your check on the Turn has deceived your opponent into thinking that you had a worse hand than hers. You probably gained a bet. Your opponent was thinking on level 2, "What does my opponent have?" You were thinking on level 3, "What does my opponent think I have?" You thought your opponent thought you had her beaten. In order to use this information to maximize your potential profit, you decided to check to make her change her mind from thinking she is beaten to thinking she is ahead. Thus you gained a big bet that other players might not have gained.

This play can only succeed against some players. Players with discipline who can think on level 3 are more likely to fold after you check-raise them on the Turn. They can deduce that they are beaten, and are more willing to fold. Against passive players who are afraid to bet (because they fear a check-raise) but are not afraid to call a bet, you should bet rather than check.

Changing Your Play for Deception

Deception can be a useful tool in poker. It is nice when opponents think you have one hand but you actually have another, as it may lead them to play incorrectly. An example of deception was presented above, where a check on the Turn convinced your opponent to think she had the best hand. Bad players make incorrect decisions all the time and do not need others to deceive them. They deceive themselves and often call you down when they are unlikely to have the best hand. Against players who play correctly, you should vary your play now and then. Play the same hand differently in the same situations if you can do so without giving up much edge. This makes your opponent think twice on future hands; so you might benefit not only on the hand in question, but in future hands as well.

Suppose you are in the big blind and hold A9o. Everyone folds to the button, who is a good player. The button raises and the small blind folds. In a situation like this, reraising and calling are close in value. It is nice to mix up your play by sometimes reraising and sometimes calling, so your opponent will not have a good handle on what you have after you reraise.

Continuing on with the hand: suppose you called the pre-Flop raise.

Your hand: A9o
Flop: A-Q-3 rainbow

You check and your opponent bets. A check-raise might scare off an opponent who does not have an A. Since you should also check-raise sometimes when you have KJ and JT with the same Flop (for a gutshot straight draw), you also need to check-raise sometimes when you do flop an A. (See Chapter 9 "Semi-Bluffing.") When you are check-raising without the A in future hands, your opponent may assume you do have an A and fold if he does not have one. If you play drawing hands and made hands differently, you allow astute players to deduce the strength of your hand. For example if you always check-raise when you have an A in this spot, but never when you have a straight draw, then your opponent knows to fold a hand like QJ after you check-raise. On the other hand if you never check-raise when you have a weak A, but always check-raise with the inside straight draw, then your opponent can feel comfortable calling you with the same QJ hand. Mixing up your play puts your opponent on the defensive; he cannot be sure exactly what you have.

Varying your play is more useful when hands frequently go heads-up. With more players battling through the River for the pot, deception becomes less important than having the best hand. Thus varying your play is more valuable in shorthanded games than in full games, and more useful in higher-limit games than in lower-limit games.

When you vary your play, you may look dumb once in a while. In the above scenario with a Flop of A-Q-3, if you had check-raised with KJ and lost the hand, being forced to show it down on the River might make it look as though you were gambling it up and taking unnecessary risk. In a situation like this some observers may think you are on tilt or playing poorly, and decide that you are a habitual bluffer. When this happens, try to use it to your advantage. Play tighter and semi-bluff less in upcoming hands, because the observant opponents are going to be more likely to give you action when you have a hand.

Some players take this idea too far and play a wild and crazy game to establish an image of a maniac. They surely increase their expected value (see Chapter 3 "Expected Value") on future hands when they do get back to playing correctly, but they might be losing too much on the current hand in order to establish that wild image.

Do not change your play if doing so would give up too much expected value on the current hand relative to the possible expected value you might receive on future hands. A good way to vary your play is to play differently in situations where there is not much difference in edge no matter how you play. This way you do not lose the edge, but gain the benefit of being more unpredictable to your opponents.

Playing the Players

Playing against the same players all the time

If you play against the same players all the time, you should have a good grasp before you sit down at the table of how they play the game. This is nice, but the other players have a good idea of your play as well. If you are a sharp observant player, you will be able to take advantage of familiarity more than average players can. You have an extra edge over them that you would not have if they were strangers. Against players who are not observant, you do not need to vary your play, since they keep making the same mistakes over and over without adjusting to your play. Against players who are observant and adjust their play based on your play, you can vary your play to keep them off guard. Play normally until the hand becomes heads-up, and then decide then whether varying your play is worthwhile against the specific opponent in that hand.

Playing against unknown players

It is difficult to play against unknown players. It is unclear how they play, and you are forced to size them up quickly so you can make decisions when you are in a hand against them. Sometimes your quickly formed opinion of a player is wrong; and you make an incorrect playing decision based on that wrong opinion. But the more you play against opponents, the more feel you get for how they play.

Questions to ask yourself about unknown players to help you make initial judgments:

1. How observant are they?

Watch where their eyes are looking. If they are watching every player's movement like a hawk, they are more likely to be sharp than if it looks like they are daydreaming when they are not involved in a hand.

2. Are they thinking?

Sometimes it is easy to tell if someone is thinking. Players who think are usually the sharper players. Players whose actions all seem automatic are probably not thinking as much. The better players have learned to act quickly and not appear to be thinking, so it is sometimes difficult to tell who is thinking and who is not.

3. How old are they? Are they male or female?

Generally, younger players tend to be more aggressive than older players. Men are more aggressive than women at the poker table. Without knowing anything else about them, use these stereotypes as an initial basis for sizing up the player.

4. How many hands are they playing?

After a few hands, recall how many hands each player has played. For example: after five hands, a player who has limped in and seen each Flop is probably loose. A player who has folded every hand may be a tight player, or at least not loose. If a player has raised in three of the five hands, and won all three with strong starting hands, then the information about the raises is not useful. Many players, both good and bad, raise with good starting hands. Do not interpret winning three out of five pots as indicating a good player.

When will a player play tighter than usual?

A loose player may sometimes play tighter than normal, for instance when she has rallied from a significant loss to a point that is close to even or slightly ahead. She is now cognizant of that break-even point and is more risk-averse than normal. She does not want to get back into the red after having had to battle to get ahead. Another time this can happen is when a player has a decent win and is about to leave, racking his chips and looking like he is waiting until the big blind arrives before leaving. With a nice win, he does not want to give winnings back; at the same time he does not want to give up on the positive expectation of getting "free" hands when not in the blinds.

When will a player play looser or more aggressively?

A player who has few chips left may play looser and more aggressively than usual, looking to get even. Her thought process might be that after she has lost so much, any extra loss does not make a difference. For most people the difference between losing $2,100 and losing $2,300 seems smaller than the difference between losing $100 and losing $300, though the difference is $200 in both cases. The value of money has changed for the losing player; her current loss has clouded her judgment. The losing player with this mentality does not mind throwing in extra chips. Watch for it, and adjust accordingly. Be more inclined to bet when you think your edge is small, and to call her down more often than you normally would.

Examples of adjusting play based on your opponent

Following are examples of when to play the same hand differently, depending on your opponent, when it is heads-up on the River.

Example 1

You have AK. You open-raise pre-Flop on the button and the big blind calls. You have been betting all along and getting called. By the River the board is T-4-2-7-7 with no flush possibilities. It is checked to you on the River. Should you check or bet?

Your hand: AK
Board: T-4-2-7-7

If your opponent is a calling station, you should consider betting. Although he calls with any pair, he may also call with a worse A-high hand, such as AJ, A8, A3. Against a calling station you do not mind betting since you will get called down by a worse hand. But if your opponent will fold to a bet, then you should check. This can occur if the player was on a draw with a hand like A3 (gutshot straight draw with one high card) and called on the Flop and Turn. You should not bet against this player because you cannot count on him calling without a pair (whereas a calling station might call without a pair). If the player will not call without a pair, then you cannot gain any value by betting.

Example 2

You have QJ in the big blind. A loose, aggressive player has raised in middle position. You call, along with a couple of other players.

Your hand: QJo
Flop: K-T-9 rainbow

You flopped a straight and there are no flush draws; you are happy! You decide to play your hand strong on the Flop because you think there is a good chance you will get paid off, since there are high cards on the board.

Turn: 3

The Turn cannot improve another player's hand over yours, and you bet. Everyone folds except the original raiser, who calls.

River: A

Consider check-raising. Your opponent is an aggressive player; and a check by you in this spot might make her think you are afraid of the A—that you might have a hand like KQ or KJ. An aggressive player with an A bets with a hand like AQ or AJ. She would be on a straight draw with either of those hands, and might be thinking an A was an out as well. Even with a worse hand, such as QQ or JJ, she may consider betting in the hopes that you will fold a split pair of K's or call with only a split pair of T's. Calling stations do not press their edge like the aggressive players do. Check-raising against calling stations works less often because they often check, even with an A. Against calling stations and passive players, betting out on the River is the best option.

Game Selection

The first level of the game-selection decision is the limit. If you want to play $20-$40 or higher, it does you no good to learn that the least talented players can be found at a $3-$6 game. But a $10-$20 game filled with bad players may be more profitable than a $20-$40 game filled with decent players.

Once you have the limit in mind, your choice should depend on the quality of the players. The best games are the ones with many predictable and loose players. The worst games are the ones with many unpredictable, aggressive, and sharp players. If there are multiple tables at the same limit and you have a choice of tables, then scout the talent at the tables. See if you know any of the players. Try to choose the table that looks the softest. Sometimes you may prefer the table with the sharpest player. A sharp player may have gone through the same game-selection decision, and may have chosen the table that looked softest. That table might be the easiest to beat, even with the best player in the house.

If the casino does not offer you a choice, then the above paragraph is moot. Many casinos have more than one table at the same limit with one game as the main game and the other games as the must-move games. The idea of the must-move games is to protect the main game from breaking up due to the spreading of additional games. When the casino has this rule, players cannot freely move from one table to another.

The only time you should consider choosing a tougher game if there are two or more games at the same limit is when you want to go through the experience of playing against a tougher lineup. This may help you prepare for when you move up in limits. For example if you usually play $10-$20 and are thinking of moving up to $20-$40, consider playing the toughest $10-$20 game in preparation for the $20-$40 game. Giving up edge in that session may be worthwhile for the education and experience.

Seat Selection

You have positional advantage over whoever sits to your right. Whoever sits to your left has positional advantage over you.

When making a decision on where to sit at the table, the key is not how well or poorly the other players play, but rather the other players' styles and levels of aggressiveness. In general you want the unpredictable and aggressive players to your right because players to the right have to act before you do most of the time. You can see the unpredictable players act before you act, which reduces the ambiguity in their game. You prefer to have the predictable and tight players to your left, acting after you. Though they see how you act and have positional advantage over you most of the time, do not be concerned. The predictable and tight players play fewer hands, and thus are in pots against you less often than unpredictable and aggressive players.

If a predictable player raises after you have bet, your decision is easier than when an unpredictable player raises you. When a predictable player raises, you have a good idea what cards the raise represents. A raise by an unpredictable player, on the other hand, can mean a wider variety of cards. He could have the nuts or be semi-bluffing or bluffing. He could be raising for a free card or have top pair. It is more difficult to pinpoint the hand of an unpredictable player, so you prefer to have him act before you. The information in the actions of an unpredictable player is more valuable than the information in the actions of a predictable player.

See Chapter 6 "Position" for more on the value of position.

CHAPTER 3
EXPECTED VALUE

You are in a restaurant looking at a menu. You see two entrees that you like equally, but one is cheaper. You decide to order the cheaper one. You have just made a decision by comparing the expected value of the two entrees.

You are driving on a highway during rush hour. Your lane seems to be going slower than the lane to your left. The first chance you get, you switch over to the left lane so you can get home faster. You have just made a decision based on the comparison of the expected value of the two lanes.

You are playing poker. The pot is big, but your hand is mediocre. On the last round of betting, you say "Aw what the heck, I'm going to call. The pot is huge." You have just made a decision based on the perceived expected value using information about the strength of your hand and the pot size.

Expected value is a concept that all people use in their daily lives, sometimes without being conscious of it. Whenever there is a choice, expected value can be useful in making a decision. Sometimes the values are not purely monetary. The value could be based on happiness, a term that academics like to call utility. Usually there is no need to use a formula to calculate the expected value of a decision. There are cases where this calculation gives a result that is counterintuitive, or shows why a certain idea is correct or incorrect. It can also help to pinpoint factors to consider in Hold'em.

Expected value (EV) is a term used to describe the value of an event averaged over all possible outcomes. It is a way to describe situations that can have many different results. Consider a basketball player at the free throw line. If Lebron James has made 750 free throws out of 1,000 attempts, a fair estimation of his chance of making his next free throw is 75%. The EV of the number of points scored with one free throw attempt is 0.75. James either makes the free throw and scores one point or misses the free throw and scores no points; but on average, with one free throw, he is expected to score 0.75 points. The concept of EV is used throughout this book to demonstrate the value of certain poker plays and ideas. This chapter introduces EV, and shows how it is calculated and how it can be used.

Calculating EV

To calculate the EV of an event, take all possible outcomes and assign each of them a probability and a result. The sum of the probabilities equals 100%. The sum of each individual result multiplied by its probability equals the EV of that event. If the EV of the event is a positive number, the event has a positive expectation or positive EV. If the EV of the event is a negative number, the event has a negative expectation or negative EV.

Here's an example with a roll of a single die. You roll a fair die, and each of the six numbers on the die has an equal chance of coming up. If the die comes up 1 through 4, you win $3. If the die comes up 5 or 6, you lose $3. Below are the probabilities of each roll and the results:

Die	*Prob.*	*Result*	*Prob. x Result*
1	1/6	+ $3	+ $0.50
2	1/6	+ $3	+ $0.50
3	1/6	+ $3	+ $0.50
4	1/6	+ $3	+ $0.50
5	1/6	- $3	- $0.50
6	1/6	- $3	- $0.50
Total	6/6	N/A	+ $1.00

The last column shows the multiplication of the Probability and the Result columns. Add all the numbers in that column to get the result, the EV of a roll: +$1. You expect to make $1 per time the die rolls. However on any given roll your win will not be $1. You will either win $3 or lose $3. This information can be written as a mathematical equation:

EV of rolling one die = 1/6 x (+$3) + 1/6 x (+$3) + 1/6 x (+$3) + 1/6 x (+$3) + 1/6 x (-$3) +1/6 x (-$3) = $1.00

The EV equations used in this book are formatted into a chart like the one below. The Action column shows the event, the Computation column shows the math work and the Result column shows the answer. Below is the above equation formatted this way.

Action	*Computation*	*Result*
Roll one die	1/6 x (+$3) + 1/6 x (+$3) + 1/6 x (+$3) + 1/6 x (+$3) + 1/6 x (-$3) + 1/6 x (-$3)	+$1.00

In mathematics the order of operations is to do everything within parentheses first (in this case there are no operations within parentheses), then multiply and divide, and then add and subtract. In the EV equation for rolling one die, multiply 1/6 x (+$3) to get +$0.50, and do the same for each term before adding all the terms together.

Look at another chart. If the roll is a 1, you win $100; but you lose $1 with any other number. This is a great game for you, provided your opponent is not cheating. This shorter equation is simpler than writing out each term.

Action	*Computation*	*Result*
Roll one die	(1/6 x $100) + (5/6 x -$1)	$15.83

There is no need to write out each of the rolls from 2 through 6 in the Computation column because they all have the same result: a loss of $1. The solution for the equation is $15.83. You expect to make $15.83 on average per roll of the die. Losses outnumber wins; on average you lose five out of every six rolls. But the win amount overwhelms the loss amount by so much that you have a positive expectation of $15.83 on average per roll.

Here's an example in Hold'em. You are playing $10-$20 Hold'em, and the pot is $80 after the Turn. You have an open-ended straight draw, and you are 100% sure your opponent has a hand that you cannot beat unless you make the straight. But if you do catch the straight, you will win. You believe there is a 17% chance that you will make your straight and a 83% chance that you will not. (Chapter 4 "Outs" and Chapter 5 "Pot Odds" go into further detail on how to estimate your chances of winning and losing.)

Your opponent bets $20 and you must decide whether to call or fold. You have $20 left in your stack; so if you call you cannot lose more or win more on the River, as you are all-in. If you call and win, you win $100. If you call and lose, you lose $20. Figure out if calling has a positive EV.

Action	*Computation*	*Result*
$10-$20 problem	(17% x $100) + (83% x -20)	+$0.40

You expect to make $0.40 by calling. The EV of folding is $0 since you would not be risking any more and would have no reward. $0.40 is greater than $0, so calling is the correct decision.

The chips you have already put into the pot are a sunk cost. They belong to the pot and not to you. You have equity in the pot as long as you still have a chance to win the hand. When you do EV calculations, treat the chips as belonging to the pot.

If you make this play several times: sometimes you will win $100; but more often you will lose $20. On average you expect to make $0.40 per hand. At the poker table these calculations can be difficult to do in your head. Chapter 5 "Pot Odds" presents a simpler way to make the pot-odds calculations to make a correct decision.

Poker players, whether they realize it or not, are always trying to put themselves into situations where they have positive EV. Good players are able to distinguish between situations with positive EV and situations with negative EV. When the situation has positive EV, they get involved. When it has negative EV, they get out. Bad players are not able to distinguish between positive and negative EV, so they often get involved when they have negative EV; and sometimes they get out when they have positive EV. The core purpose of this book is to help you identify the difference in Limit Hold'em between situations which have positive EV and negative EV. Once you identify the positive EV situations, your goal is to identify the play that maximizes the EV.

EV Quiz and Answer

Question 1

You have a fair coin, one that is expected to come up heads 50% of the time. You are told that you win $5 if you flip two tails in row; but if at least one of the flips is a head, you lose $2. What is the EV of this game?

Answer

First figure out the chance of getting two tails in a row. (See Appendix C: Probability and Odds Conversions for more information.) 50% x 50% = 25%

Second convert this number to the probability you will not get two tails in a row (which means at least one of the flips is a head). 100% -25% = 75%

Last multiply the probability with the corresponding result. You get an EV equation of:

EV = (25% x $5) + (75% x -$2) = $1.25 - $1.50 = -$0.25

Action	*Computation*	*Result*
EV for Quiz 1	(25% x $5) + (75% x -$2)	-$0.25

On average you lose playing this game, at the rate of $0.25 per game.

Question 2a

You roll a fair die, and you receive a dollar amount equal to the outcome of the roll. If you do not have to pay anything to roll the die, what is the EV of one roll?

Answer

Action	*Computation*	*Result*
EV for Quiz 2a	(1/6 x $1) + (1/6 x $2) + (1/6 x $3) + (1/6 x $4) + (1/6 x $5) + (1/6 x $6)	+$3.50

Question 2b

If you roll the die five times, what is the cumulative EV of all five rolls?

Answer

Action	*Computation*	*Result*
EV for Quiz 2b	+$3.50 x 5	+$17.50

Question 3

You are the decision-maker at a pickup basketball game, and you care only about winning. Your team is down by two points and there is one possession left in regulation. You know that if the game goes to overtime you have a 55% chance of winning, since your team is slightly better than the other team. You are sure you have only one shot (no offensive rebounds, no second chances, no fouls). Your team has a 30% chance of making a three-point shot (which would win the game) and a 51% chance of making a two-point shot (which would tie the game and send it to overtime). Draw up one play; do you go for a three-point shot or a two-point shot?

Answer

To solve this problem, compare the EV of taking a two-point shot with the EV of taking a three-point shot. Assign a value of 1 to winning and 0 to losing.

If you decide to go for a three-point shot, there is no need for an overtime. Your team either wins the game or loses the game on the last shot. The EV of going for three = (probability you make the three x 1) + (probability you do not make the three x 0).

If you decide to go for a two-point shot, you will go to overtime if you make it since the game will be tied. To find the probability that your team wins the game, multiply the probability of making the two-point shot by the probability of winning the game in overtime. The EV of going for two = (probability you make the two x probability you win in OT x 1) + (probability you make the two x probability you lose in OT x 0) + (probability you do not make the two x 0)

Action	*Computation*	*Result*
EV of going for three	(30% x 1) + (70% x 0)	+0.30
EV of going for two	(51% x 55% x 1) + (51% x 45% x 0) + (49% x 0)	+0.28

The EV analysis says you should go for three because the EV of going for three is higher than the EV of going for two (0.30 to 0.28).

Question 4a

You are playing $10-$20 Hold'em, hold three-of-a-kind on the River, and there is a straight possibility on the board.

Your hand: A♣A♥
Board: A♠K♥Q♣T♥3♦

You have one opponent, who bets $20. You estimate a 70% chance that your opponent has a J for the straight and a 30% chance you have the best hand. The pot is $90 after your opponent bets. Should you call or fold?

Answer

Action	*Computation*	*Result*
EV for Quiz 4a	(30% x $90) + (70% x -$20)	+$13.00

Calling has a positive EV of $13; so you should call.

Question 4b

What if the pot is $50 after your opponent bets?

Answer

Action	*Computation*	*Result*
EV for Quiz 4b	(30% x $50) + (70% x -$20)	+$1.00

The EV is $1.00, which is positive; so you should call.

Question 4c

What if the pot is $50 after your opponent bets and your estimate of her having the J for the straight is 80% instead of 70%?

Answer

Action	*Computation*	*Result*
EV for Quiz 4c	(20% x $50) + (80% x -$20)	-$6.00

The EV of calling is negative. You should fold.

Question 5

You are playing $10-$20 Hold'em. On the Turn you have four cards to a flush draw. The facts:

- You know with certainty that if you do not make your flush draw you lose the hand.
- You know with certainty that if you do make the flush draw you win.
- There are 46 unknown cards left in the deck (you have two in your hand and you can see four on the board). Of those cards, 9 give you the flush and the other 37 do not.
- After your opponent bets, the pot contains $100.
- It is $20 to you and, coincidentally, that is all you have left. There will be no betting on the River since you are all-in if you call.

Should you call or fold?

Answer

There are 46 unknown cards left in the deck; and 9 of them give you a flush while the other 37 cards do not. You have a 9/46 chance of winning and a 37/46 chance of losing. If you win, you win $100; if you lose, you lose $20.

Action	*Computation*	*Result*
EV for Quiz 5	(9/46 x $100) + (37/46 x -$20)	+$3.48

The EV is positive; so you should call.

CHAPTER 4
OUTS

The number of outs is the key to the probability of winning a hand. If you know the number of outs you have, you can figure out if you have proper pot odds to stay in a hand. Without that knowledge you are guessing, and your decisions will not be optimal. This chapter shows how to identify your outs and how to count them. Chapter 5 "Pot Odds" builds on the material in this chapter.

Outs and Non-Outs

In this book, outs are individual cards that help a hand, whether they improve a second-best hand to the best hand or keep the best hand ahead of other hands. If you are ahead, receiving an out means your hand remains the best hand. If you are behind, receiving an out improves your hand to make it the best hand.

Non-outs are all cards that result in a hand being other than the best, whether the best hand is overtaken by another hand or a second-best hand does not improve to the best hand. If you are ahead, a non-out is a card that improves another player's hand to a better hand than yours. If you are behind, receiving a non-out does not improve your hand relative to the best hand. If a card improves your hand but any other hand is still better than yours, then that card is not an out. For example the River may improve your hand from one pair to two pair; but if your opponent simultaneously improves from a better pair to a better two pair, your improvement does not help your relative position. The card that improved your hand was a non-out, as it did not improve your hand to the best hand.

The term *live outs* is often applied to outs that give you the best hand (or allow you to keep the best hand) as opposed to outs that improve your hand without making it the best. In this book, cards that improve your hand without elevating it to the best hand are considered non-outs; so there is no need to distinguish between outs and live outs. All outs are good, and all non-outs are bad.

Example of the concept of outs

On the Turn you have four cards to the nut flush; you have two suited cards in your hand and there are two cards of the same suit on the board. (A nut hand is the best hand possible given the board.)

Your hand: A♠K♠
Board: Q♠7♠3♣2♦

If you make your flush, it will be the nut hand, provided no one has a full house. There are no straight flush possibilities since the gap between the Q♠ and the 7♠ is too wide. Any of the nine remaining spades will give you a flush; and out of those nine, seven do not pair the board and will give you the nut hand. Two of the flush cards will pair the board (3♠ and 2♠) and give you the best possible flush, but not necessarily the nut hand. You know that the seven flush cards that do not pair the board are definitely outs because they offer no possibility of a full house or a four-of-a-kind. (There must be a pair on the board for anyone to have a full house or a four-of-a-kind.) If the flush card that comes on the River pairs the board, there is a chance that another player made a full house when you made your flush. That card was not an out if it simultaneously improved another player's hand to a full house, even if it improved your hand to a flush.

There are 52 cards in a deck. In this example you know six cards before the River card is dealt: you know the two cards in your hand and the four cards on the board. You do not know the other 46 cards (52-6 = 46). If you have 9 outs, the other 37 cards in the deck (46-9 = 37) are non-outs. If the 3♠ or the 2♠ would give another player a full house at the same time it gives you a flush, then you have 7 outs and the other 39 cards are non-outs.

Table 1
Count of Unknown Cards

Round	*Unknown Cards*
Flop	47
Turn	46

Unknown Cards

The concept of the number of unknown cards might be confusing since there are fewer than 46 cards undealt after the Turn. If ten players receive two cards each, that is 20 cards. With another four cards on the board after the Turn, there are 28 cards that nobody has seen. The dealer burned a card before the Flop and another before the Turn, so there are 26 cards left in the deck.

However you have seen only six cards. You do not know what the other players' holdings are, and you do not know what cards were burned. Any particular card might have been dealt to another player or burned, or might remain in the deck. If you do not know which cards were dealt to other players or burned, you cannot make any assumptions about them. It is usually correct to assume 47 unknown cards after the Flop and 46 after the Turn.

Sometimes you can be sure of an opponent's two hole cards based on the play of the hand. In such rare cases you can do the calculations on the basis of 45 unknown cards after the Flop and 44 after the Turn, as shown in table 1.

Counting Outs

Poker is a game of imperfect information. The process of counting outs is a combination of art and science. If the opponent's cards were known, it would be pure science, as the number of outs and non-outs would be a simple matter of counting the cards and doing the necessary math. It might be unusual to know an opponent's exact two cards, but good players often have an idea of what their opponents hold based on how they play. Players who read an opponent's hand with precision are able to pinpoint their own outs and non-outs with a high degree of certainty.

Figuring out how many outs you have is as much art as science. Know how your opponent plays. If your opponent is a maniac and is likely to bluff or semi-bluff, then you probably have more outs. If your opponent plays like a rock, then you probably have fewer outs since a rock would enter the pot only with premium hands.

Tips for counting outs

Try to get a general idea of the cards that your opponents hold by observing their playing styles, as well as their actions so far in the hand. If you know how an opponent plays, then you have a better idea of whether you are ahead or behind, and what your outs are.

If you are certain you are ahead, it is not necessary to count your outs in a Limit Hold'em game. When you are behind, you need to know the likelihood of improving your hand to one that outranks your opponents' hands. There will be times when you are not sure if you are ahead or behind. In those cases you need to know how many outs you have if you are behind and how many outs your opponents have if you are ahead, so you can estimate the chances that you are ahead.

If you are behind figure out which cards can improve your hand to one that is better than your opponents' hands. Once you have identified the exact cards that can improve your hand, count them. For example if you have a flush draw and you know your hand will be a winner only if you catch the flush, then figure out how many undealt cards are of the same suit as your flush draw. If you have a flush draw, you have four cards of the same suit: either two in your hand and two on the board, or one in your hand and three on the board. Since there are 13 cards of the same suit in a deck, there are nine cards remaining of the suit you need; and that would be the number of outs you have, provided no one hits a full house or a four-of-a-kind simultaneously.

Table 2
Count of Outs, Unknown Cards, and Non-Outs

Round	*Hand*	*Outs*	*Unk Cds*	*Non-Outs*	*Prob*[a]
Flop	Flush Draw	9	47	38	19.1%
Flop	Two Overcards	6	47	41	12.8%
Turn	Straight draw	8	46	38	17.4%
Turn	One Overcard	3	46	43	6.5%

[a] prob is probability of hitting on the next card

Once you have an idea of how many outs you have, you can figure out how many non-outs you have. The number of non-outs is the number of unknown cards minus the number of outs. You should usually assume there are 47 unknown cards on the Flop and 46 unknown cards on the Turn. Subtract the number of outs from the number of unknown cards on the appropriate round to figure out how many non-outs there are, as shown in table 2.

Terminology

Drawing dead

A hand that has no outs is *drawing dead.*

Example

Player 1: Q♠9♠
Player 2: A♣A♥
Board: A♠A♦K♠K♦

Player 2 has four A's. Player 1 cannot improve to a winning hand regardless of the card that comes on the River, so Player 1 is drawing dead.

A common example of drawing dead is when a player has overcards to the board on the Turn, while another player has two pair. In that case the best the River card can do for the player with overcards is to improve his no-pair hand to one pair, which does not beat two pair.

Example

Player 1: AKo
Player 2: 87o
Board: T-8-7-3 rainbow

Player 1 is drawing dead; no River card can give her a better hand than Player 2's hand. The only way Player 1 can win this hand is if Player 2 folds to a bluff by Player 1. Avoid putting money into the pot when you are drawing dead. Encourage your opponents to put as much money in the pot as possible when they are drawing dead to you.

Drawing thin

A player with only 1 or 2 outs is said to be *drawing thin.*

Example

Player 1: Q♣J♣
Player 2: A♠A♥
Board: A♣A♦K♣K♦

Player 1 can make a royal flush, which is better than Player 2's four A's. Only the T♣ can give Player 1 a royal flush; so Player 1 is drawing to 1 out, or drawing thin.

Great draw

Sometimes you can have a hand that is a favorite to win but is not leading at the moment.

Example

Player 1: Q♥J♥
Player 2: 2♣2♦
Board: T♥T♠9♥3♣

Player 1 has 25 outs and 19 non-outs, and currently has the worse partial hand. Player 2's pair of 2's is the best hand at the moment; but Player 1 is favored to win this match-up. Player 1's outs:

- Any Q or J gives Player 1 a better two pair. (6 outs)
- Any 9 or 3 will give Player 1 a better two pair because of the higher kicker. Player 2's pair of 2's would get counterfeited with a higher two pair on the board. (6 outs)
- Any heart will give Player 1 a flush. (7 outs, because the 2♥ is not an out since it gives Player 2 a full house and you have already counted the 3♥ previously)
- Any K or 8 that is not a heart will give Player 1 a straight. (6 outs)

It is usually difficult to know when you are in such a great situation. If you held Player 1's cards, you could not be sure your opponent had 2♣2♦; but you should know that unless your opponent already has a full house, you have a great chance of winning the hand.

Thinking About Outs

Before the Flop

With only two cards there are normally too many possibilities and not enough information to tell how many outs you have.

One hand is easier than others: a small pocket pair. Conventional wisdom is that the small pocket pair has 2 outs to hit a set on the Flop; but a small pocket pair has more than one way to win.

After the Flop

Once the Flop comes, you have a better idea of how many outs you have; but you are not certain until you get more information about the other players' hands through the betting.

Example

Your hand: A♣T♣
Flop: T♠7♥4♦

There is a good chance you have the best hand with top pair and the best kicker. The chart below shows the number of outs and non-outs that your AT has against other hands with the given board of T-7-4. Against Opponent 1 your hand is second-best.

Opp	*Opp Hand*	*Your Outs*	*Your Non-Outs*	*Second-Best Hand Needs*
1	JJ	5	40	A♠A♥A♦T♥T♦
2	Q♦T♥	42	3	Q♣Q♠Q♥
3	Q♣J♣	39	6	Q♦Q♠Q♥J♦J♠J♥
4	9♣8♣	37	8	J♣J♠J♥J♦6♣6♠6♥6♦

Although the usual assumption is that there are 47 unknown cards on the Flop, the chart above reflects 45 unknown cards. The chart is comparing two hands. You know seven cards (three cards on the board and two each in the two players' hands), which means there are 45 unknown cards left in a 52 card deck.

Against Opponent 1 holding JJ, you need to hit an A or a T to overcome the higher pair. There are three A's and two T's left, so you have 5 outs. With 45 unknown cards, you have 40 non-outs. ATs is a large underdog against JJ.

Opponent 2 with QT must hit a Q in order to beat your AT. If he does not improve to two pair of Q's and T's, he cannot beat your AT since you have a higher kicker. There are three Q's left in the deck; so the second opponent has 3 outs, and those outs for him would be non-outs for you. (If the Turn and the River are both 7's or both 4's: both of you would have the same full house, and the kicker would no longer matter. That possibility is so small that you can ignore it on the Flop when counting outs.) The remaining 42 cards are non-outs for him but outs for you. ATs is a major favorite against QT.

If you are involved against two or more players, then you have to count the total number of outs and non-outs you have against all the opponents as a group. If you are ahead and the outs that your opponents have overlap, then you may not be worse off playing against two opponents instead of one. You may even be better off, depending on the cards they hold. Say your two opponents are Opponent 2 and Opponent 3 in the chart above. Opponent 2 holds Q♦T♥ and Opponent 3 holds Q♣J♣. Separately, Opponent 2 has 3 outs (three Q's), and Opponent 3 has 6 outs (three Q's and three J's). Together they have 5 outs (two Q's and three J's). Since each hand has a Q, there are only two Q's left in the unknown cards. Opponent 2's outs are the 2 Q's, as they would make Q's and T's. Opponent 3's outs are the three J's. (The Q's are not outs because a Q on the board would give Opponent 2 a better hand.) Compare this situation to playing the hand heads-up against Opponent 3, who would have 6 outs. Not only are there fewer outs for your opponents when their hands have a card in common, but you also have the added benefit of getting two players to put money into the pot instead of one.

Unfortunately when you are involved against two or more players, they often have non-overlapping outs. If your opponents were Opponent 2 and Opponent 4, they would have 11 outs combined. Against those two hands, you can add their outs together since they are not looking for the same cards. Knowing two other players' hands means the number of unknown cards is 43, and your outs total 32. You have a lower chance of winning the hand against both Opponent 2 and Opponent 4 than if you were in a heads-up situation with either of them; but the increased size of the pot makes up for it.

If you are the favorite to win the hand, it is not as important to know the number of outs you have. Your focus is on getting the other players to put in as much money into the pot as possible.

Sometimes you think you are ahead but you are actually behind. Other players playing aggressively may mean trouble. In the above example an opponent could have an overpair with AA, KK, QQ, or JJ, in which case you could have as many as 5 outs (against KK, QQ or JJ) or as few as 2 outs (against AA).

It is possible to catch your out on the Turn only to have your opponent catch an out on the River. If you can catch on the Turn and lose on the River, you may have fewer effective outs than you think. This is one of the reasons why it is usually a good idea to be conservative about the number of outs you think you have.

After the Turn card

All of the issues that were brought up on the Flop also apply on the Turn; but now you do not need to be concerned with getting redrawn if you catch your out, since there is only one card left to come. All you need to be concerned about is how many outs and non-outs you have. This is the last point in the hand where you are concerned with outs and non-outs. Once the River card comes, the hands are set; and no hand can overtake another hand with a future card.

Outs that are not outs; and when a blank is an out

In Hold'em sometimes a card that improves your hand also improves an opponent's hand. In such a case you may think the card is an out for you when it may not be at all.

Example

Your hand: A♠K♣
Board: Q♣8♦7♠2♥

If your opponent has a pair, then you might have 6 outs, as any A or K would give you the top pair with top kicker. But if your opponent holds a card that matches both the board and one of your hole cards (in this case, an A or K), then you have 3 outs. In the above hand if your opponent has A♣2♦, then your only outs are the three K's left in the deck. Although an A improves your hand to a pair of A's, it improves your opponent's hand from a pair of 2's to two pair, A's and 2's.

Another frequent problem: a card that gives you a pair also gives another player a straight. A card that you thought was an out might actually be an out for her. It may be that you were ahead and she was doing the chasing.

Example

Your hand: A♣9♦
Board: K♣T♠2♦2♥

If your opponent holds Q♣ J♠: then an A is an out for her, not for you, as it gives her a straight. You are ahead on the Turn; and more cards than you expected can come on the River to give you the best hand. It might not look like that from the play of the hand, especially if your opponent was betting or raising with the straight draw on the Flop.

Identifying and Counting Outs

Assume you have perfect information and know your opponent's cards. This makes it easier to figure out how many outs you have. Use this assumption on the Turn when there is one more card to come, the River card, and you are not worried about catching your hand only to get redrawn at a later round. You also do not need to worry about what happens if you miss on the Turn and catch on the River.

The chart below shows several examples of your hand, your opponent's hand, the board, the number of outs and non-outs, and the specific cards that are outs for your hand. Look at the hands of the two players and the board and try to count the outs for your hand before looking at the last three columns.

Your	*Opp*	*Board*	*Outs*	*Non-Outs*	*Cards That Are Outs*
J♥T♥	A♣K♦	K♥8♠6♥4♠	9	35	A♥, Q♥, 9♥, 8♥, 7♥, 5♥, 4♥, 3♥, 2♥
J♥ T♥	K♣K♦	K♥Q♠7♣3♦	8	36	A♣, A♦, A♥, A♠, 9♣, 9♦, 9♥, 9♠
A♣A♦	K♠Q♠	K♣Q♣J♠7♠	10	34	A♥, J♣, J♦, J♥, T♣, T♦,T♥, 7♣, 7♦, 7♥
9♠8♠	J♠J♣	A♣9♣7♦6♦	13	31	T♣, T♦, T♥, T♠, 9♦, 9♥,8♣, 8♦, 8♥, 5♣, 5♦, 5♥, 5♠
A♣K♦	Q♣Q♦	J♣8♦3♠2♥	6	38	A♦, A♥, A♠, K♣, K♥, K♠
T♠9♠	A♠K♠	Q♠J♠T♣9♣	5	39	8♠, T♥, T♦, 9♥, 9♦

Note that the total number of unknown cards for each hand in this chart is 44. Normally the assumption is 46 for the number of unknown cards on the Turn. In this chart the opponent's hand is known, and that cuts the unknown cards from 46 to 44. When you know the opponent's hand, you have perfect information; and figuring out the odds of winning the hand becomes a pure mathematical exercise. It is easy to compare the probability of winning the hand to the pot odds and make the decision to call or fold. Perfect information is rare.

Counting each individual card can be tedious. For certain draws it is easier to generalize the number of outs. As a general rule if you think your hand becomes the best hand if you hit your draw, you can assume the number of outs shown in table 3. The "Rule" column shows the rule of thumb for outs with one card to come.

Sometimes you have a combination of more than one of these types of draws. You could have a flush draw and a straight draw at the same time, which could increase the number of outs to 15.

Example

Your hand: J♣T♣
Board: Q♣-9♣-x-x

In this case any club will make a flush and any K or 8 will make a straight. There are nine clubs left in the deck, as well as eight straight cards (four K's and four 8's). However the K♣ and the 8♣ were already

Table 3
Outs With One Card to Come

Type of Draw	*Rule*	*Prob*
Flush draw	9	19.6%
Open ended or double inside straight	8	17.4%
Overpair versus two pair	8	17.4%
Two overcards versus one pair	6	13.0%
Middle pair versus Top pair where the kickers are different	5	10.9%
Inside straight draw	4	8.7%
One overcard versus one pair	3	6.5%
Pocket pair versus a higher pair	2	4.3%

counted when you counted the nine clubs, so there are only six more cards that will make a straight. In total 15 cards will make either the straight or the flush.

Counting the outs for a straight draw

With an open-ended straight draw there are 8 outs. An open-ended straight draw has two different ranks that will make the straight; and each rank has four cards.

Example

Your hand: JT
Flop: Q-9-x

Any K or 8 makes the straight. There are four cards of each rank; so there are eight cards left in the deck that will make the straight, for 8 outs. (With an inside straight draw there are 4 outs, as there is only one rank that can fill your straight.)

With a straight draw, see if the board allows for a possible flush draw. Another player having a flush draw while you have a straight draw reduces your outs from 8 to 6 or 4 to 3, since you can make the straight while that player makes his flush.

Counting the outs for a flush draw

A flush draw has 9 outs (assuming you already have four cards to the flush). There are 13 cards of the same suit in the deck. If you have four of them, there are nine cards of the same suit left.

Example

Suppose you have two hearts in your hand and there are two hearts on the board.

Your hand: A♥ 3♥
Board: T♥ 9♠ 8♠ 2♥

From the betting thus far and the composition of the players, you are sure that someone else already has a straight; so you must hit your flush in order to have a chance to win the hand. Any heart gives you a flush; and since you have the A♥, it would be the nut flush. There are 13 hearts in a full deck. You have two hearts in your hand and there are two on the board; thus there are nine hearts left in the rest of the deck. With

46 unknown cards and 9 outs, the remaining 37 cards are non-outs. (The 9 and the 37 are the crucial numbers in the method of comparing the number of outs to the expected pot size presented in Chapter 5 "Pot Odds.") The probability of hitting the flush is 9/46, which is 19.6%.

If you are drawing to a flush that is not the nut flush, be aware of the possibility that someone is simultaneously drawing to a higher flush, crippling your hand.

Counting the outs when you have overcards

If you have two overcards, pairing either of them may be an out for your hand.

Example

Your hand: AKo
Your opponent's hand: QJo
Board: J-8-3-2 rainbow

You have 6 outs. There are three A's and three K's left in the deck. If any of them come on the River, your hand is best.

Sometimes your opponent has one of your outs counterfeited. Hitting that card would improve your opponent's hand as well as your own, so you have fewer outs than you were hoping for. For example if the opponent's hand were AJ instead of QJ, the remaining two A's would no longer be outs for your AK; and your only outs would be the three K's.

In the heat of the battle at the poker table you do not have perfect information and you do not know your opponent's exact hand. It is possible you are ahead and your opponent has a hand like T9, going for a straight draw.

If you know your opponent well, her actions give you a good idea of her possible cards. Say you know she would not raise with a straight draw, but would raise with the top pair and a good kicker. In that case she could have a hand like AJ, KJ or QJ. If she has QJ, then your AK has 6 outs. If she has AJ or KJ, then your AK has 3 outs. As a rule of thumb, estimate the expected number of outs to be 4 in cases like this, a compromise between the different possibilities. With few outs, the typical correct decision is to fold. This depends on the pot size; but rarely is the pot big enough to warrant continuing. However this is only true if you are fairly sure your opponent has a pair and is not on a draw. Knowing how your opponent plays made hands versus drawing hands is useful in such situations.

Counting the outs when you have a split pair vs. an opponent's higher split pair

A split pair uses one card from the board and a hole card.

Example

Your hand: ATo
Flop: J-T-3 rainbow

In this case you have a split pair of T's. If you suspect your opponent has a split pair of J's, then you may think you have 5 outs (three A's and two T's). However if his kicker matches your kicker, then you have 2 outs (two T's). For example if your opponent has AJ for a split pair of J's, when you hit your A for two pair he will simultaneously hit his two pair. His two pair would be better than yours (A's and J's versus A's and T's). You would have the two remaining T's as outs. You would prefer that your opponent have JT for two pair instead of AJ for one pair. If he has JT and already has two pair, you have 3 outs (three A's), which is more outs than you have if he has AJ. In this case you prefer your opponent to have what appears to be a stronger hand, because you have a better chance of drawing out against two pair of J's and T's than of drawing out against one pair with the same kicker as yours.

Counting the outs when you may have additional outs

If you are on a straight draw or a flush draw, you may have another opportunity to win by pairing one of your cards. Usually you will not be sure if pairing one of your cards will be an out; so estimate the expected number of extra outs.

Example

Your hand: A♠T♠
Board: K♠9♠7♣2♥

You have 9 outs for the flush. If your opponent has a pair and does not have an A or T as a kicker, then you may have up to 6 additional outs. If she has KQ: then any A is an out for you, giving you 3 additional outs with your flush draw. If she has AK: then an A is not an out for you, and you have 9 outs. If she has 98 for a pair of 9's: then both the A and the T are outs for you, giving you 6 additional outs with your flush draw, for a total of 15 outs.

As a rule of thumb assume that half of the overcards you may have to the board are outs, because pairing your overcard may or may not give you the winning hand.

In the hand above with A♠T♠ as your hand, the rule of thumb would give you 1.5 additional outs along with the flush draw. Consider yourself to have 10.5 outs: 9 outs for the flushes and 1.5 outs for the A, which is half of the three remaining A's. This is an estimate; but it is better than assuming the three A's are outs, and better than assuming none of them are outs.

The betting of the hand may give you additional information to make an estimate that is better than the rule of thumb. If the betting has been strong from the beginning, then it is likely that you have no additional outs. The number of players also makes a difference. With more players the likelihood of any overcard being an out decreases. If one opponent has KQ: another opponent could have A9, in which case neither the A nor the T would be additional outs.

Counting the outs when there is a chance you are drawing dead

There are times when you are not sure if you are drawing dead or drawing live.

<u>Example</u>

Your hand: Q♣J♠
Flop: K♥T♣T♦

It may look as though you have 8 outs, since there are eight cards that can make your straight (four A's and four 9's). If your opponent already has a full house or four-of-a-kind, then you are drawing dead. Rarely will your opponent have two perfect cards for a full house or better, but it can happen. If he does not currently have it, you could make your straight on the Turn only to see him draw a full house on the River to beat you. Or he could hit a full house at the same time you hit your straight. If you could be drawing dead or get redrawn, assume you have fewer outs.

As a rule of thumb: subtract 1 out from the straight, and assume 7 outs. Adjust the expected number of outs accordingly, bsaed on the betting of the hand.

Counting the outs when there is a chance you are ahead

Sometimes you are not sure whether your hand is ahead or behind. If it is behind, it may have a chance to improve.

Example

Your hand: J♠T♣
Board: Q♠J♣9♥3♦

If you are behind to a split pair of Q's, you could have as many as 13 outs (8 outs for the straight, two J's and three T's). But you may be ahead if your opponent has T9, in which case you have 2 non-outs to lose (two 9's), and 8 non-outs to push the hand after you both make the same straight. There is also a chance that she already has a straight with KT, in which case you have 3 outs to push the hand. These situations make it difficult to know exactly how many outs and non-outs you have. Being able to read your opponents well makes it easier to estimate the number of outs you have, as you can pinpoint their hands with more accuracy.

When you have a pocket overpair, a pair on the board may decrease your opponent's outs

Assume you have an overpair in your hand. You think your opponent has one pair with a kicker that is different from your cards, for 5 outs.

Example

Your hand: AA
Your opponent's hand: JT
Flop: T-6-3 rainbow.

Your opponent's outs are three J's and two T's, for a total of 5 outs. However if the Turn pairs the board with a card that he does not have, then his outs drop to two, the two T's. Continuing with the Flop above: if the Turn is a 6 and the River is a J, then the board is:

Board: T-6-3-6-J

Your opponent has two pair of J's and T's, and a useless third pair with the 6's on the board. You have a higher two pair: A's and 6's.

It may be difficult to tell if your opponent's outs were reduced by the pairing of the board on the Turn, or if he caught three-of-a-kind; but you might be able to get a read on his hand. Players are more likely to play T than a 6; so trip 6's are unlikely, but possible. You would not expect a solid player from a non-blind or non-stealing position to hold a 6, with the exception of A6s or maybe 76s. It would be less of a surprise to see a calling station flip over a hand like 86o.

Counting outs on the Flop: runner-runner straights and flushes

A runner-runner straight draw or flush draw occurs when you have three to a flush or straight on the Flop, and catch a perfect card on both the Turn and the River to turn your hand into a flush or straight.

Example

Your hand: A♠3♠
Flop: A♣9♠8♣

You have three cards to a spade flush. If both the Turn and the River cards are spades, then you have a runner-runner flush. Hitting a runner-runner draw does not happen often but the possibility should not be completely discounted when counting outs. If you assume the runner-runner flush draw is the best hand: you can figure out the probability of it occurring, and then convert that into the appropriate number of outs.

One way to look at it is: a fourth flush card will come on the Turn 10/47 of the time, giving you 9 flush outs on the River. The other 37/47 of the time a fourth flush card will not come on the Turn, and you will have no flush outs on the River. Thus 10/47 x 9 is the expected value (EV) of the number of flush outs that you will have on the River.

Action	*Computation*	*Result*
EV of the number of flush outs on the River	10/47 x 9 outs	1.91 outs going into the Turn

Another way to look at it is to compute the probability of hitting a runner-runner flush draw, and then multiply that by the number of unknown cards to get the number of outs. The chart below shows the results. Notice that the answers are the same.

Table 4
Outs for Runner-Runner Flush Draw

Highest Hidden Flush Card	*Estimated Number of Outs*
Highest possible	2
2nd or 3rd highest	1.5
All others	1

Action	*Computation*	*Result*
The probability of hitting a runner-runner flush draw	10/47 x 9/46	4.16%
Converting 4.16% into the equivalent of outs	4.16% x 46	1.91 outs

You may catch the runner-runner flush but not have the best hand if someone else had a higher flush. So as a rule of thumb, choose a number of outs for runner-runner flush draws that depends on the highest card of that suit in your first two cards.

Table 4 shows estimated outs for runner-runner flush draws.

With this information you can add the expected outs for a runner-runner draw to your "main" draw.

Example

Your hand: K♠9♠
Flop: A♠9♣2♦

If you think one of your opponents has an A, then you have 5 outs (three K's, two 9's) not counting the flush draw. Your K♠ will give you the nut flush if the board gets two more spades; so you can add 2 outs for the runner-runner flush draw, for a total of 7 outs.

More ways to catch runner-runner straight draws

1. When you need one perfect card, then one of two cards

Your hand: JT
Flop: K-T-3

Table 5
Outs for Runner-Runner Straight Draw, One Perfect Card Needed

Action	*Computation*	*Result*
The probability of hitting a runner-runner straight draw with one perfect card needed	(4/47 x 8/46) + (8/47 x 4/46)	2.96%
Converting to outs	2.96% x 46	1.36 outs

In this case you need to catch a Q on the Turn, and then either an A or a 9 on the River. You could also first catch the A or 9 on the Turn and then catch the Q on the River. In either case you need the Q to make your straight.

The probability of hitting a runner-runner straight draw with one perfect card needed is shown in table 5.

If you believe your opponent has a hand like AK, you can consider three J's and two T's as outs. With the runner-runner straight draw possibility, you can add another 1 out for a total of 6 outs. Adjust 1.36 outs downward to 1 out because of the chance that you might hit your hand on the Turn only to see your opponent draw a higher hand on the River.

2. When you need two cards, but you have more options

Your hand: T9
Flop: J-T-6 rainbow

In this case you can make a runner-runner straight with any of these card combinations on the Turn and then River: KQ, QK, Q8, 8Q, 87, 78. Each of these combinations has a 0.74% chance of happening (4/47 x 4/46). Since there are six combinations, the total chance of hitting the runner-runner straight is 6 x 0.74% = 4.44%. The equivalent in terms of outs is 2.02, as shown in table 6.

These combinations can be dangerous. Even if you catch, someone else may have caught a higher straight. For example using the above hole cards and Flop, if you catch a K on the Turn and a Q on the River: you would make a K-Q-J-T-9 straight, but a player with an A would have

Table 6
Outs for Runner-Runner Straight Draw, Maximum Options

Action	*Computation*	*Result*
The probability of hitting a runner-runner straight draw when there are more ways	4/47 x 4/46 x 6	4.44%
Converting to outs	4.44% x 46	2.02 outs

a higher straight. As a rule of thumb, count all runner-runner straight draws as 1 out instead of 2. This may be on the conservative side, but it is easier to count the outs on all runner-runner straight draws as the same. There are already a lot of things to consider when playing a poker hand at the table; and this tiny difference is small enough to ignore.

KQ with a Flop of J-8-3 may be better than AK

If you have AK and do not hit a pair on the Flop, you may have fewer outs than when you have two overcards without an A, like KQ. You are more likely to get counterfeited with an A since many players like to play hands that contain an A (such as A8), but will not play with any hand that contains a K or Q (such as K8 or Q8).

Flop: J-8-3 rainbow

Players are more likely to play with AJ or KJ than with QJ, and with A8 than with Q8. If your opponent has made a split pair on the Flop, you are more likely to have 6 outs with KQ than with AK. If you hit your pair when you have AK, the probability that someone else hit two pair at the same time is higher than if you hit a pair with KQ. This does not mean that KQ is a better starting hand than AK. In situations like this, AK needs to be careful.

Chapter 5 "Pot Odds" shows how to use this information, along with the information on the expected pot size, to figure out if continuing with the hand is worthwhile.

Quiz: Counting Outs

Question 1

You are last to act on the Turn.

Your hand: 3♠2♠
Flop: A♠5♣K♦
Turn: 9♥

There are three other players in the hand on the Turn. How many outs do you have?

Answer

With three other players it is almost impossible for a 3 or a 2 to be an out for you, as you should be confident someone else has a pair if not better. You should count this hand as having 4 outs; the four 4's give you the nut straight.

Question 2

You checked and your opponent bet on the Turn.

Your hand: Q♠8♣
Flop: J♣T♦3♠
Turn: 4♣

You suspect your opponent has a J but you are not sure of her kicker. How many outs do you have?

Answer

You can make a straight with a 9; that is four outs. If your opponent does not have QJ, then three Q's become outs for you. There is a chance she has a Q. To be conservative assume two-thirds of the time that a Q is an out, and count the three Q's as 2 outs. When these are added to the 4 outs for the straight, you have an estimated total of 6 outs.

Question 3

You are in the big blind. There is one limper. The small blind calls and you check.

Your hand: T♣3♣
Flop: J♣6♦2♠

Everyone checks on the Flop.

Turn: 4♣

The Turn gives you a flush draw and an inside straight draw. The small blind bets out, and can be presumed to have at least a pair of J's. How many outs do you estimate you have?

Answer

You have nine clubs to make the flush and three other 5's to make the straight (one of the 5's is a club, which was already counted as one of the nine clubs). It appears you have 12 outs.

CHAPTER 5
POT ODDS

Pot odds is the ratio of the size of the pot to the amount you have to put into the pot to stay in the hand. For example if the pot is 7 big bets, and you must call 1 big bet in order to stay in the hand, you are getting pot odds of 7:1.

The bet you are contemplating does not count as part of the pot in the calculation of pot odds. In the above example where the pot contains 7 big bets, your call will increase the size of the pot to 8 big bets.

Casinos sometimes use the term *for* when discussing odds. They may offer 9 for 1 to the public on a wager. This is commonly seen at a dice table and on parlay cards in sportsbooks. If the odds offered are 9 for 1, then the casino pays a total of 9 if the player wins. Included in that 9 is the 1 that the player wagered. Thus the player won 8. 9 for 1 is the same thing as 8 to 1.

Outs and Pot Odds

The reason you count the number of outs is to have something to relate to the pot odds to decide how to play your hand. If you know the numbers of non-outs and outs, then you can compare the ratio of them to the pot odds to see if you should be staying in the hand.

Odds Notation

There is more than one way to display odds. For example 7 to 1 and 7:1 mean the same thing. The amount that can be won is on the left side, while the amount that is risked is on the right side. If the odds are 6:1, 6 is the amount that you will win if you win; and 1 is the amount you will lose if you lose.

It is usually easiest to have the lower number in the ratio be 1. If winning is worth 10, and losing is worth -2, then the odds are 10:2. This can be reduced to 5:1 by dividing both sides by 2.

When the event is more likely to occur than not, then the number on the right side is larger. For example if you are betting on a big favorite where you are trying to win 1 but might lose 2, the odds are 1:2.

From the pot odds you can compute the probability of winning that you need in order to have a break-even decision. Divide the number of bets it will cost you to call by what the pot size will be after you call. X to Y has a break-even probability of Y/(X+Y). Example: 7:1 pot odds breaks even at a probability of winning of 1/(7+1) = 1/8.

Table 7 shows pot size and winning percentages. "Pct needed" means the winning percentage needed to break even on the bet.

If the expected winning percentage of your hand is greater than the winning percentage needed for a break-even decision, then you have positive expected value (EV) to stay in the hand. If the expected winning percentage of your hand is less than the winning percentage needed to break even, then you have negative EV to stay in the hand.

Break-even probabilities can be converted to odds. Breaking even with the probability A/B requires pot odds of (B-A) to A. For example a break-even probability of 1/5 requires pot odds of (5-1) to 1, which can be expressed as 4 to 1 or 4:1.

Example

Assume you have 10 outs and 30 non-outs, and the pot is 5 big bets. Also assume it will cost you 1 big bet to see the last card, at which point you will know if you are a winner. Compare the pot odds to the ratio of non-outs to outs. If the ratio of non-outs to outs is smaller than the pot odds, then staying in the hand is a positive EV play.

Table 7
Pot Size vs. Winning Percent Needed

Pot Size	*Bet to Call*	*Pct Needed*
4	1	20.0%
5	1	16.7%
6	1	14.3%
7	1	12.5%
8	1	11.1%
9	1	10.0%
10	1	9.1%
7	2	22.2%
8	2	20.0%
9	2	18.2%
10	2	16.7%

In the example the pot odds are 5:1 (5 big bets in the pot and 1 big bet required to call). The ratio of non-outs to outs is 30:10 or 3:1. Since the pot is offering you odds greater than the ratio of non-outs to outs, staying in the hand is a positive EV play.

Alternatively the numbers can be calculated as percentages. Pot odds of 5:1 means the winning percentage for breaking even is 1/6 or 16.7%. If you have 30 non-outs and 10 outs, then you have 10/40 or 25% chance of hitting an out. Looking at the percentages gives same result: staying in the hand has a positive EV.

A tougher example

The above numbers are easy to compare because the calculations yield integers, but the numbers can be more complicated. Suppose the pot is 7 big bets, and there was a raise so you have to put in 2 big bets to call. You have 37 non-outs and 9 outs. Should you call?

This math is tougher because the numbers are not as simple as in the previous example. Compare the ratios and see if 7:2 (the pot odds) is greater than 37:9 (ratio of non-outs to outs).

It is easier to compare two ratios if you convert them to have a common number on the right side of the ratio. The easiest number to use for the right side is generally 1. Converting a ratio to the form x:1 involves converting the numerator to a decimal.

In the example pot odds of 7:2 becomes 3.5 to 1; and non-outs to outs of 37:9 becomes 4.1 to 1. Since the pot is offering 3.5 odds and you need 4.1 to break even, calling is not worthwhile. This method is not an easy mental exercise for most people.

Another way to do the calculation is to convert the ratio into a percentage. The pot odds of 7:2 becomes 22.2% (2/9), while the chance of hitting an out becomes 19.6% (9/46). You arrive at the same conclusion: the winning percentage needed for a break-even decision is higher than the one you have, so you should fold. This method is also not an easy mental exercise for most people.

Although both of these methods are correct, neither method is easy to put into action at the table. Both are difficult when there are many other issues to think about. This chapter shows a method that is more practical to use at the table, because the computations are easier to do, but without sacrificing significant accuracy.

Implied Pot Odds and Expected Pot Size

Understanding this method requires an introduction to the concepts of implied pot odds[a] and expected pot size.

Implied pot odds describes the total pot odds you expect to have at the end of the hand, after all the chips that will be in the pot are in the pot.

Here is an example. There are 6 big bets in the pot when you make a decision to call a bet on the Turn, and you are confident your opponent will call if you hit your out and bet on the River. Therefore you will win 7 big bets if you win your hand; 7 big bets is the expected pot size (EPS).

The EPS does not include the bets that you have yet to put in yourself, although it does count the bets that you have put in already. In this example the current pot on the Turn is 6 big bets and the pot odds are 6:1; but that information is not as relevant as the EPS. The EPS is 7 big bets, and the implied pot odds are 7:1. The size of the expected pot may make a difference in your decision.

[a] David Sklansky introduced the concept of implied pot odds in his book *Hold 'em Poker*.

The method presented in this book relies on the EPS. Instead of converting into odds and looking at the implied pot odds, you estimate the EPS and leave it at that. With that number you can make correct calculations in your head while at the table.

Information needed

In order to apply pot odds analysis at the table, you need the following information:

- The pot size and the expected pot size
- The amount you are risking
- The number of outs you have
- The number of non-outs you have.

Chapter 4 has already covered how to count the number of outs and the non-outs. The focus in the next two sections is on how to count the pot and the EPS.

Counting the pot in bets, not dollars

It is easiest for most people to think of the pot and the pot odds in terms of bets instead of dollars. There are two ways to do this. One way is to count in small bets on the pre-Flop and Flop round, and then convert that into big bets for the Turn and River rounds. If there are 6 small bets in the pot after the Flop, convert that to 3 big bets (2 small bets equals 1 big bet).

Another way is to count every round in terms of big bets, so there is no need to convert small bets to big bets at any point. Each small bet is counted as half of a big bet.

Either way achieves the same goal. Counting the pot in terms of bets instead of dollars saves one step. If there are 6 big bets in the pot on the River and your lone opponent bets, making the pot 7 big bets, you are faced with a decision to call or fold. If you call, you are risking 1 big bet in order to win 7 big bets. The pot odds are 7:1. You would have to win this hand 12.5% (1/8) of the time in order to make calling a break-even decision. In a $30-$60 game if you are counting in terms of dollars, you count $360 in the pot on the River and another $60 from your opponent, making the pot $420. Your call is $60. To convert that to pot odds, divide $420 by $60 to get 7:1.

The Mechanics of Counting the Pot

Understanding pot odds means relating the size of the pot to the bet you make. To know the size of the pot, you must count the pot. This takes practice. You can back-count the pot by replaying the action in your mind, but that causes three problems. First it slows the game and takes your concentration off the play of the hand. Second other players may catch on to what you are doing, as it is easy to give accidental visual clues that you are counting the pot. Third you may be too lazy to count the pot when you are not in the hand, so you may not know if another player has made a mistake on pot odds or is even taking pot odds into consideration. How well an opponent's actions match up with pot odds is useful information. Counting the pot in progress takes discipline and practice, but is worth the effort to gain an advantage over your opponents.

Another way to count the pot is to count the bets as they go into the pot, converting them to big bets. After the blinds have been posted, there are 0.75 big bets in the pot: a quarter of a big bet for the small blind and half a big bet for the big blind. A call brings the pot to 1.25 big bets. If the next player raises by putting 2 small bets or 1 big bet into the pot, the total pot is 2.25 big bets.

You can also count the bets in the pre-Flop round by counting the number of players who see the Flop and adjusting for the number of raises. If four players are in the hand and there was one raise, then there are 4 big bets in the pot if both blinds are in the hand, since each of the four players would have put in 1 big bet total. If both blinds have folded, but there are four other players who see the Flop for one raise, then there are 4.75 big bets in the pot.

In the pre-Flop round you can round the quarter bets to the nearest integer. Round 4.75 big bets to 5.0 big bets and 4.25 big bets to 4 big bets. This causes a small loss in accuracy due to rounding, but ensures fewer mistakes.

The small bet on the Flop is half a big bet. On the Flop you can use either way to add to the size of the pot.

On the Turn, count the bets as they enter the pot. This is the time when pot odds come into play, and you will want to know the total quickly.

On the River there are fewer reasons to count the pot. You may want to keep track of the pot in order to make a decision to call or fold.

The additional bets that go into the pot on the River normally should not affect your decision.

In a low-limit game, instead of counting the small blind as half of a small bet, you may not want to count it at all. The rake in a low-limit game is usually close to the amount of the small blind. You can think of the rake as going directly into the dealer's tray rather than into the pot. The examples used in this book assume there is no rake; you may need to adjust for the rake in the games you play.

DIPO: "Do I Have Pot Odds?"

Once you have gathered all the information required, you can figure out whether you have the pot odds you need to stay in. You don't need a complicated algebraic formula. Make the decision in your head with relative ease with the "Do I have Pot Odds?" or DIPO method. The DIPO method is easier to use during the Turn when there is only one more card to come and thus there are fewer variables than at the Flop. DIPO can also be used during the betting on the Flop.

To use the DIPO method, compare two numbers: the Good Number and the Bad Number.

- The Good Number: the EPS times the number of outs
- The Bad Number: the number of non-outs.

If the Good Number is greater than the Bad Number, then you have the pot odds you need to stay in the hand. If the Good Number is less than the Bad Number, then you do not and would be well advised to fold.

It is easy to see the advantages of using DIPO. You are able to put yourself in a position where you no longer have to size up the pot compared to the strength of your hand. You also do not need to backtrack and count the pot after the fact, which could take your concentration away from other factors of the game. If you count the pot size at a later point, you may unknowingly give a tell. If you let other players know you are counting the pot, they may deduce that you do not have a made hand and are on a draw, which is information you should conceal. DIPO is easier to implement than counting the pot in terms of dollars and calculating the pot odds relative to the probability you will win the hand. The drawback of DIPO is that it takes discipline and practice. Fortunately most poker players do not have the discipline to think at the table. If you do, you have an advantage over most of your competition.

The following section explains the math behind the method. For most people this method is easier than comparing pot odds to the ratio of non-outs to outs because multiplication is easier than division.

The Math Behind DIPO

Understanding the math is not essential to using DIPO; so don't worry if you don't understand this section.

- EPS = Expected Pot Size (not counting any bets you will put into the pot in the future)
- Outs = Outs
- NOuts = Non-Outs
- Cards = Outs + NOuts (all the cards that are unknown to you)
- Bet = The bet you are facing.

Assumptions: It is the Turn and there is one card left to come. Someone has bet and it is up to you to call or fold. (Disregard raising for now.) You are sure that if you hit any of your outs, you have the winning hand. You are also sure that if you do not hit any of your outs, you have a losing hand so you will fold on the River without losing any more bets.

The equation for the expected value (EV) of calling the bet is:

EV of calling = EPS x Outs/Cards - Bet x NOuts/Cards

If this number is positive, then you have positive EV in calling the bet. If it is negative, then you have negative EV in calling the bet and should fold.

These algebra calculations may be too complicated to do in your head when you are sitting at the poker table, so simplify the problem to a comparison. Compare the term [EPS x Outs/Cards] to the term [Bet x NOuts/Cards].

When the first term [EPS x Outs/Cards] is greater than the second term [Bet x NOuts/Cards], the answer to the EV-of-calling equation is positive. Conversely when the second term is greater than the first term, the answer to the EV-of-calling equation is negative. You should call if the EV of calling is positive, so you should call if the first term [EPS x Outs/Cards] is greater than the second term [Bet x NOuts/Cards].

In comparing these terms, cancel out the common variable Cards. You are left with comparing [EPS x Outs] to [Bet x NOuts].

When there is 1 bet to you and you close the action on the Turn (meaning there are no players left to act after your call, so you cannot be raised), then you know that the variable Bet equals 1. You are left with the comparison of EPS x Outs versus NOuts.

You do not care how large the difference is between the two terms. All you care about is whether the first term is greater than the second term. When there is more than 1 bet, compare the first term to NOuts x the Number of Bets instead of just to NOuts. This is discussed with an example later in this chapter. Abdul Jalib created a similar method.

Examples and Issues of Using DIPO on the Turn

The easiest way to illustrate the use of DIPO is on the Turn with your action closing the betting, so that no one can raise behind you.

Example 1

You are the big blind.

Your hand: A♠T♣
Flop: K♣Q♠4♥
Turn: 3♦

Any J gives you the nut hand, as there are no flush possibilities. If a J comes on the River, there are no full house or four-of-a-kind possibilities. There has been enough betting that you suspect someone has a hand like AK, AQ, KK or QQ, so an A is not an out for you. You are confident you have 4 outs: the four J's. Before the Turn there were 9 big bets in the pot and two other players in the hand. The first player to act on the Turn bets. The second player calls, which brings the pot up to 11 big bets. If you call you close the betting, and the dealer deals the River card. You suspect that if you hit your straight you will get at least 1 more big bet out of them, and possibly more.

Use a conservative EPS of 12 and apply the DIPO method. Recall that the Good Number is the EPS times the number of outs, and the Bad Number is the number of non-outs.

DIPO Method	*Computation*	*Result*
Good Number	12 x 4	48
Bad Number	46 - 4	42

The Good Number is greater than the Bad Number, so you can call knowing you are being offered value to try to get lucky.

Example 2

It is down to you and a lone opponent.

Your hand: A♠K♠
Flop: Q♦8♠3♣
Turn: 2♥

You are sure your opponent has a pair, and possibly an A or a K as a kicker. If both of your cards are indeed outs, then you have 6 outs. If one of your cards matches your opponent's kicker, then you have 3 outs. There is also a small chance your opponent is semi-bluffing with a straight draw like JT or J9, in which case you are ahead and have more outs. Taking everything into consideration, including how the player plays, you estimate that you have about 5 outs. Since there are 46 unknown cards on the Turn, 5 outs means 41 non-outs (46 - 5).

If the EPS is 7 bets, then:

DIPO Method	*Computation*	*Result*
Good Number	7 x 5	35
Bad Number	46 - 5	41

It is close, but not worth a call. Poor players repeatedly put themselves in a position where they are getting the worst of it by calling in spots like this. During a session in which this type of decision comes up a few times, the loss in edge may seem negligible if the player gets lucky and hits a couple of these draws. Over the long run, regularly staying in hands with negative EV is disastrous.

But if the EPS is 9 big bets, then:

DIPO Method	*Computation*	*Result*
Good Number	9 x 5	45
Bad Number	46 - 5	41

A call is correct, having positive value. The increase in the EPS has changed the correct decision from folding to calling.

The correct estimation of the number of outs is crucial. If the number of outs were 4, then with an EPS of 9, a call would not be good. If the number of outs were 6 instead of 5, then even if the EPS were only 7, a call would be worthwhile. To make good decisions in situations like this: be able to read your opponents' hands well so you can evaluate the number of outs you have, and know your opponents' playing habits so you can pinpoint the EPS.

Example 3

You are the cutoff with A♠K♠. Two players limp in front of you and you raise. Both blinds fold; but both limpers call. Going into the Flop there are three players and 4 big bets.

Your hand: A♠K♠
Flop: Q♠7♣3♦

The first player checks. The second player bets. You decide to call with your overcards. The first player folds. Going into the Turn there are two players and 5 big bets.

Turn: 2♦

You are sure you are beaten. The player who bet on the Flop is known to bet his hand and hardly ever bluff. He could have limped in with hands such as AQ, KQ, QJ, QT. There are no legitimate straight or flush draws, so he is unlikely to be bluffing. You suspect you need at least an A or a K to win the pot, and that may not even be good enough. With the chance that your opponent has AQ or KQ, an A or a K may give him two pair. You have 6 outs if your opponent does not hold an A or K kicker, or 3 outs if he has one of those cards. He could also have a set (three-of-a-kind with a pocket pair in his hand and the third card on the board), which would mean you have no outs and are drawing dead. Having already thought about situations like this previously, you estimate that your expected number of outs is 4.5. (More on this estimate below.)

Your opponent bets on the Turn, making the pot 6 big bets. If you hit your hand and win, you expect to win another big bet on the River for a total of 7 big bets.

DIPO Method	*Computation*	*Result*
Good Number	7 x 4.5	31.5
Bad Number	46 - 4.5	41.5

You decide to fold because you do not have the pot odds you need to call. If you were aggressive and estimated that you had 6 outs, then the Good Number would be greater than the Bad Number.

DIPO Method	*Computation*	*Result*
Good Number	7 x 6	42
Bad Number	46 - 6	40

With an estimate of 6 outs, you would think you had the pot odds to call. This shows how critical it is to be able to count the number of expected outs correctly. Doing so in this spot allows you to make the correct decision.

Why the estimate of 4.5 outs on average? The reason is that your opponent has about a 40% chance of having AQ or KQ, a 55% chance of QJ or QT and a 5% chance of a set. Given that you have AK and there is a Q on the board, there are three A's left and three Q's unaccounted for; thus there are nine ways for him to have AQ. Since you have the A♠ in your hand and the Q♠ is on the board, that leaves the following A's and Q's in the rest of the deck: A♣, A♦, A♥, Q♣, Q♦, Q♥. There are nine ways to get AQ with these cards: A♣Q♣, A♣Q♦, A♣Q♥, A♦Q♣, A♦Q♦, A♦Q♥, A♥Q♣, A♥Q♦, A♥Q♥. The same analysis can be used for KQ; it results in nine ways for KQ as well. Your opponent has a higher chance of having QJ or QT because you do not hold either the J or T. There are three Q's, four J's and four T's left; so there are 12 ways for him to have either QJ or QT. For your opponent to have a set he needs 77 or 33, for which there are three ways each.

You are not worried about a set of 2's since the 2 on the board did not show up until the Turn. You profile this opponent as conservative. A conservative player would not have bet pocket 2's on the Flop.

Hands	*Ways to Make*	*Fraction*	*Percentage*
AQ	9	9/48	19
KQ	9	9/48	19
QJ	12	12/48	25
QT	12	12/48	25
77	3	3/48	6
33	3	3/48	6

With those numbers, your opponent has a 38% chance to have AQ or KQ (19% + 19%), a 50% chance to have QJ or QT (25% + 25%), and a 12% chance to have 77 or 33 (6% + 6%). Most players with a set will check-raise, or wait until the Turn to raise, rather than bet into the field on the Flop. They are looking to trap other players, especially a late-position pre-Flop raiser. Therefore bump the estimate up to 40% for AQ or KQ and 55% for QJ or QT, and down to 5% for 77 or 33. In order to make these estimates, assume that this player is equally likely to limp in with AQ, KQ, QJ or QT. Tighter players are more likely to have AQ or KQ than QJ or QT.

If your opponent has AQ or KQ, then your AK hand has 3 outs. If he has QJ or QT, you have 6 outs. Against a set you have 0 outs. You can use an EV formula to calculate the number of outs you have.

Action	*Computation*	*Result*
Exp Outs	(40% x 3) + (55% x 6) + (5% x 0)	4.50 outs

On average, expect the number of outs to be 4.5 against the normal player. Coincidentally if you ignore the chance of being up against a set, 4.5 is exactly halfway between the optimistic view (6 outs) and the pessimistic view (3 outs). This is useful because in situations like this you can use the halfway point to estimate the number of outs you have; that is an easy process and yet should get you close to the right answer. Keep in mind that against tighter early-position players, the expected number of outs should be lower since they are less likely than an average player to limp in with QTo in this situation. If the player check-raises, then bump up the chance that he had a set. In both of these situations (a tight early-position player and a check-raiser), estimate 4 outs instead of 4.5 outs.

Using DIPO on the Flop

The chapter has discussed using DIPO on the Turn with one card still to come. Applying DIPO on the Flop is useful as well, although it is not as accurate. However the losses in accuracy are minuscule compared to the increase in effectiveness of DIPO over other methods. The times when DIPO might be slightly less accurate than the EV method are when the solutions are close to break-even. If you understand the issues and pitfalls of using DIPO on the Flop, its benefits outweigh the small loss in accuracy compared to the EV method.

When using DIPO on the Turn, look at the Turn/River dynamic. Consider the additional bets you expect to win on the River if you hit your hand; and consider the outs and non-outs with one card left to come. To use DIPO on the Flop, look at the Flop/Turn dynamic in the same way that you looked at the Turn/River dynamic on the Turn. Without thinking further ahead to the River, you keep the ease of use of DIPO without sacrificing much accuracy.

Issues to consider when using DIPO on the Flop

- Be careful when you count the number of outs. You could hit your out on the Turn and get redrawn on the River. For example you could complete a flush draw on the Turn only to see your opponent hit a full house on the River. This possibility means you should veer toward the conservative side when counting outs.
- Do not go further than the Turn when counting the EPS. It is easy to get carried away and count too many bets in the EPS if you extrapolate the hand all the way out to the River. If you catch your hand on the Turn and you bet accordingly: other players may fold, thus not paying you off on the River. Counting all the bets through to the River sometimes leads to decisions that are too aggressive.
- If you use DIPO on the Flop and miss, do not hesitate to use DIPO again on the Turn. Think of the chips you put into the pot on the Flop as a sunk cost. That money no longer belongs to you; it belongs to the pot.
- Think in terms of small bets on the Flop since that is usually the amount you have to put in to call. You must use the same unit bet size in the Good Number and the Bad Number in order to compare them correctly.

Example of using DIPO on the Flop

You and two other players remain in an unraised pot. You are on the button.

Your hand: 8♥7♥
Flop: A♥9♥2♠.

The first player bets and the other player folds. You have a flush draw;. Should you call?

Using the DIPO method and considering the Flop/Turn dynamic (and leaving out the River) gives the following:

- Outs: 9 outs for the flush. (You should err on the side of caution. Do not add in the other possible outs, such as runner-runner straights or two pair.)
- Non-outs: 38. (On the Flop there are 47 unknown cards as opposed to 46 on the Turn. 47 - 9 = 38.)
- Expected pot size: On the Flop there are four small bets. You expect to gain another 2 small bets on the Turn.
- Bet you must call: 1 small bet.

DIPO Method	*Computation*	*Result*
Good Number	6 small bets x 9	54
Bad Number	47 - 9	38

The Good Number is bigger than the Bad Number, so your hand is worth a call. Notice that you are using small bets for both the Good Number and the Bad Number, so they are comparable. If your flush does not come on the turn, go through the same analysis for the Turn/River dynamic.

This may be confusing because it seems that if you miss the flush on the Turn, you are putting in a total of 3 small bets (1 on the Flop and 2 on the Turn) to see an EPS of 8 small bets (4 on the Flop, another 2 on the Turn and 2 on the River). If you use these numbers, then the Good Number is lower than the Bad Number. The Good Number is 9 x 8 = 72. The Bad Number has to be multiplied by 3 small bets, making it 114. From this perspective it looks as though calling is not worthwhile.

The confusion is here: instead of having 9 outs, you have many more because if you do not hit the flush on the Turn, you could hit it on the River. You have the equivalent of about 16 outs, because you have two chances to hit. The way to get the equivalent of 16 outs is that you have a 9/47 chance of hitting the flush on the Turn. If you miss, which you will 38/47 of the time, you have a 9/46 chance of hitting it on the River. The math shows that you have a 35% chance of catching the flush either on the Turn or the River. That translates to about 16 outs (35% x 46 = 16.1). If you substitute 16 outs for 9 outs in the Good Number, the Good Number is 16 x 8 = 128, making it bigger than the Bad Number and showing the worth of calling the Flop and Turn. Doing it this way is more complicated. Look at the Flop/Turn dynamic first before going on to think about the River. Using the DIPO method for the Flop/Turn dynamic by itself is easier and is correct also.

Comparing this to an EV formula where you think through the Turn and River rounds, you get:

Action	*Computation*	*Result*
EV of calling (words)	(Prob hit Flush on Turn x EPS) + (Prob hit Flush on River x EPS) + (Prob of no Flush x 3 small bets)	N/A
EV of calling (numbers)	(9/47 x 8) + (38/47 x 9/46 x 8) + (38/47 x 37/46 x -3)	+0.85

There are rare cases (when the EV is close to zero) when using DIPO instead of the EV formula on the Flop results in different solutions. These mistakes are minor and should not happen often. They give reason for being conservative when counting outs on the Flop. The bottom line is that the ease of using DIPO on the Flop outweighs these small concerns.

DIPO on Flop, DIPO on Turn, Two Different Decisions

You have AKo (an A and a K of different suits) on the button. Everyone folds to you and you raise. Both blinds call. There are three players seeing the Flop for 6 small bets.

Your hand: AKo
Flop: Q-8-2 rainbow

The action is checked to you and you bet. The small blind check-raises and the big blind folds. The decision is whether to call or fold if you expect 4.5 outs on average (an estimate made in a similar problem earlier in this chapter). You expect that if you call and catch an A or K, your opponent will bet once. The EPS is 5.5 big bets or 11 small bets. (There were 6 small bets before the Flop. Your bet on the Flop made it 7 small bets. The check-raise made it 9 small bets. You expect to make another big bet on the Turn if you catch.)

DIPO Method	*Computation*	*Result*
Good Number	4.5 x 11	49.5
Bad Number	47 - 4.5	42.5

The Good Number is greater than the Bad Number; so calling is a good decision.

Turn: 6

A total blank. Your opponent bets again, making the pot 5.5 big bets. You suspect that if you catch your out on the River, you will win another big bet; so the EPS is 6.5. Now you should use big bets instead of small bets in the DIPO method, because now calling takes 1 big bet instead of 1 small bet.

DIPO Method	*Computation*	*Result*
Good Number	4.5 x 6.5	29.25
Bad Number	46 - 4.5	41.5

You should fold. The bet got too expensive compared to the pot size, making the pot no longer worth pursuing.

Myth: Never Draw to an Inside Straight

The common wisdom of "Never draw to an inside straight" may not be wise all the time. The following is an example of when drawing to an inside straight is correct.

Example

You are in the big blind and you have J♠T♠. The pot gets raised in early position and many other players cold-call the raise. You call the raise when it gets to you. A total of seven players see the Flop for 2 small bets each.

Your hand: J♠T♠
Flop: 8♣7♦3♠

You check. The pre-Flop raiser bets. Three players call. You call as well. Five players see the Turn with a total of 9.5 big bets in the pot.

Turn: A♥

You are sure that someone has either an A or a higher pair than J's; so you know the only card you can win on is a 9 to give you the nut straight. Since there are no flush possibilities, you do not need to be worried about hitting your straight and losing. You have 4 outs; any 9 gives you the nut hand. You check and the pre-Flop raiser bets. Everyone else folds. There are 10.5 big bets in the pot. If you hit the straight, you are likely to win another bet; so you estimate the EPS to be 11.5 big bets. There are four cards that give you the winner and a total of 42 cards that make you muck on the River.

DIPO Method	*Computation*	*Result*
Good Number	4 x 11.5	46
Bad Number	46 - 4	42

The DIPO method shows that the Good Number is greater than the Bad Number; so a call is worthwhile. The general advice to never draw to an inside straight is bad advice in this case.

When There is a Raise and More Than 1 Bet to Call

Instead of 1 bet, there are sometimes 2 bets to call on the Turn. This can happen if there is a bet from one player and a raise from another player. The number of bets can increase because other players can raise after you have called a bet. This discussion will focus on the situation when you know there are 2 bets.

The assumption in the DIPO method is that you have to call 1 bet. If there are 2 bets, then you need to make an adjustment by doubling the Bad Number. Only if the Good Number is greater than the doubled Bad Number are the pot odds good enough to justify a call. If you must call 3 bets to stay in the hand, multiply the Bad Number by 3 and make the same comparison versus the Good Number. If there is a bet and a raise, it may be prudent to adjust the number of possible outs you have, as two players are indicating they have strong hands.

Example

You are on the button with A♠K♣. By the Turn there are three spades on the board and you have the nut flush draw with your A♠.

Your hand: A♠K♣
Flop: J♠6♠2♠
Turn: 3♥

Given the betting pre-Flop and on the Flop, you are convinced you need to catch a spade on the River to win the hand. There are two other players left in the hand. From the betting you are sure one player has a flush already and the other player has a set. The player with the set is first to act, and bets. The player you suspect has a flush raises. Assume there are 14 big bets in the pot due to heavy betting pre-Flop and on the Flop. You expect the original bettor to call the raise. You expect to gain one additional big bet on the River if you catch your flush, as it will be obvious to the other players that you hold the A♠. With this information you calculate that the EPS will be 16 big bets if you win. Normally you would think you had 9 outs since there are nine flush cards left. But you suspect the raiser on the Turn already has two spades for a flush, leaving seven spades for 7 outs. You are sure the original bettor has a set; so the 3♠ is not an out for you since it would give him a full house. This reduces your outs to 6. There are normally 46 unknown cards on the Turn; but given your ability to pinpoint the other two players' hands, the number of unknown cards to you is 42. You have all the information to apply DIPO.

DIPO Method	*Computation*	*Result*
Good Number	16 x 6	96
Bad Number	Non-outs x Bets to Call = 36 x 2	72

The Good Number is larger than the Bad Number. It is worthwhile to call and hope a non-pairing spade comes on the River.

Observing Other Players While Counting the Pot

Use the DIPO method even when you are out of a hand. You can observe the actions of the other players to see if they have a good understanding of pot odds.

Example

Pre-Flop action

A passive player limps in middle position. The small blind completes. The big blind checks. Three players see the Flop for 1 bet each, bringing the pot to 1.5 big bets.

Flop action

Flop: K♣8♠5♦

Everybody checks.

Turn action

Turn: 2♥

Both blinds check and the passive player bets. The small blind folds and the big blind calls.

River action

River: A♦

Read my lips and eyes: this player gave himself away

I was playing in a friendly $20-$40 game in San Francisco when this situation came up. I was involved in a pot with a player I thought was decent and fairly tight. On the Turn I was in last position without a pair and I was a worried that the tight player had a pair. I knew that he thought I played a solid, tight game as well. This piece of information was crucial to the way I played the hand.

I held Q♠J♠. On the Turn the pot was relatively small, and the betting was relatively tame. The cards were:

My hand: Q♠J♠
Flop: K♣T♠7♣
Turn: 2♥

My opponent checked and I bet, hoping he would fold. And if he didn't, I had a chance of hitting my straight. Then I saw something interesting. He was staring at the pot; then his eyes started to dance around the table, and his lips were moving! It was obvious at that moment that he was counting the pot size, by backtracking the previous action and counting every bet that had gone in up to this point. After he was done, he called. Right there I knew he could only be on a draw, either a club flush draw or a straight draw. In either case I knew that if he did not catch his draw on the River, I could steal the pot with a bet, even if I had nothing.

A blank came on the River. He checked. I bet my no pair. He flashed me A♣J♦, grinned, and said: "I thought I had 7 outs. I can never hit against you" and mucked his hand. I smiled back at him, nodded my head and happily scooped in the pot. If he had not given away the fact that he was on a draw, I might have given up and checked, thinking he would call a River bet anyway. However once he gave himself away, I was confident the pot was mine. This hand illustrates how counting the pot size at the time you need the information may hurt you if others can detect that is what you are doing.

The big blind bets and the passive player calls. The big blind turns over 4♠3♠ for a straight. He picked up an open-ended straight draw on the Turn. He needed to hit the straight to have any chance of winning, because the passive player would not bet without a pair. The big blind should have counted 8 outs and 38 non-outs going into the River. There were 1.5 big bets going into the Turn; and the bet by the passive player made it 2.5 big bets. The big blind, expecting the passive player to call a bet on the River, should have estimated the EPS at 3.5 big bets.

DIPO Method	*Computation*	*Result*
Good Number	8 x 3.5	28
Bad Number	46 - 8	38

The big blind's call on the Turn had a negative expectation. Knowing that might allow you to revise your opinion of this person as a poker player.

More on Pot Odds

In lower limits the pot usually has more big bets since more players are seeing the Flop, making it usually correct to go for flush draws and open-ended or double inside straight draws. (Inside straight draws need to be careful.) Without knowing the size of the pot or the pot odds, most low-limit players make these decisions correctly because the pot almost always affords them enough to call. They have not done the math to figure out the odds; but they have a sense that it is correct to chase. With overcards or other hands that are behind, it is unclear whether chasing is a correct decision. That is when these players make mistakes. Because they play such hands incorrectly, it is difficult for winning lower-limit players to win at a higher limit, where the pot is usually smaller and it is less often correct to chase.

In middle- and high-limit games, going for straight or flush draws regardless of pot size is a problem. If you are counting the pot size and notice a player drawing on the River without having correct odds, you have discovered a weakness in that player's game.

DIPO works better when you are *closing the betting*, meaning you are the last to act on that specific round and no one can raise after you have called. If there is another player behind you, and a player in front of you has bet, your pot odds calculations may be off because the player behind you may raise. You are expecting to put in 1 bet. If a player behind you raises, then you will have to put in an additional bet to see the next card.

When the pot is large, the risk of raising and putting in more bets is compensated for by the increase in EV after an opponent who had outs folds. If the pot is small, the risk of putting in more bets may not be compensated for adequately by the increased chance that others will fold.

If you are drawing to the nut flush or the nut straight, you can usually assume that you will have the best hand if you hit your draw, with a few exceptions. But if your draw is not to the nut flush or the nut straight, then decrease the number of outs you have estimated in case someone else hits a higher flush or straight when you hit yours. This is more likely to happen when there are three to a flush on the board and you hold one card of that suit in your hand.

When you are ahead

What about when you are ahead and your opponent is on a flush draw? Then you have 37 outs and 9 non-outs on the Turn, as any card that does not make a flush for your opponent keeps you ahead. You don't need information on the exact numbers of outs and pot odds if you are ahead, since it is clear you should be involved in the pot.

Analysis of thinking in reverse may be useful when you can control how much your opponent has to put into the pot to see the River card, as you can in No-Limit Hold'em and Pot-Limit Hold'em. In Limit Hold'-em the bet size is fixed and you have little control over the number of bets your opponent makes, so you have little control over the pot odds he faces. In No-Limit Hold'em and Pot-Limit Hold'em you can manipulate the pot odds; for example you could bet enough to force a flush draw to fold.

When you are ahead on the Flop, and then fall behind on the Turn

There are situations where you are ahead on the Flop, fall behind on the Turn, and have a chance to catch up on the River. A typical situation occurs when you flop two pair and your opponent picks up a straight or flush on the Turn, but you have a chance to pick up a full house on the River. Depending on how sure you are that your opponent has a straight or flush, you may need to fold on the Turn and forgo your draw for the full house.

If you have two pair against a straight or flush, then you have 4 outs. You need the EPS to be greater than 11 big bets in order for a call to be correct. Almost every player calls in this spot in the hopes of catching a full house. When you are 100% sure your opponent has a straight or flush, a fold is correct if the EPS is less than 11. However what if you are only 90% sure your opponent has a straight or a flush? What if there is a chance your opponent has top pair or a lower two pair than yours? In that case you have 10% chance of being ahead. Your opponent has maybe 4 outs against you, which means you have 40 outs. Using those probabilities, you have 7.6 expected outs as the equation below shows.

Action	*Computation*	*Result*
Expected Outs (words)	(Outs when ahead x Percentage ahead) + (Outs when behind x Percentage behind)	N/A
Expected Outs (numbers)	(40 x 10%) + (4 x 90%)	7.6

With these assumptions you need the EPS to be bigger than 6 for a call. It is not unusual for a pot to be bigger than 6 big bets. Although most people do not think in these terms when they have two pair after the Turn, their call against a possible straight may be correct if the opponent could be bluffing, semi-bluffing, or playing a worse hand.

Quiz: Pot Odds

Question 1. Exposed hand

You are on the button, with A♠K♠. There is one limper in middle position. You raise. Both blinds and the limper call. There are four players seeing the Flop and the pot is 4 big bets.

Your hand: A♠K♠
Flop: A♦J♥6♠

Everyone checks to you and you bet. Two players call. There are three players seeing the Turn and the pot is 5.5 big bets.

Turn: 5♣

The first player bets and is all-in. The second player folds, making it heads-up. Before you act, the first player exposes his cards and shows 6♣5♠ for two pair and says: "Look, I know you have AK. I have two pair. I have you beaten. I just put in all my chips and I don't want to suffer another bad beat. I'm having a bad night. Just fold and give me the pot."

Question

Should you call or fold?

Answer

Once the first player has bet on the Turn, there are 6.5 big bets in the pot. You count your outs, which are any A, K, or J's. (A J would give you two pair, A's and J's, which is better than your opponent's two pair of J's and 6's.) There are two A's left, three K's left and three J's left, for a total of eight cards. You can see eight of the cards (your two cards, the first player's two cards and the board's four cards), which means there are 44 unknown cards left. Eight of those cards give you a winner; the other 36 give you a loser.

DIPO Method	*Computation*	*Result*
Good Number	8 x 6.5	52
Bad Number	44 - 8	36

The Good Number is greater than the Bad Number, so there is value in calling. You should say to the first player: "Sorry buddy, but I gotta see the River," throw your chips in and hope for the best.

Question 2. The Turn

It is the Turn with four players still in.

Your hand: A♠2♠
Board: K♠J♠4♣3♦

There are 5 big bets in the pot. The first player bets. The second player raises. The third player folds. Neither remaining player has impressed you as a maniac, so you suspect that both their hands are legitimate. The first player's demeanor tells you she is going to call and not reraise. You are sure you will lose if a pair comes on the River, as one of your opponents will make a full house. You expect to get at least one caller on the River, and if you are lucky, perhaps two callers for multiple bets.

Question

Should you call?

Answer

You have 7 outs for a flush. Two spades pair the board and give someone a full house, so those are not outs. You also have 3 outs to make a straight; the fourth 5 is a spade, which you have already counted. That makes a total of 10 outs. At the moment the pot contains 8 big bets and you expect the initial Turn bettor to call, making it 9 big bets before the River. If you hit your draw, you expect to win at least 1 more big bet.

DIPO Method	*Computation*	*Result*
Good Number	10 x 10	100
Bad Number	(46 - 10) x 2	72

The Good Number is higher than the Bad Number, so you should call.

Question 3. You are in the big blind

You are in the big blind with four other players left on the Turn. There are 5 big bets in the pot before the betting on the Turn

Your hand: K♠Q♣
Board: A♣Q♠T♣3♠

The small blind bets and it is up to you to act.

Question

Should you call?

Answer

The most aggressive way to approach this problem is to assume you have 6 outs (two Q's for trips and four J's for straights). However there are ways you can lose if you hit one of these cards. There are two flush draws on the board. Someone could already have a straight. Someone could hit a full house if you hit trip Q's. There are two cards, J♦ and J♥, that would give you the nut hand. There are 6 big bets and you can probably get more bets if you hit your hand. There are two players left to act. If you call, one of your opponents could raise, making you put in another big bet to see the River. With the most aggressive numbers, 6 outs, an EPS of 8 big bets, and no raises behind you, DIPO looks like this:

DIPO Method	*Computation*	*Result*
Good Number	6 x 8	48
Bad Number	46 - 6	40

That result indicates you should call. However that result is based on aggressive assumptions. It would be more realistic to adjust your outs downward and allow for the possibility that you may have to put in more than 1 bet. More realistic estimates might be 4 outs and having to put in 1.5 big bets, which means a player behind you has a 50% chance of raising. With these variables you can increase the EPS since another player appears to be in for the ride if you do hit your hand. With realistic assumptions, the hand is clearly a fold.

DIPO Method	*Computation*	*Result*
Good Number	4 x 10	40
Bad Number	40 x 1.5	60

Question 4. T♣3♣ in the big blind

The following problem was presented in the quiz section of Chapter 4 "Outs." You have T♣3♣ in the big blind. There is one limper. The small blind calls. You check.

Your hand: T♣3♣
Flop: J♣6♦2♠

Everyone checks on the Flop.

Turn: 4♣

The Turn gives you a flush draw and an inside straight draw. The small blind bets out; and you are sure he has at least a pair of J's. How many outs do you estimate you have?

Question

Should you call?

Answer

The answer to the number of outs is 12 (see the answer in the quiz section of Chapter 4). There were 1.5 big bets in the pre-Flop round and no bets on the Flop. On the Turn the small blind made 1 big bet. If you expect he will call on the River, then you can expect 3.5 big bets.

DIPO Method	*Computation*	*Result*
Good Number	12 x 3.5	42
Bad Number	46 - 12	34

This may look as though it is worth a call. However if the small blind is 50% to call your bet on the River, then it becomes closer.

DIPO Method	*Computation*	*Result*
Good Number	12 x 3	36
Bad Number	46 - 12	34

It is close, but worth a call.

CHAPTER 6
POSITION

Hold'em is a fixed-position game. With the exception of the blinds in the pre-Flop round, the early-position players have to act first in every round. Before the late-position players have to act, they are able to see the actions of the players in early and middle position. This information is valuable; and good players use it to their advantage. Good players play the same cards differently in different positions, whereas bad players ignore their positional advantages or disadvantages and play the same cards the same way regardless of their position.

The Value of Position

Suppose you have a mediocre hand. You are the second player to act and there are four players left in the hand. If the first player bets, you are in a bind. You do not know if a player after you will raise, call or fold. You are not sure of the expected pot size or how much it will cost to see the next card. You may think your hand is strong enough to play against the first player and 1 bet, but not against two players and a raise. If you know a player behind you was planning to raise, you may fold as you do not want to stay in for 2 bets. Without knowing what the plans of the players behind you are, your decision is tough. On the other hand if you are the fourth and last player to act in the hand, you have a better idea of how to proceed. You will have seen the second and third players act. If they both fold, you know there cannot be a raise behind you as no one

Table 8
Pre-Flop Positions, Seven Players Min

No. of Players	*7*	*8*	*9*	*10*
Blinds	1, 2	1, 2	1, 2	1, 2
Early Position (including under the gun)	3, 4	3, 4	3, 4, 5	3, 4, 5
Middle Position	5	5, 6	6, 7	6, 7, (8)
Late Position (including the cutoff and the button)	6, 7	7, 8	8, 9	(8), 9, 10

can act after you act. If either the second or third player raises, then you can fold since you would prefer not to see the next card for 2 bets. Being the last to act allows you to gather more information before acting.

General Positions in a Full Game

Table 8 shows the positions of each player pre-Flop in seven-handed to ten-handed games. (Shorthanded games are treated in Chapters 17 and 18.) The numbers in the table refer to the positions of the players. 1 means the player is first to act; 2 means second to act; etc.

Note: The eighth player in a ten-handed game could be considered in middle position or late position, depending on how aggressive and loose the ninth and tenth players play.

In Chapter 12 "Starting Hands," position with regard to the pre-Flop round is discussed in detail. Throughout the rest of the book, the advantages and disadvantages of different positions are discussed as they pertain to the issue at hand. Following are general comments on the different positions.

Early position: the small blind, the big blind and the player under the gun

Players in early position are at a positional disadvantage because they have less information about the quality of the other players' hands before betting; and they are likely to be at a positional disadvantage throughout the whole hand. Players in early position must be more selective with starting hands. In the later rounds, early-position players are more exposed to strategies being used against them, such as semi-bluffing, raising for free cards and raising for a free showdown. These strategies can be used only on players who act ahead of you.

The blinds have the benefit of seeing everyone act before they have to act in the pre-Flop round; but they have the disadvantage of having to act first in all subsequent rounds, as well as being required to put money into the pot before the cards are dealt. Many players call a raise from the blind position in the pre-Flop round because they believe they are already partially invested. This thinking is flawed. The chips they have put up as their blinds are a sunk cost, and should be thought of as part of the pot. The old adage about throwing good money after bad applies here. Base your decisions on the chips that are going to go from your stack into the pot. Treat the chips that you have already put into the pot as part of the pot, and not as part of your bet.

The small blind is at a positional disadvantage to all other players. If everyone folds to the blinds, then the small blind is at a significant disadvantage to the big blind. The big blind can often call a raise with mediocre cards. The small blind cannot do that, due to having to put in more money than the big blind; and the big blind is getting better odds. When any player other than the small blind raises, the big blind is getting at least 3.5 to 1 to call (1 small bet from the big blind, 2 small bets from the raiser, and a minimum of half of a small bet from the small blind). If there are other players involved in the hand, then the big blind has greater odds to call. The small blind, however, has to act before the big blind. The small blind has to put in 1.5 small bets to see a raise, and has to act without knowing what the big blind will do. If the big blind folds after the small blind calls the raise, then the small blind was calling with odds of 3.5 to 1.5 (2.33 to 1). These odds are worse than the big blind's. If the big blind calls after the small blind, then the small blind is getting odds of 3 to 1. By calling, the small blind is offering the big blind 5 to 1 to see the Flop.

If there are many players who have invested 2 bets, then there is a smaller difference between the small blind's position and the big blind's. When the hand looks as though it will be contested by two or three players, the small blind's position is weak compared to the big blind's. This is more relevant in shorthanded games, and is discussed in further detail in later chapters.

The big blind has better reasons to call a raise and see the Flop than the small blind has. As mentioned previously, if there is only one raise: the big blind is getting 3.5 to 1 or better to see the Flop. The big blind can play hands such as 98s or 76s that other positions should not. The big blind's poor position after the Flop can be enough to negate the advantage of having to put in only 1 more small bet to see the Flop after a raise. For example a tight early-position player raises and the big blind holds a hand such as A9o. Since many players raise with hands like AK or AQ, an A hitting the board is not necessarily good for the big blind. A hand like JTs has more drawing possibilities and may be better than a hand like A9o. A drawing hand like JTs matches up better against AK than A9o would.

Even though players in early position are at a positional disadvantage, there are strategies they can use due to their position that other positions cannot. One of those strategies is check-raising. An early-position player can check-raise to get more money into the pot or to try to knock out players if it is a late-position player who makes the initial bet on the Flop. Since the check-raise is one of the few advantages that early-position players enjoy, they should use it often when they think they have the best hand and there is evidence that a player in late position will bet if checked to.

The first player to act also has first chance to bluff into the pot on a later round in a hand where all the other players have shown weakness.

Example

Two limpers call. The small blind folds. You check in the big blind.

Your hand in the big blind: T3o
Flop: Q-5-2 rainbow

Everyone checks on the Flop.

Turn: 5

You have a nice opportunity to be the first player to bluff into the pot. Unless one of the other players was slowplaying his hand on the pre-Flop round or the Flop, being the first to bluff has value.

Middle position

Middle-position players have some of the disadvantages of the early-position players and some of the advantages of the late-position players. Middle-position players can see the actions of the early-position players, but have a few players behind them yet to act. In the pre-Flop round, middle-position players can open-raise with a few more hands than early-position players can, since there is a smaller chance that a player in a later position has a better hand (because there are fewer players in a later position); but their list of raisable hands cannot be expanded much beyond that of the early-position players.

After the Flop the relative position of the middle-position player is the most prone to change. If a middle-position player raised pre-Flop and everybody behind him folded, but one or both of the blinds call, then the middle-position player is last to act in all subsequent rounds. On the other hand if the only player to stay in the hand with the middle-position player is a late-position player, then the middle-position player is first to act after the Flop. A player's position may not be static throughout a hand; and this affects the middle-position player most.

Late position: the cutoff and the button

The button is the last to act on all rounds with the exception of the pre-Flop round. The button has the greatest positional advantage of any player at the table, seeing how everyone else acts before having to act. The cutoff player is to the right of the button. If the button folds, then the cutoff becomes the "button" in the sense of being last to act on all subsequent rounds. Any player who becomes last to act on the Flop and beyond becomes the de facto button.

Players in late position have the best chance to apply the strategy of raising for free cards, since they have the option to check on the Turn when acting last. A player in early position would have to act first on the next round, so that strategy would not have the same effect. Players in late position can also apply the free showdown semi-bluff raise. This strategy is a raise on the Turn with the intention of checking on the River and showing down the hand if it does not improve, but betting if it does improve. These strategies are discussed in later chapters of this book.

The Value of Acting Last

The value of any position is tough to determine. Simulations against reliable opponents can provide estimations. It is possible to see the value of position without a simulation by using a sample hand against a simple opponent. Here is an example.

Your hand: T9s
Board: T-8-5-3-Q rainbow

Assume your opponent is loose and passive. Such an opponent normally will not bet except with a strong hand, in which case he usually beats you. Since he is loose, he is willing to call with many hands that others would raise or fold. When you have a better hand, you will win money because he will call.

You are not sure whether you have the better hand since this opponent would play in the same passive manner with a bad hand as with a pair of T's with a better kicker than you have.

Though your opponent is passive, you can count on him to bet if he caught something good on the River. In this hand you can count on him to bet if he caught a straight or a top pair of Q's. Assume he will not check-raise.

If your opponent did not improve on the River, then it does not matter in this hand whether you act first or last.

If your opponent caught a straight or a top pair of Q's on the River....

....and you act first, then you have to bet because he will call with worse hands as well. He is more likely to have a worse hand than a better hand.

....and you act last, then you have the opportunity to see what he does first. If he bets, you can fold and save a bet that you would have lost had you acted first.

Here are hypothetical percentages for the types of hands your opponent might have.

25%: A missed draw
50%: A worse hand than yours, but strong enough to call a bet
12.5%: A slightly better hand than yours
12.5%: A much better hand than yours

If he has a much better hand than yours, such as J9 for the straight, he will happily bet or raise. If he has a slightly better hand than yours, such as JT, he will check or call.

Here is a table that shows how much you will win or lose on the River when you act first and when you act last.

Opponent's Hand	*Prob.*	*You Act First*	*You Act Last*
A missed draw	25%	0	0
A worse hand than yours	50%	1	1
Slightly better hand	12.5%	-1	-1
Much better hand	12.5%	-1	0

If your opponent bets on the River, fold; you are not worried about a bluff.

If your opponent checks on the River, bet. The probability he has a worse hand than yours is greater than the probability he has a better hand.

If your opponent has a much better hand than yours, it is because the River card improved his hand to either a straight, two pair or a top pair of Q's.

With these assumptions you can quantify the value of your position in this hand.

EV when you act first: (25% x 0) + (50% x 1) + (12.5% x -1) + (12.5% x -1) = +0.25

EV when you act last: (25% x 0) + (50% x 1) + (12.5% x-1) + (12.5% x 0) = +0.375

The value of acting last in this hand is worth 0.125 big bets (0.375 - 0.25). Situations like this occur frequently. Gaining an extra 0.125 big bets here and there adds up.

Decision making is easier when you act last than when you act first. You have more information when you act last. The advantage in acting last is present in all hands. The strategy of check-raising can reduce that positional advantage somewhat.

More on Position

Position can change from round to round

Positional advantage can change on any single round. Suppose you are first to act on the Turn and three other players are still around. You decide to check a mediocre hand, and the next player bets. If there are no raises, then when the action gets back to you, you have perfect information about that round. There cannot be a raise after you. You have given yourself a positional advantage, the value of which depends on your cards, the board, the players and the situation. Nevertheless your position on this round is stronger than that of the third-position player, who must act before the other players. If you suspect that a player who acts after you will bet, then you may be able to use that information by gaining positional advantage on that round. (You will revert back to early position in the next round.)

Position can be relative

A player's position is relative to the other players. If you raise in the under-the-gun position and everyone folds except the blinds, you are in last position relative to the other players and you have the same positional advantage that you would have on the button. If you raise in middle position and two players in late position call, then you are in relatively early position because you act first on future rounds.

The importance of position when dealing with pot odds

Chapter 5 "Pot Odds" showed why there is value to being the player to close the betting. The number of bets you have to put into the pot cannot increase after the last player has acted. If there are 10 big bets in the pot and you are last to act, then you know you are getting 10:1 pot odds to call. Being in a later position relative to the bettor means being more sure of the pot odds.

A player after you might raise after you call; then if you want to continue with the hand, you have to put an additional bet into the pot. That affects your estimate of the number of bets you have to put into the pot and whether you have the pot odds you need to call. In an early position you can be surprised to end up with pot odds that are lower than you thought they would be.

CHAPTER 7
RAISING FOR FREE CARDS

Raising for a free card is a strategy used by a late-position player on the Flop to show strength when on a draw.[a] When the strategy works, the early-position players check to the late-position player on the Turn. Then you as late-position player can choose to bet if you have made your draw or check if you have not, thereby gaining a free card. (You may choose to bet again if you have not made your draw, but that bet on the Turn would be considered a semi-bluff.) Also there is the added value of the possibility that the early-position players will fold to a raise on the Flop.

Example of raising for a free card on the Flop with a flush draw

Your hand: 4 ♦3 ♦
Your opponent's hand: T ♥9 ♥
Flop: K ♦9 ♦5♣

[a] The assumption in this book is that the bet doubles on the Turn. In games where the bet remains the same on the Turn, the strategy of raising for a free card is not applicable.

There are two players left on the Flop. Your opponent acts first and bets with the middle pair of 9's. You raise with a diamond flush draw and your opponent calls. You have 9 outs to make a flush.

Turn: 8♠

Your opponent checks, thinking his middle pair is not the better hand after you raised on the Flop. You do not have anything yet, and are hoping to catch the flush; so you check. (If your opponent is weak and you think he might fold a middle pair, you should bet as a semi-bluff.) The Turn is your "free card," since you do not have to put in a bet though you are behind. By raising on the Flop, you used a small bet to convince your opponent to check on the Turn. If your opponent had bet on the Turn, it would have forced you to put in a big bet to see if you could catch a flush on the River. Not having to put in a bet on the Turn is helpful if the flush does not come. If the flush does come on the Turn, you can bet after your opponent checks.

If there is a chance your opponent will fold to a raise on the Flop, then there is added value in raising for a free card. But if your opponent does not fold on the Flop after you raise, then raising for a free card does not change the probability that you will win the hand; it changes the amount that you win or lose. Assuming your free-card raising strategy goes as planned and your opponent does not fold, you win 1 small bet more if a flush card comes on the Turn. If the flush comes on the River instead, then you win 1 small bet less. If it doesn't come at all, then you lose 1 small bet less. If your opponent cooperates by checking the Turn after you raise the Flop, then the expected value (EV) of raising is greater than the EV of calling when you have a flush draw.

Following is a chart showing the results of raising or calling on the Flop, depending on when the flush comes. The amount won or lost is in terms of big bets and counts the bets from the Flop through the River. This chart assumes:

- You are against one opponent.
- If you raise: your opponent calls your raise on the Flop and checks to you on the Turn.
- If you call: your opponent keeps betting until a third flush card comes, and then checks with the intention of calling if you bet.

When Flush Comes	*Probability*	*Expected W/L if you Raised on the Flop*	*Expected W/L if you Called on the Flop*
Turn	19.15%	+3[a]	+2.5[d]
River	15.82%	+2[b]	+2.5[d]
Never	65.03%	-1[c]	-1.5[e]
EV		+0.24[f] big bets	-0.10[g] big bets

NOTES:

[a] 2 small bets on the Flop, 1 big bet on the Turn, 1 big bet on the River—total 3 big bets

[b] 2 small bets on the Flop, 0 big bet on the Turn, 1 big bet on the River—total 2 big bets

[c] 2 small bets on the Flop, 0 big bet on the Turn, 0 big bet on the River—total 1 big bet

[d] 1 small bet on the Flop, 1 big bet on the Turn, 1 big bet on the River—total 2.5 big bets

[e] 1 small bet on the Flop, 1 big bet on the Turn, 0 big bet on the River—total 1.5 big bets

[f] EV of Raising = (19.15% x 3 + 15.82% x 2 + 65.03% x -1) = 0.24

[g] EV of Raising = (19.15% x 2.5 + 15.82% x 2.5 + 65.03% x -1.5) = -0.10

Against an opponent who plays into your hands, the EV of raising on the Flop is +0.24 big bets ($9.60 in a $20-$40 game). The EV of calling is -0.10 big bets (-$4.00 in a $20-$40 game), a difference of 0.34 big bets. The negative EV of calling does not tell the whole story. Only the amount won or lost on the Flop and after is counted in this chart. If the previous bets were added in, then calling and raising would both have positive EV. If the pot size after your opponent has bet on the Flop is 5 big bets, then the EV difference is +0.34 big bets (+1.99 for raising versus +1.65 for calling). In comparing the EV of raising and the EV of calling, the pot size previous to the bets on the Flop is not relevant. If the opponent plays the same way regardless of the pot size, the EV of raising with a flush draw is exactly +0.34 big bets greater than the EV of calling. If the pot size is 100 big bets, then the EV difference is also +.34 big bets

(+35.21 and +34.87). The pot size is not the key variable to this strategy; the key variable is how your opponent acts.

A passive opponent then checks on the Turn, giving you the free card. A more aggressive opponent may reraise on the Flop or bet out on the Turn; and that could change the value of raising for a free card. These counter-strategies to the free-card raise are discussed in the next section.

Counter-Strategies to the Free-Card Raise

Although raising for a free card is a powerful strategy, there are counter-strategies. A sharp player who can detect an opponent's free-card raise can use these counter-strategies to thwart that plan. The following are counter-strategies against the free-card raise. The late-position player is denoted as LP and the early-position player is denoted as EP.

1. Reraising on the Flop

If there is a draw on the Flop and you are sure the LP is a player who will raise with a draw to get a free card, then consider reraising on the Flop. This thwarts the free-card strategy, as it makes the free-card raiser put in more bets. Instead of the card being free, it's expensive for the LP.

2. Betting on the River after the free-card raiser has checked on the Turn.

If the LP checks on the Turn after she does not catch her draw, then it is easy for the EP to see that the LP was on a draw after she raised on the Flop. As a counter-strategy, the EP can bet on the River if it does not look as though the River card filled a draw. If the EP was on a draw himself, he can bet out with nothing and win the pot because the LP has a busted draw. On the other hand if the EP has a made hand, he can check and hope the LP bluffs, since he thinks the LP will not call a bet. If it looks as though the River completes a draw, then the EP can have more confidence that he is beaten, and can check with the possible intention of folding.

Type of Draw by LP	*Outs*	*EV of Free-card Raise when EP Checks on Turn*	*EP Bets on Turn*	*EV Calling on Flop*	*BE Pt* [a] *for Raise*
Flush	9	+1.99	+1.50	+1.65	69.5%
Straight	8	+1.69	+1.15	+1.33	65.7%
Overcards	6	+1.06	+0.41	+0.67	59.9%
Lower Split Pair	5	+0.73	+0.04	+0.33	57.6%

[a] The break-even point for raising is the probability of the EP betting on the Turn that would make the EV of a free-card raise the same as the EV of calling. It assumes the EP has a better hand and the LP raised on the Flop.

3. Betting out on the Turn

After the LP raises on the Flop, the EP can bet out on the Turn and force her to put in more chips than she was hoping to. There is value for the EP in waiting until the Turn to bet instead of reraising on the Flop because he can see if a dangerous card has come on the Turn.

There can be value for the LP in raising for a free card, depending on how likely the EP is to employ the counter-strategy of betting on the Turn. The value to the LP of raising for a free card is determined by how often an EP with the better hand bets out on the Turn after the LP raised on the Flop. If the EP bets on the Turn all the time, then the LP's free-card raise strategy will backfire. If the EP never bets out on the Turn, then the LP's strategy will work. The chart above shows how often the EP has to bet out as a percentage in the Break-even Point column. The break-even point is determined by the number of outs the LP is drawing to. The fewer outs the LP has, the lower the break-even point. The chart assumes the pot size was 5 big bets before the LP raised on the Flop.

The EV of the free-card raise depends on the frequency with which an EP with the better hand bets on the Turn. The chart above shows that if the EP always checks on the Turn after the LP raises for a free card on the Flop, then the EV of raising for a free card is significantly higher than the EV of calling. For example if the LP has a straight draw with 8 outs, the EV of a free-card raise if the EP always checks on the Turn is +1.69. If the LP calls on the Flop, then her EV is +1.33. In that case a free-card raise has gained the LP +0.36. This is true in all situations, no matter the type of draw by the LP, although the value of raising for a free card varies depending on the number of outs the LP has.

If an EP with the better hand can play back and bets out on the Turn, then the EV of the free-card raise for the LP is lower than the EV of calling on the Flop. For example if the LP has a flush draw with 9 outs, the EV of the LP's free-card raise if the EP bets on the Turn is +1.50. If the LP calls on the Flop, then her EV is +1.65. In that case a free-card raise is worse by 0.15. The value of raising for a free card is based partially on the EP's aggressiveness.

The EP's aggressiveness can be expressed as the probability that he will bet on the Turn with the better hand after being raised on the Flop. The break-even point is shown on the chart. For example if the LP raised on the Flop for a free card with a flush draw, the EP has to be willing to bet on the Turn with a better hand less than 69.5% of the time for the LP's free-card raise to be a better option than calling on the Flop. The chart shows that the fewer outs there are, the lower that break-even point needs to be. With fewer outs for the LP, the EP does not have to be as aggressive on the Turn to thwart the plan of the free-card raise.

Key Points on Raising for a Free Card

There are a few key points to consider regarding raising for a free card. You should use the free-card raise less often against aggressive players than passive players. Passive players check on the Turn more often, giving you the benefit of raising for a free card. Aggressive players bet on the Turn more often and make your free-card raise backfire.

For "advertising" value it can be useful to raise for a free card against observant, aggressive players if you play against them regularly. An observant, aggressive opponent who thinks you will raise for a free card will play back against you as she would against anybody else in that situation. You should use that information and raise her when you have a made hand but it looks as though your raise was a free-card raise (such as when there are two cards of the same suit on the Flop). If you never raise for a free card against her, then she may not play back at you when you have a made hand because she may think your raise is more likely to be with a made hand than a draw. You may be giving up a bit of edge when you raise for a free card. You will be able to gain that edge (and hopefully more) back against her during the hands when you are raising with a made hand.

Against an aggressive player in EP who may think you are raising with a draw, you should play aggressively when you have a made hand in LP. The aggressive EP plays back at you, thinking you are on a draw. When you have a made hand, you can win more bets from a player in EP who reacts aggressively to your raise.

Against players in LP who are constantly raising for free cards on the Flop and then checking on the Turn when they have not made their draw yet, you should bet on the Turn more often.

Against aggressive players in LP who are raising for free cards on the Flop and continuing with semi-bluffs on the Turn, you can wait for the Turn to check-raise them.

Straight Draw Free-Card Raises

With open-ended or double inside straight draws on the Flop, a raise in late position has the same benefits as a free-card raise with a flush draw. It also has the added benefit of deception because straight draws are more difficult to read than flush draws. (This is discussed further in the section titled Reading Straight Draws in Chapter 16 "Reading Hands.") This play is especially useful when there are two cards to a flush on the Flop. A flush card on the Turn or River may scare your opponents since your actions up to that point have been consistent with a player holding a flush draw. Thus you may have an easier time in bluffing.

Example

Your hand: J♠T♠
Flop: 9♥8♥2♣

You have an open-ended straight draw, but there are two hearts on the board. A raise in late position may look like a raise for a free card with a flush draw. If a straight card that is not a heart comes on the Turn or the River, it is more difficult for your opponents to see that you have made your draw. You could win an extra bet that you might not have if there had not been a flush draw possibility. If you do not catch the straight, but a third flush card comes on the Turn or the River, you may have an easier time bluffing against perceptive players. They are more likely to give you credit for catching the flush draw, given your play up to that point.

Overcard Free-Card Raises

There are two situations where you might raise with overcards on the Flop. The first is when there is a chance that you can win the pot with a raise on the Flop. Most players do not fold to a raise on the Flop after they have bet; so do not count on this happening often. The second situation is when the pot is relatively big, and a raise to get a free card may have value. With overcards to the board you have at most 6 outs against an opponent who has a pair. If your opponent has two pair or better, then your overcards give you close to 0 outs. (A runner-runner draw is your only out.) If you have 9 or 8 outs, the pot odds usually are high enough to justify staying to the River to see if you make the draw; but 6 outs might not be enough. This is why the pot needs to be bigger for a free-card raise with overcards.

Example

You have A♣K♣ in last position. Two players limp. You raise. Both blinds and both limpers call. Five players see the Flop for 5 big bets.

Your Hand: A♣K♣
Flop: J♦8♠3♥

The first player checks and the second player bets. The other players fold. You may consider raising since the pot is relatively big. It is worthwhile to stay in the hand and see if an A or K comes on the Turn. A raise may give you a chance for a free card and let you see the Turn and River for 1 more small bet. Your raises pre-Flop and on the Flop tell the rest of the table that you have a premium hand such as AA or KK. Getting reraised usually means your opponent is not worried about playing against an overpair; he is more likely to have two pair, trips, or a premium pair.

Raising into Multiple Opponents

If you flop a drawing hand (especially if it is the nut drawing hand) in a multiple player pot and another player seems to have a solid made hand, raising is questionable. You should avoid raising if it makes everyone fold except for the player with the solid made hand, thus changing the pot from multiple player into heads-up. Your chance of hitting your draw remains the same whether you are playing against multiple players or only the solid made hand. Since the solid made hand is likely to stay in through the River and cannot be bluffed out, you must hit your draw in order to win the hand. You want as many players in the pot as possible so you can win more by hitting your draw. A raise on the Flop that scares out all other opponents except the solid made hand would defeat that purpose. On the other hand the player with the solid made hand would be happy to reraise your raise in the hopes that everyone else will fold, because her equity increases when others fold.

Example

Flop: J♣ 9♠ 3♣
Your hand: A♣ 4♣ (nut flush draw)
Solid made hand: K♦ K♠ (overpair)
Third hand: J♥T♥ (top split pair, with runner-runner straight draw)

Hand	*A*	*B*
A♣ 4♣	46.2%	46.3%
K♦ K♠	39.1%	53.7%
J♥T♥	14.7%	N/A

Column A shows the likelihood of the hand winning if all three hands stay in through the River. Column B shows the likelihood of the hand winning if J♥T♥ folds after your raise. The numbers come from twodimes.net.

If the J♥T♥ folds due to your raise, the K♦K♠ benefits by "eating up" the J♥T♥'s equity. The K♦K♠'s chance of winning the pot increases from 39.1% to 53.7%, while your nut flush draw increases by a mere 0.1%. Your drawing hand did not increase its chance of winning the hand. With the third player folding, you will win a smaller pot if you do win.

If you are confident the third player will call a raise, then raising is worthwhile as you are getting 2:1 with a hand that wins 46% of the time.

More Flush Draw Free-Card Game Theory

If your early-position opponents can play back at you after you raise for a free card, then it may be useful to raise in situations where it looks like you might be going for a free card when you are not, such as when there are two cards to a flush on the board and you have a made hand such as trips, top pair, two pair or an overpair. Consider raising on the Flop instead of waiting to raise on the Turn, to cause sharp opponents to think you are raising for a free card. When they try to use counter-strategies (such as reraising on the Flop or betting on the Turn if a third flush card does not come), you can raise them again.

Example

You hold top pair and are in late position (relative to the other players still in the hand).

Your hand: A♣T♥
Flop: T♠5♠3♣

Against an early-position opponent who may think your raise on the Flop means a free-card raise with a flush draw, you should not slow-play this hand on the Flop. Even if there are flush draws on the Flop, you should probably play the hand aggressively since there are three possible overcards to your hand. You should raise on the Flop and hope that a non-flush card hits the Turn. Your opponent may then feel comfortable betting on the Turn, not wanting to give you a free card. You can raise him again on the Turn, gaining an extra small bet over what you would have by not raising on the Flop but waiting for the Turn to raise. After you raise them on the Flop, most opponents will not bet out on the Turn with a hand like JT, fearing a higher kicker. Decide which opponents will bet out on the Turn with a weaker T (or lower pair) as a counter-strategy against a free-card raise, and which opponents will bet out with a set or two pair. In this case you are not trying for a free card; but you can use your opponent's knowledge of the strategy to your advantage.

CHAPTER 8
BLUFFING

A bluff is a bet or raise that has little chance of winning if called. Bluffing is an important part of Limit Hold'em. Some people who do not play much poker think bluffing is the most important concept in the game. This is a mischaracterization of the game. People probably overestimate the importance of bluffing in poker because bluffing is what makes poker special. Bluffing cannot be used in many other competitive games, such as craps, blackjack, billiards or chess. People often refer to poker when they discuss bluffing in other aspects of life. For example during the 2004 NFL Draft, Chris Mortensen of ESPN described the trade negotiations between the New York Giants and the San Diego Chargers for Eli Manning as a game of poker because both sides were trying to bluff and not show their hands.

To bluff successfully, you need to know the right time to use the tool. In most low-limit games bluffing is pointless since most players call with weak hands rather than fold. In middle- and high-limit games, where players are more willing to fold, bluffing becomes an effective tool and can be used strategically. The value of bluffing depends on the players and the situation. Some opponents do not care how you play because they have already predetermined whether to call or fold based on their own holdings. They have not taken the second step of trying to analyze what you have. Against those opponents, your decision about whether to bluff should be based solely on what you think they have.

Against opponents who play better and who try to deduce your cards from your play of the hand up to that point, the bluff decision is more difficult. You need a good handle on the cards they hold; and you need a good idea of what *they* think *you* have.

The decision about whether to bluff does not depend on how many chips you have put into the pot yourself in previous rounds. Those chips are a sunk cost. They are no longer your chips; they belong to the pot. What you should care about is the equity you have in the pot.

A bluff does not need to win the pot a majority of the time to be a winning strategy. If the pot holds 9 big bets, risking 1 big bet to try to win the pot is worthwhile if the chance of a bluff being successful is more than 10%.

Bluffing can be quantified. For example if the probability of winning a 10-big-bet pot by bluffing is 15%, the expected value (EV) of a bluff is:

Action	*Computation*	*Result*
EV of bluffing	(15% x 10 big bets) + (85% x -1 big bet)	+0.65 big bets

If your opponent calls 85% of the time, then 85% of the time you show your bluff cards and look foolish. During the 15% of the time that your opponent folds a better hand than yours, you take the money and no one sees what you did.

Bluffing Against One Opponent

Now examine bluffing on the River against one opponent. You are in last position and your opponent has checked to you. The scenarios you can face:

1. You have a good to strong hand.
2. You have a mediocre hand.
3. You have a below-average hand.
4. You have a poor hand.

Situation 1 is simple. You have a good to strong hand. You should be betting and hoping your opponent calls and loses more chips to you. This is not a bluff.

Situation 2 is more complex. You have a mediocre hand, one that could be a winner or a loser. Think about whether it is worthwhile to make a *value bet*. Your cards are not a lock, but you think there is value in making a bet because you believe your hand is likely to be the best hand. This bet is not a bluff.

In Situations 2, 3 and 4, you need to consider both the size of the pot and your opponent's thoughts on the size of the pot. In Situation 2 if the pot size is large, you should be more inclined to bet; your opponent will be inclined to call with a worse hand, believing she is getting relatively large pot odds in case you are bluffing. In Situations 3 and 4 a bigger pot rewards you more handsomely for a successful bluff than a smaller pot would. But your opponent may be aware of the relative pot size as well, and may be more inclined to call your bet when the pot is bigger.

Situations 3 and 4, when you have a below-average or a poor hand, are the situations when bluffing can come into play. The following are examples of bluffing in Situations 3 and 4.

Example of Situation 3: betting a below-average hand

Assumptions

- You have a 25% chance of having the best hand.
- If you bet, an opponent with a better hand folds 40% of the time and calls 60% of the time.
- If you bet, an opponent with a worse hand folds 100% of the time.
- The pot size is 5 big bets.
- Your lone opponent has checked on the River and you are last to act.

EV of checking

The pot size is 5 big bets. If you do not bet, you have a 25% chance of winning the hand and a 75% chance of losing the hand. The EV of checking in this hand is:

Action	*Computation*	*Result*
EV of checking	(25% x 5) + (75% x 0)	+1.25 big bets

In this example if you check you expect to get 1.25 big bets on average.

EV of betting

The assumptions state that when you have the best hand (25% of the time), your opponent does not call a bet. When your oppponent has a better hand (75% of the time) and you bet, your opponent folds 40% of the time and calls 60% of the time.

When you have the best hand: there is no increased value to betting compared to checking. When you have the best hand and you bet, your opponent folds; so you win no extra bets. (This is not the case in all situations; but it is the case in this example.) The extra value you gain by betting lies in your having the worse hand, with your bet making your opponent fold a better hand. However in this example you are not sure if you have the best hand; so it is unclear whether you are bluffing.

The EVs of the different scenarios are:

Action (when you bet)	*Computation*	*Result*
You have the best hand	25% x 5	+1.25
Opp has better hand & folds after you bet	75% x 40% x 5	+1.50
Opp has better hand & calls after you bet	75% x 60% x -1	-0.45
Total EV of betting		+2.30

When you bet, you have an EV of +2.30 big bets. In this example betting is better than checking because an EV of +2.30 big bets is better than an EV of +1.25 big bets.

If the numbers are different, a bluff might be unwise. Change the assumptions: instead of folding a better hand 40% of the time, your opponent will fold a better hand 10% of the time and call 90% of the time. Then the EV equation becomes:

Action (when you bet)	*Computation*	*Result*
You have the best hand	25% x 5	+1.25
Opp has better hand & folds after you bet	75% x 10% x 5	+0.375
Opp has better hand & calls after you bet	75% x 90% x -1	-0.675
Total EV of betting		+0.95

In this case the EV of betting is +0.95 big bets, which is worse than the EV of checking (+1.25 big bets). Your decision about whether to bluff depends on how likely your opponent is to call when holding a better hand.

Example of Situation 4: you have a poor hand

When you have a poor hand and almost no chance of winning the pot outright, the calculations are similar. You can assume you have 0% of winning if you check, but a 20% chance of your opponent folding if you bet. If you also assume the pot contains 5 big bets, then the EV formulas are:

Action	*Computation*	*Result*
EV of checking	0% x 5 big bets	+0.00
EV of bluffing	(20% x 5) + (80% x -1)	+0.20

With these numbers it is clear that bluffing is the better option as you gain +0.20 big bets. But if the frequency of your opponent folding is lowered to 10%, then bluffing is the worse option. The EV formula is:

Action	*Computation*	*Result*
EV of bluffing	(10% x 5 big bets) + (90% x -1 big bet)	-0.40

You have the math. You still need to learn the skill of pinpointing the frequency with which your opponent folds. If the folding frequency number were simple to obtain, then poker would be easy for those who are adept at math. You could plug the number into an EV formula like the ones above and know the right move. Alas in real life it is difficult to assess folding frequency. Putting a percentage on how frequently an opponent calls or folds is a tough skill to learn, but one that experience can teach. Pay attention to the other players to see how they play. Pick up on their tendencies. The main way to gain this skill is through experience, observing your opponents and thinking about the game.

Another example of a bluff attempt against one opponent

You are in the big blind holding A♦8♣. Everybody folds to a player one to the right of the cutoff seat, who raises. Everybody else folds and you call. There are two players and 2.25 big bets in the pot.

Flop: 8♠7♠6♣

You check. The pre-Flop raiser bets. You check-raise. She re-raises. You call. Going into the Turn the pot is 5.25 big bets.

Turn: 2♣

You check and hope your opponent is on a spade draw, also checking. Instead she bets. You are afraid that she has an overpair and has you down to 5 or 2 outs. (If she has KK you have 5 outs: three A's and two 8's. If she has AA you have 2 outs: the two 8's.) There is also the possibility that she holds a hand like K♠Q♠ that gives her many outs. Her actions of raising on the Flop and betting on the Turn as a semi-bluff are reasonable if she holds those hands. With two overcards and a flush draw, she may have thought she had 15 outs; so she did not mind reraising on the Flop. Many times such players will also continue to bet on the Turn, in the hope that you will fold. If you do not fold, they have many outs. It is unclear exactly what hand she has. You may be the favorite or the underdog. You decide to call her bet.

But the important decision is what to do on the River. You have an opportunity to bet out if a T, 9 or 5 hits the board, whether or not it is a spade. A spade helps you; if she has a flush, she will raise your bluff and you can fold knowing that you are beaten, thus losing the same amount as if you had checked and called her bet. If she has an overpair instead of a flush, the 9♠ is going to look dangerous to her. You may be in the hand with a spade draw or a straight draw, or have hit two pair. If she views you as a good player, she may be afraid that a bet on the River by you is intended to save the hand from being checked down on the River. It will look as though you got there with a draw. Whether a bluff is correct depends on your estimate of the chance that your opponent will fold with an overpair.

There are two important points here. One is that your bluff does not have to succeed all the time to be profitable. The frequency with which a bluff has to be successful depends on the size of the pot. The bigger the pot, the less often a bluff needs to be successful for it to be correct. Getting called once or twice making a bluff like this does not necessarily make it a bad bluff. On the other hand if you are bluffing into players who are incapable of folding a J♦9♦ with a scary board of 9♠8♠7♠6♣2♣, then a bluff attempt is throwing your money away. If your opponent is incapable of folding a better hand, then bluffing is foolhardy. This is one of the differences between low-limit games and middle-to high-limit games. Since players in the low-limit games often call with hands that do not warrant calling, bluffing has less value.

Bluffing with a small chance to win

Should you bluff if you have a small chance to win? Two situations:

Situation 1

You are last to act on the River. The pot is 7 big bets. Your opponent, who you think is loose, has checked.

Your hand: A♠4♠
Board: K♣8♠7♥3♣2♠

You raised pre-Flop and bet on the Flop and on the Turn, hoping your opponent would fold. You think there is a 15% chance that he has a worse hand than yours—specifically, a busted straight draw—in which case if you check, you win the pot. However because your opponent is loose, he will call you with any pair most of the time. 5% of the time he folds a better A-high and you steal the pot from him. In total he will fold 20% of the time. The EV tables show that with these assumptions, checking is better than betting.

Action	*Computation*	*Result*
EV of betting	(20% x 7) + (80% x -1)	+0.60
EV of checking	(15% x 7) + (85% x 0)	+1.05

Checking yields a higher EV than betting, so checking is better. Betting reduces your EV by 0.45 big bets.

Situation 2

Everything is the same as Situation 1, except instead of having A♠ 4♠, you have a worse hand.

Your hand: 6♣5♣
Board: K♣8♠7♥3♣2♠

You were betting all along with a straight draw on the Flop, and then a flush draw on the Turn; but you have nothing on the River. If you check, there is zero chance you will win. However your opponent has the same hand as in Situation 1. Since the action is the same, he is willing to fold 20% of the time. 5% of the time he is folding a better hand than A♠4♠. The other 15% of the time he is folding a worse hand than A♠4♠. 15% of the time when he folds, his hand is better than your 6♣5♣ in

Situation 2. In this case a bet gives you 20% chance of winning with the worst hand possible. You are raising your chance of winning from 0% to 20% in Situation 2, compared to 15% to 20% for Situation 1.

Action	*Computation*	*Result*
EV of betting	(20% x 7) + (80% x -1)	+0.60
EV of checking	(0% x 7) + (85% x 0)	+0.00

Betting increases your EV by +0.60. A bluff is worthwhile, having a greater value than checking.

In general the worse your hand, the more valuable the bluff. As shown in Situation 1, if your hand has a chance of winning, a bet may have negative value compared to checking. If your opponent understands this concept: then you should call more often after he bets, since he may be betting because he has no other way to win.

Keep in mind that if the assumptions were changed, bluffing could be a worse option than checking. If there were a 10% chance that the opponent would fold a better hand, then bluffing would have negative value.

Action	*Computation*	*Result*
EV of betting	(10% x 7) + (90% x -1)	-0.20
EV of checking	(0% x 7) + (90% x 0)	+0.00

Bluffing when your opponent has a 10% chance of folding is a losing play. When deciding whether to bluff, remember that the lower your chance of having the best hand, the more value there is in bluffing. Balance that with the fact that the lower the chance that your opponent will fold a better hand, the less value there is in bluffing. The mathematical calculations are impossible to do at the poker table; but you can make these decisions by understanding the players and the situations. These calculations illustrate how changing factors affect whether bluffing is correct or incorrect.

Summary

Bluffing in Context of Recent Plays

The decision about whether to bluff should not be based on one hand in isolation, but rather within the context of recent plays that you have made. Players who think you bluff too frequently will call you often. If that happens, bluff less. When you bluff unsuccessfully and have to show down the losing hand, other players pick up on your play and may feel more comfortable calling you in other hands, believing you are likely to be bluffing.

Other players may also start thinking you bluff too much if you have recently won a few hands without showing your cards; and this may lead them to calling you more in the future. Whether you had legitimate hands or were bluffing is irrelevant to them. You may need to reduce your frequency of bluffing. On the other hand if you have not been involved in many hands recently, or have shown down good hands when you did win pots, you may be able to take advantage by bluffing slightly more frequently. If you have not played many hands recently, other players give you more credit after you do enter a pot, thinking you are less likely to be bluffing since they judge you to be a tight player.

You should seek balance when you bluff. Bluff the amount that causes your opponents to think you are not bluffing when you are, so they are more likely to fold. In order to bluff successfully, you cannot bluff too frequently.

Bluffing Against Multiple Opponents

It is difficult to bluff successfully against more than one opponent. The chance of at least one player calling your bluff is higher when there is more than one opponent. The pot is usually bigger since there were more players in previous rounds. A larger pot size makes calling more worthwhile. With more opponents, the probability increases that one of them has a legitimate calling hand. With that said, there are certain situations where a bluff against multiple opponents may work with a high enough percentage relative to the pot odds to make it worthwhile.

Situations where it may be profitable to risk a bluff against more than one opponent usually occur when there is a straight draw or a flush draw on the board. If you believe one of your opponents has a busted draw on the River, then bluffing into two players is the same as bluffing into one player, since the player with the busted draw can be discounted (although the other player may be more likely to call since the pot is probably bigger). If there is a draw on the board and a card that looks as though it has completed a possible draw on the River, then a raise may make them think you drew the card you needed. You have to hope that neither of the players were on a draw themselves, as they would be likely to call with a made draw.

Bluffing on the Flop while on the button

Sometimes you call in late position after several other players have already limped in. Whether or not you are on the button is unimportant, as long as all the players to your left have folded (which in effect makes you the button as you are last to act after the Flop). If the Flop comes with one high card and two low cards, such as Q-3-2, and everyone checks to you, then you have a nice opportunity to bluff regardless of the cards you hold. A player with a Q would probably have made a bet along the way; so if everyone checks to you, there is a higher chance that no one has a Q. Q-3-2 is a better Flop for bluffing than three low cards would be, because loose players may be willing to call with any two overcards, such as K9 and A8, with a Flop of three low cards. But with the Q on the board, players with hands like K9 and A8 think they have one overcard. Players with JT think they have no overcards, so they are more likely to fold to a bet. Players who call are likely to have a straight draw, such as 54, A5, or A4, which means you should keep betting if they check and no other low card or A appears.

Bluffing on the Turn with a ragged board

When there are no pre-Flop raises and no bets on the Flop with a weak board, the first player to bet usually wins the pot. If it is checked to you on the Turn, consider betting to steal the pot regardless of your own holdings. A check on the Flop by a player who willingly entered the pot after the blinds had checked implies one of two things: that player either has a monster hand and is slowplaying, or has nothing and will be willing to give up the pot to a bet. If you are in one of the blinds, then you can represent a hand more easily with a ragged board.

Example

You are in the big blind with a weak hand. A middle-position player limps in and everyone else folds to the small blind, who calls. You check.

Your hand: 7♠2♣
Flop: 8♣5♠3♦

This is a ragged Flop and you do not have anything—no pair, no straight draw. You are ready to give up on the hand if someone bets. To your surprise, everyone checks on the Flop.

Turn: 5♥

Bet if the small blind checks. Since you were in the big blind and involuntarily in the hand, the other players give you more credit for having cards that match the ragged board. The board pairing decreases the chance that any players have a pair (other than the 5's on the board) because if they did not have a pair on the Flop, they do not have a pair on the Turn. A player who did have a pair on the Flop probably would have bet. A steal bet on the Turn with all this weakness and a ragged board is a worthwhile venture.

If the small blind bets on the Turn, the hand becomes more interesting. A small blind who is a sharp, aggressive player may take this opportunity to bluff and steal the pot; so it may be correct to raise as a re-bluff or a re-steal. But if the small blind is a dull, passive player, then her bet is less likely to be a bluff and you should give up. You should bluff a player who may be bluffing, but not a player who could hold only a legitimate hand.

How Often Should You Bluff?

This is a tough question, and cannot be answered by a simple percentage. Say you know that you bluff 10% of the time. This information does not really tell you anything. You could be bluffing at the wrong time, so all your bluffs are worthless and 10% is too high. Or you could be bluffing at the exactly perfect times, in which case 10% is not too low. Instead of looking at how often you bluff, look at the times when your bluffs are called or not called.

If your bluff is never called, that may seem great, implying that you are bluffing at opportune times and getting the best of your opponent when you do bluff. However since the success rate for bluffing does not need to be high for it to be profitable. Perhaps you are not bluffing enough if you never get your bluffs called. You may be missing out on bluffing opportunities and choosing the times when the chances of bluffing successfully are the highest. Similarly if you never see any busted bluffs after you call, it may mean you are folding too often.

Inducing a Bluff

Inducing a bluff [a] is making an opponent bluff when he otherwise would not have bluffed. To induce a bluff, you usually need to act weak so that your opponent thinks he has a chance of making a successful bluff. When inducing a bluff works, opponents bluff when they otherwise would not have called a bet. Inducing a bluff works in two situations:

- You are last to act on the Turn and you check in the hopes that your opponent will bet out on the River.
- You are first to act on the River and you check to your opponent.

Inducing a bluff on the River with a check on the Turn when you are last to act

The circumstances required to make this play successful:

- You are heads-up.
- Your opponent has checked.
- You are last to act on the Turn.
- You are not sure if you are ahead or behind.
- Your opponent is aggressive, and can be counted on to sense weakness and bet on the River if you check on the Turn.
- If your opponent has a better hand, he calls a bet; but if he has a worse hand, he does not call.
- There are few free cards possible.
- You can stomach a bad beat.

Example

You are on the button and you open-raise with a mediocre hand. The big blind calls. The Flop gives you a pair, but also has an overcard.

[a] David Sklansky was the first to write about inducing a bluff, in *Hold'em Poker*.

Your hand: K♣9♣
Flop: A♣K♥8♦

Your opponent checks to you and you bet. She calls.

Turn: 5♠

On the Turn after your opponent checks, you consider checking to induce a bluff on the River. You could be behind if your opponent has a pair of A's. If the Turn were a heart or a diamond, you would have more reason to bet because of the higher chance that your opponent would call if she picked up a flush draw. If the Turn were a club (giving you a flush draw of clubs), then you would have more incentive to bet because if you were behind you would have many outs on the River.

Inducing a bluff: "Chapter 20"

In the early 1990s I was an options trader for a proprietary trading firm. Often some of the traders would get together for home poker games. Here's a story that I thought was funny at the time; and I chuckle to this day thinking about it.

I had received my copy of *The Theory of Poker* by David Sklansky the night before and read it cover to cover. The next day I used one of the lessons I learned from the book. I managed to induce a bluff from my opponent, a talented young trader named Ian Schaad. I knew he would fold to my bet, as I pegged him on a missed draw. I also thought he would attempt a bluff if I checked, because it would look as though my hand was weak. The plan worked to perfection. I checked. He bet. I called and won the pot as he showed a missed straight draw. As I was scooping the pot, I looked over at Ian and said: "Chapter 20." He looked puzzled and asked me what I meant. I said: "Chapter 20, Inducing a Bluff," and pointed to *The Theory of Poker* which I had on the table next to me. Boy! Did he look perturbed! He was able to get his revenge on me a couple of days later as he induced a bluff out of me. He quickly said, "Chapter 20" back to me. This story serves as a fond memory of those games, along with the story of another friend, Dean Potashner, who nicknamed his couch "King's sofa." He used the money he won from me in a particular session to buy the couch.

The last criterion on the list is having the ability to stomach a bad beat when trying to induce a bluff. Every once in a while when you try to induce a bluff with a check on the Turn in last position, you allow your opponent to catch a miracle card and beat you. She might have folded if you had bet on the Turn. Instead she got lucky and caught on the River due to the free card you gave her. You have to be able to live with that if you are going to try to induce a bluff with a check on the Turn.

In the example above, an opponent with QJ, QT or JT could think you have a pair of A's or K's on the Flop, and not raise. But she may decide to call on the Flop in the hopes of catching a straight on the Turn. When the Turn comes and she does not have the straight yet, the increased bet size on the Turn may convince her to fold since she has only 4 outs. When a Q, a J or a T hits on the River, call if she bets because she may be betting with a pair. (If a Q hits and she had QJ or QT, she may bet because she may think she has the best hand since you checked on the Turn.) You may not feel good if she catches her inside straight and takes the pot because you were trying to induce a bluff from her.

A side effect of checking on the Turn is that you might induce a call on the River, rather than a bluff. In the example above if your opponent has bottom pair, she might not call if you bet again on the Turn (after raising pre-Flop and betting on the Flop), because you look strong. When you check on the Turn, she may think there is a chance she has the best hand with bottom pair. While her hand is not good enough to bet on the River, she may think it is good enough to call a bet from you on the River. Instead of inducing a bluff, you have induced a call that she would not have made if you had bet on the Turn.

Inducing a bluff on the River when you act first

The circumstances required to make this play successful:

- You are first to act on the River.
- You believe your opponent was on a draw and missed.
- Your opponent is aggressive enough to bluff when shown weakness.

If you are first to act on the River and think your opponent is on a draw that missed, a bet will do you no good because your opponent will not call. A check is better, since he may bluff and you can win a bet from him that you would not have won by betting on the River, since he would not have called. This can occur when there are two cards of the same suit on the Flop and your opponent raises. On the Turn he checks after you check, implying he was on a flush draw and is not there yet. On the River if the flush card does not come, you may decide that checking with the intention of calling (or raising) is the best way to win an extra bet.

Example

You are in the big blind and get raised by an aggressive player on the button. You call the raise. Tthe two of you see the Flop heads-up.

Your hand: K♠J♠
Flop: K♥Q♥5♣

You check-raise with your top pair and good kicker. After you check-raise, your opponent reraises. Her possible hands are:

- A better made hand (with AA, KK, QQ, AK, KQ, 55)
- A worse made hand (AQ, QJ, KT)
- A draw (JT, A♥5♥).

Turn: 7♦

You check. Your opponent checks. It appears that she was on a draw, or has a worse made hand, such as AQ or QJ. Here is what can happen when a blank comes on the River, with the possible hands your opponent could have:

1. She has a better hand (AA, KK, QQ, AK, KQ, 55). If a heart does not come on the River, so there is no possible flush, a bet by you is usually followed by a raise. If you check and call her bet, you lose the minimum. If you bet, you lose 1 or 2 bets (depending on whether you called a raise). If you check with the intention of calling, you lose 1 bet.

2. She has a worse made hand (AQ, QJ, KT). If she checked on the Turn, she is worried that you have a better hand. If you bet on the River, she calls and you win 1 bet. If you check, she is likely to bet and you win 1 bet. Either way you have a chance of winning 1 bet.

3. She has a busted draw (JT, A♥5♥). If you bet, she folds since she has no pair. If you check, she may bet because your weakness may have given her the hope that she can win the pot with a bluff bet on the River. If you bet, you win 0 bets. If you check with the intention of calling, you have a chance of winning 1 bet.

In all three cases, checking and calling is superior or equivalent to betting. You are not completely sure what you are up against—a better hand, a worse made hand or a draw—but checking and calling is the dominant strategy in all three cases.

This only works well against some opponents. A passive opponent is less likely to bluff on the River. A calling station will call on the River with hands she would not bet, such as a split pair of 5's. Consider the aggressiveness of your opponent when making this type of play. The more aggressive your opponent, the more you should try to induce a bluff out of her. The more passive she is, the more you should bet and the less you should try to induce a bluff.

Example with EV

Assume you are sure you have the best hand. For example you have the top set and there are no possible straights or flushes on the board. You are heads-up on the River and you are first to act. You estimate that your opponent has a missed draw and probably will not call if you bet. You estimate his calling percentage to be 10%. However you know he is a sharp player. If you check, there is a chance that he may bet, hoping to steal the pot. You estimate the chance of him betting if you check to be 20%. Since you are sure you have the best hand: if he bets you will raise, at which time he probably will fold.

Action	*Computation*	*Result*
EV of Betting	10% x 1 big bet	+0.10
EV of Checking	20% x 1 big bet	+0.20

If your perception of the situation is correct and these probabilities are right, then check and try to induce a bluff. In practice instead of plugging numbers into an equation, you often have to rely on your "feel" for your opponent and the situation.

To Bluff or To Induce a Bluff

Situations come up in which you are not sure if you have the best hand, so you are not sure whether you are in a position to bluff or to induce a bluff. If you are behind, then you can consider bluffing. If you are ahead, then you might consider inducing a bluff. These situations are complex, and your play depends on your estimate of your opponent.

If your opponent is a calling station, bet when you have a hand instead of trying to induce a bluff. A calling station is more likely to call your bet than to bet once you have checked. But if a calling station raises after you bet, you should consider folding. Don't bluff against a calling station.

If your opponent is tough and sharp, tend to check and call when you have a hand. You are less likely to get a tough, sharp player to call with a second-best hand. But you may induce a bluff from a sharp player whose only chance to win the pot is by bluffing.

Calling a Bluff

There are two ways to catch a bluff. One way is to look at the physical behavior of the player and see if there is a sign that tells you the person may be bluffing. Picking up tells is a valuable poker skill, because a tell can indicate whether to call another player's bet. Tells are beyond the scope of this book. See Appendix B: Other Sources for Limit Texas Hold'em for resources on tells.

The other way to catch a bluff is to deduce from the board and your opponent's actions whether there is a chance she could be bluffing. If the opponent likes to raise with draws, a missed draw on the board may mean she was raising with a draw on previous rounds and is bluffing on the River. Some players like to bet after everyone else checks. If you can identify these players, you can call them in spots where you think they are betting because of the perceived weakness of their opponents. This takes experience and observing how other players play. Be alert and attentive at the table to build this skill.

CHAPTER 9
SEMI-BLUFFING

A semi-bluff is: a bet or a raise before the River in the hope that your opponents fold; but if they call, you still have a chance to improve on the next card. The term was coined by David Sklansky. When you semi-bluff, you have two ways to win the hand. If there is no chance that a future card can make your hand the best, then you are bluffing, not semi-bluffing.

An example of a semi-bluff on the Turn in a middle-limit game:

Your hand: A♣K♣
Your opponent's hand: J♦J♥

Pre-Flop: A decent player open-raises in middle position with a pair of J's. You are on the button and you reraise. Everybody else folds and the JJ calls.

Flop: Q♣8♦3♥

Your opponent checks. You bet. He raises. You call.

Turn: 2♣

Your opponent bets. You have a flush draw along with two overcards to the board. If you knew your opponent's hand exactly, you would know that you have 15 outs: 9 for the flush, 3 for an A and 3 for a K. A raise by you on the Turn is a semi-bluff because you are hoping your opponent folds. If he does not fold, you have a good chance of getting lucky on the River.

When you raise on the Turn, your opponent must consider that you might have a hand such as AA, KK, QQ, AQ, KQs, or 88. Based on your actions thus far (reraising pre-Flop, betting and calling a check-raise on the Flop, and raising on the Turn), along with his opinion that you are a solid player, any good opponent would be aware that he could be beaten when he has a pocket pair of J's. He has to consider folding, given his cards and the game situation. If he does call, you might still get lucky on the River by catching an A, a K or a club.

To semi-bluff you must think there is a chance your opponent will fold. If your opponent is a calling station who would never fold, then a semi-bluff is not a useful strategy because you are an underdog to win a showdown.

To compare the expected value (EV) of calling or semi-bluff raising, consider several things:

- The chance that you will have the best hand by the River is 15/44 (you have 15 outs with a total of 44 unknown cards in this example, assuming you know your opponent's hand).
- If you raise on the Turn, your opponent will fold 20% of the time and call 80% of the time.
- If you raise on the Turn and do not hit your hand, you will not bluff on the River.
- If you raise on the Turn and do improve on the River and you then bet, your opponent will call half the time.
- After your opponent has bet, there are 6 big bets in the pot.
- If you call and win, you expect to make 7 big bets. (You expect your opponent will check and call your bet 100% of the time on the River.) If you call and lose, you expect to lose 1 bet. (You will fold on the River if you do not catch.)
- If you raise and your opponent folds, you will win 6 big bets.
- If you raise and win on the River, you expect to make 7.5 big bets on average. (When your opponent sees a danger card on the River, you expect him to call half the time and fold half the time.) If you raise and lose, you expect to lose 2 bets.

The EV of calling on the Turn:

Action	*Computation*	*Result, EV*
Calling	(15/44 x 7 big bets) + (29/44 x -1 big bet)	+1.73

The EV of raising on the Turn when your opponent folds 20% of the time:

Action	*Computation*	*Result, EV*
Semi-bluff Raising on the Turn	(20% x 6 big bets) + (80% x 15/44 x 7.5 big bets) + (80% x 29/44 x -2 big bets)	+2.19

The EV of semi-bluffing (+2.19) is greater than the EV of calling (+1.73). With these assumptions the semi-bluff is justified. The strategy has increased your EV.

But what if you estimated your opponent's folding percentage incorrectly? What if he is a calling station and would never fold in a situation like this? If he is this loose, then you have cost yourself money with a semi-bluff raise. You are more likely to lose this hand than win; and you have chosen a strategy that will put more money into the pot.

Action	*Computation*	*Result, EV*
Semi-bluffing against a player who never folds	(0% x 6 big bets) + (100% x 15/44 x 8 big bets [a]) + (100% x 29/44 x -2 big bets)	+1.41

The EV of semi-bluffing against a calling station (+1.41) is lower than the EV of calling (+1.73). The semi-bluff may backfire! When it is used against the wrong opponent, it can do more harm than good. This is the main reason why semi-bluffing is almost useless in low-limit games. Players in low-limit games are more likely to call than players in the middle- or high-limit games. Thus players who semi-bluff too often in low-limit games are costing themselves money. They scratch their heads wondering why a play written about in well-respected poker books does

[a] An opponent who is loose enough never to fold on the Turn will also never fold on the River. If you raise on the Turn and bet on the River, your opponent will call both bets.

not work for them. The concept itself is not flawed; but they are applying it in the wrong situations.

Break-Even Point of Semi-Bluffing

In the previous section you saw how semi-bluffing against an opponent who folds 20% of the time is a good play. Semi-bluffing against an opponent who never folds is a bad play. With that information you can derive how likely it must be that the opponent will fold in order for the EV of semi-bluffing and calling to be the same. In the above example that break-even point is 10.3%. If the opponent folds 10.3% of the time after you raise on the Turn, then semi-bluffing and calling have the same EV.

This chart summarizes the EV of semi-bluffing based on your opponent's folding frequency.

Action	*Computation*	*Result, EV*
Semi-bluffing against a player who never folds		
	(0% x 6 big bets) + (100% x 15/44 x 8 big bets) + (100% x 29/44 x -2 big bets)	+1.41
Calling on the Turn		
	(15/44 x 7 big bets) + (29/44 x -1 big bet)	+1.73
Semi-bluffing against a player who folds 10.3% of the time		
	(10.3% x 6 big bets) + (89.7% x 15/44 x 7.5 big bets) + (89.7% x 29/44 x -2 big bets)	+1.73
Semi-bluffing against a player who folds 20% of the time		
	(20% x 6 big bets) + (80% x 15/44 x 7.5 big bets) + (80% x 29/44 x -2 big bets)	+2.19

The break-even points are different with different pot sizes and different numbers of outs. If the pot size is larger, the break-even point is lower and you can semi-bluff more often. If you have fewer outs, the break-even point is higher and you should semi-bluff less. The two charts below show this relationship, assuming the other variables are the same as in the above example. The break-even point is the particular probability of your opponent folding to a raise on the Turn that gives raising and calling the same EV.

Pot after Opponent Bets on Turn	*Break-Even Point*
4	14.3%
5	12.0%
6 (as in above example)	10.3%
7	9.0%
8	8.0%
9	7.2%

Outs / Non-Outs	*Break-Even Point*
6 / 38	11.8%
9 / 35	11.5%
12 / 32	10.8%
15 / 29 (as in above example)	10.3%
17 / 27	9.8%
18 / 25	9.3%

The correctness of a semi-bluff raise depends on the frequency with which your opponent folds a made hand. In order to estimate this, you need a good feel for how she plays the game. You must observe her actions: see how conservative she is, how aggressive she is, how much she respects other players' raises, and how much she respects you as a player. This is a nice example of how combining the mathematical side of your brain with the social side of your brain can result in a correct analysis. If you use only the math side, you are at a loss as to whether a semi-bluff is correct since you do not have an accurate assessment of your opponent's tendencies. If you use only the social side, you are at a loss because you do not have an accurate assessment of the value of raising or calling. When you combine both sides of your brain, you can make it all work.

Unless you are an idiot savant like the character Dustin Hoffman played in *Rain Man*, you may not be able to do the math in your head. Even if you understand the concept, it is unlikely that you can do these calculations in the heat of battle at the poker table. The information presented here is useful in preparing for play at the table. It gives you an idea of how to proceed when this situation comes up. When the pot is bigger and everything else is constant (same pot odds, same folding frequency by your opponent), there is more value in semi-bluffing because a fold by the opponent has greater value. When the opponent is less likely to fold, the value of semi-bluffing goes down. Do not semi-bluff against a calling station.

Raising on the Turn for a Free Showdown

Another way to semi-bluff is when you have a decent hand on the Turn and raise for a "free" showdown. Actually the showdown is not free since you are committing 2 bets on the Turn. But in the spirit of the free-card raise on the Flop that really does save half a bet, call this a free showdown raise.

The factors to consider regarding a free showdown raise:

- Your hand has a chance to win a showdown on the River.
- If you are behind, you have outs.
- There is a chance that your opponent will fold.
- The chance that your opponent will reraise you on the Turn is low.

Now take a look at each factor.

Your hand has a chance to win a showdown on the River

This factor is important because you should not put in any extra bets if you are an underdog and your opponent is likely to call. If you call the Turn and will not call if your opponent bets on the River, then you should not consider raising here unless the other factors strongly encourage raising. You should be playing a hand with which you would be willing to call a Turn bet and a River bet anyway. So if you lose this hand, you do not lose any more than you would have anyway. This is the difference between a semi-bluff raise and a free showdown raise. The semi-bluff raise has no chance of winning a showdown if it does not improve on the River. The free showdown raise does have a chance of winning a showdown.

If you are behind, you have outs

It is important that you have a chance of being ahead; but you could be behind. You should have as many outs as possible so that if you are behind you have a chance of catching up and giving your opponent a bad beat. For example if you have KQ and the board on the Turn is K-9-8-3 you might have the best hand, but you are not sure. If your opponent has KJ or KT, then you are raising for value. If your opponent has AA, AK or K9, then you are behind with 3 outs. You are not sure if you are ahead or behind; but you are willing to see the hand through the showdown. Instead of calling on the Turn and the River, you could commit those bets on the Turn by raising. If your opponent calls your raise on the Turn, expect him to check on the River. If you catch a K or Q on the River, you can decide to bet and win a total of 3 bets (2 on the Turn and 1 on the River). If you do not improve on the River, check and see if you win on the showdown. You will win or lose the same 2 bets that you would expect to win or lose by calling both the Turn and River.

There is a chance that your opponent will fold

Whether or not your opponent has a better hand, her folding to your raise on the Turn is normally a good thing. If she is ahead and folds to your raise, you have stolen a pot from her. If she is behind, you win a hand right there on the Turn and she does not have a chance to give you a bad beat on the River. The only time your opponent folding is bad for you is when she is drawing dead or drawing thin. For example if she has two outs, you hope she calls. If she is drawing thin, but is loose enough to call a raise on the Turn, avoid giving her a free look at the River if you think she won't bet or call unless she catches a miracle card. The higher the chance of your opponent folding when she has outs, the better a Turn raise is.

The chance that your opponent will reraise you on the Turn is low

If your opponent reraises you and is ahead, then he has foiled your strategy for a free showdown. If you plan to call the River, you are risking 2 more bets by using the free showdown raise strategy. (You would have to put in a total of 4 bets semi-bluffing, compared to 2 if you play passively.) It is better to put yourself in a position where you know that a reraise on the Turn is a sign that he has a great hand and is unlikely to be bluffing. This way you can fold a marginal hand without the risk of folding the best hand. For example you have AT and on the Turn the board is A-K-J-T of four different suits. Any Q will make a straight. You decide to raise for a free showdown. A passive opponent reraises. If the pot odds warrant it, you might consider calling this raise to see if the

River brings you a full house. If the pot odds are not there, then you can fold without fearing you folded to a bluff.

Example of raising for a free showdown

Your hand: A9o
Flop: A-7-6
Turn: 5

You raise in late position before the Flop. A decent player in the big blind calls. You bet on the Flop. She check-raises. You call. You put her on a split pair of A's or a straight draw. If she has a split pair of A's, it is unclear who has the better hand since your kicker is mediocre. Three of the possible worse kickers she could have would give her two pair.

On the Turn you pick up a gutshot straight draw with the 5. You need an 8 on the River for a straight. After she bets, you raise for a free showdown on the River. If she reraises, you can fold, confident that she already has a straight, which means you have 4 outs to split the pot. If she does not already have a straight, then she has at least trips or two pair, which means you have 4 outs to win the pot. After she reraises, your chance of winning is so low that the pot odds are not good enough to make it worthwhile to see the River. If she calls, then you expect her to check to you on the River. On the River you can decide to check if you do not improve your hand, or bet if you do.

If you improve on the River, you win 3 bets (2 on the Turn and 1 on the River). If you do not improve on the River, you either win or lose 2 bets. If you call on the Turn, then if you call on the River she is likely to bet on the River; so you win or lose 2 bets. If a 9 or a 8 comes on the River, it will be tough to win 2 bets on the River, because she is likely to check and call because of the danger card on the River.

The bottom line is that you have given yourself a chance to win 3 bets while risking 2 bets by raising for a free showdown. Compare that to calling, which gives you a chance to win 2 bets while risking 2 bets. There are other factors that can change this general strategy. The chance of winning more after you improve on the River is valuable. Raising for a free showdown is discussed further in Chapter 14 "The Turn."

After the Opponent's Semi-Bluff or Free-Card Draw Has Hit

When you think the other player is bluffing or semi-bluffing, you may not mind letting him bet if you think he will fold to your raise. However sometimes you should reconsider based on the card that hits the board. If a dangerous card comes and your opponent was betting or raising with a semi-bluff, he may have made a hand. If he was not semi-bluffing to begin with, he may already have been ahead. In either case you are more likely to be behind, and should consider giving up on the hand.

Example

You are in late position with KTs. Everyone folds to you and you open-raise. The small blind and the big blind call. There are three players and 3 big bets in the pot.

Your hand: KTs
Flop: J-T-3 rainbow

Both blinds check and you bet. The small blind folds and the big blind check-raises. You know the big blind is a good aggressive player. You also know that she knows that you are a good player who has the ability to lay down a hand like A5. The big blind could be raising with any J, any T, JT, Q9, KQ, 98, A3 or 33. Many of these hands you can beat; so you call her raise. There are 5 big bets in the pot.

Turn: 5

The big blind bets and you call. The 5 is unlikely to improve her hand. Your call tells her that you have a legitimate hand, either made or drawing. There are 7 big bets in the pot.

River: Q

This Q is a dangerous card for you. If your opponent was on a straight draw, she has either hit a pair of Q's or caught her straight. With straight draws of Q9 or KQ, she has the top pair. With 98 or K9, she has a straight.

Since she is a good player, you know that she knows the Q is a dangerous card for her too. If all she has is a J or a T, she will be afraid that the Q filled your straight or gave you a higher pair. If she bets on the River and was semi-bluffing before, she has now hit a higher pair than yours or filled a straight. If she was not semi-bluffing, then she has you beaten. Even with 8:1 odds your chances look dim based on the way this hand has developed. Since your opponent should be more afraid of the Q than you are if she only has a T, she probably has something better. The only hands you can beat are an unlikely worse split pair of T's or a bluff with a hand like A3.

Another situation you will encounter, especially in shorthanded games where players semi-bluff often, is a Turn or River card that is right in the middle of a possible straight draw. For example with a Flop of J-7-3 a T, 9 or 8 are all dangerous cards, especially if you have a pair of 7's or lower. Any straight draw has either made a straight or has a higher pair than you. You may be comfortable calling an opponent you suspect of semi-bluffing when you have middle pair. But after one of these danger cards comes, it may be time to bail on the hand.

CHAPTER 10 SLOWPLAYING AND CHECK-RAISING

Slowplaying

Slowplaying is playing a strong hand deceptively so your opponents think your hand is weak. You do this by checking a hand that is strong enough to bet or calling with a hand that is strong enough to raise. A bet or raise may force your opponent to fold; whereas a check or call may convince him to commit more chips to the pot at a later point in the hand. Although slowplaying is a useful strategy, it is often misused and abused.

Slowplaying is useful if you have a hand so strong that you need other players to catch up so they can call with an improved, but losing, hand. Slowplaying is not a useful strategy if those players have a decent chance of improving to a stronger hand than yours. Slowplaying is also not useful if your opponents call your bets and raises. With opponents who call anything, slowplaying means passing up a bet or two and winning a pot that is smaller than it might have been.

Benefit of slowplaying

Against players who would have folded, slowplaying can fool them into risking more chips.

Costs of slowplaying

You may miss some bets, or give a free card to your opponent.

Examples of when and when not to slowplay

Example 1

You have Q♦J♦ and five players see the Flop for one raise.

Your hand: Q♦J♦
Flop: Q♠J♠J♣

This is a great Flop for your hand. You have a full house and there are all sorts of possible draws on the board. Your opponents could have two spades for a flush draw, a straight draw (AK, AT, KT, K9, T9, T8), or trips with the fourth J. This is a time to bet or raise as there are many ways for other players to have playable hands. They do not need to be fooled into putting their chips in; so you should bet or raise and not slowplay. A player who hits a draw on the Turn or River may think she has drawn out, and raise you. Due to the coordinated Flop and the number of players in the hand, this is not a good time to slowplay.

Example 2

You have Q♦J♦ and raise in late position. The big blind calls.

Your hand: Q♦J♦
Flop: Q♠J♠J♣

Your hand and the Flop are the same as the previous example. The difference is that you have one opponent in this hand. This is a better time to slowplay and hope your opponent improves enough to call your bets on the Turn and/or River. If the player is aware, though, you may have to bet on the Flop and hope that he calls. Most players expect you to bet on the Flop if you raised pre-Flop. They are not as scared of a bet on the Flop as they would be of a bet on the Turn. A check on the Flop may look like you are slowplaying; so you should consider betting on the Flop and then slowplaying on the Turn.

Example 3

Your hand: A♣A♥
Flop: A♠2♣3♦

If you raised before the Flop, it is usually best to bet in the hopes that another player has the fourth A or is drawing to a straight with a 4 or 5. In order to make a successful slowplay here, you need a player to catch a pair with a hand like KJ on the Turn. Players who are aware are usually careful with an A on the board, and may not call on the Turn even if they do hit a pair. Bet and hope one opponent has the fourth A.

Example 4

You have 55 in a three-way pot. Here are two different Flops: one you should slowplay and one you should not slowplay:

Your hand: 55
Flop #1: A-5-5

This is a monster hand that has almost no chance of losing. Many players play any hand with an A. So if there are two other players in the pot, they may be willing to call or raise. Slowplaying here would probably reduce the amount of your win. If you bet and everyone folds, it is likely that they had no piece of the Flop and would not have put in much after that anyway.

If the Flop has a J instead of an A, then the situation is different.

Your hand: 55
Flop #2: J-5-5

Slowplaying is a good strategy with this Flop. A player with A7 may not call a bet when there is a J on the board since she may figure you for a J and think she has 3 outs. But if she senses weakness after you check to her, she may play on. Players are more likely to play a hand containing an A than a hand containing a J. Thus a player is less likely to have a pair of J's after the Flop is J-5-5 than to have pair of A's after the Flop is A-5-5.

Example 5

You are in the big blind with J♠T♠ and call a late-position player's open-raise.

Your hand: J♠T♠
Flop: 9♣8♦7♠

You flopped the nut straight. Determine the looseness of the pre-Flop raiser. If you think he is willing to call all the way to the River with a hand like AK, consider check-raising on the Flop to take the lead. If he is willing to play aggressively with a hand like AT (open-ended straight draw with an overcard), then you should bet and raise at every opportunity. If he is more likely to give you credit and fold to your aggressive play on the Flop and Turn, then you should check and call his bets. If an A or K shows up, then a check-raise may get more money into the pot if he caught a pair.

The correct use of slowplaying depends on how your opponents play. You should slowplay against those who fold marginal hands, but not against aggressive players who like to raise for free cards. Against those aggressive players: you should bet so they can raise for the free card, and then bet again on the Turn when they are expecting the free card.

Example 6

You have AK in early position and raise pre-Flop. A couple of decent players call behind you.

Your hand: AK
Flop: A-8-4

You bet and get called by one player in later position.

Turn: 4

This is a good time to slowplay against most opponents, especially in middle- and high-limit games. Since your opponent did not reraise before the Flop, she probably did not have a big pocket pair and instead has a hand like AT. She may hesitate to raise with AT because she is afraid you have an A with a better kicker. If you check, it should give her the idea that you have a big pocket pair and are afraid that she has a split pair of A's. You can check with the intention of check-raising on the Turn or River. This slowplay works best against decent players who respect your play, yet try to get all the edge they can. You should not slowplay against opponents who are so loose that they will call your pre-Flop raise with a hand like 98. They will probably not bet after you have checked, as they have middle pair and there is a scary A on the board. You also should not slowplay against opponents who are timid and are afraid to bet a weaker pair of A's after you check to them. Players in low-limit games are more likely to cold-call a pre-Flop raise with 98 and to check a split pair of A's with a bad kicker. So slowplaying this hand is less useful in low-limit games than in middle- and high-limit games.

Check-Raising

Check-raising is a form of slowplaying. A check-raiser checks with the intention of raising after another player has bet. The check-raiser usually thinks he has the best hand at the moment. Sometimes he is check-raising to make it expensive for other players to stay in the hand.

A check-raise is a strategy that is often frowned upon in social home games. In some games check-raises are disallowed as too deceitful or cunning. If there is no negative impact on your personal relationships with the other players after you check-raise, then add check-raising to your Hold'em arsenal.

There are three situations in which you can check-raise successfully:

- You think you have the best hand and want to get more money into the pot.
- You think you can semi-bluff or bluff successfully with a check-raise.
- You think you can increase your expected value (EV) by check-raising and forcing others to fold (thus reducing the number of players contesting the pot) even if you do not have the best hand at the time.

All three rely on the expectation that someone behind you will bet after you check, because without a bet by another player, an attempted check-raise is merely a check.

The most common scenario for a check-raise is when you think you have the best hand and want to get more money into the pot. This often occurs after the Flop when you are in one of the blinds and call a late-position open-raiser's pre-Flop raise. Check-raising against a late-position player should work better than against an early-position open-raiser because a late-position open-raiser is likely to have a worse hand than an early-position open-raiser. Any pre-Flop raiser is likely to bet on the Flop when it is checked to her, especially when there are not many players left. Both an early-position raiser and a late-position raiser will bet if checked to on the Flop. On average the late-position raiser holds a worse hand than the early-position raiser, so the blind hand is more likely to have the better hand on the Flop. Thus check-raising a late-position player has more value.

Example of a check-raise vs. a late-position player

You are in the big blind with KJo and are the only player to call an aggressive player's open-raise from the cutoff seat.

Your hand: KJo
Flop: J-7-3 rainbow

You should check-raise on this Flop for two reasons.

- You probably have the best hand, so you want to get more money into the pot.
- You can count on the cutoff player to bet, since most players bet on the Flop when it is checked to them after they have raised pre-Flop.

A check-raise could either get more money into the pot or force a hand with outs to fold. If your opponent has A5, you will be happy to see him fold if you think he will not commit any more bets on the Turn or River if you call on the Flop. If you call on the Flop and you both check on the Turn, he could effectively have a free card, allowing him to see both the Turn and River without any additional bets. On the other hand if he calls your check-raise, he is making a mistake because he does not have pot odds to call with 3 outs.

Check-raising is more successful when the other player is aggressive. Aggressive players in late position raise with weak hands that other players might not play. They are almost guaranteed to bet if checked to on the Flop, especially if the hand is heads-up.

Semi-Bluff Check-Raising and Bluff Check-Raising

Semi-bluff check-raising and bluff check-raising work only against opponents who are willing to fold. They do not work as well against opponents who are willing to call you down with A-high. The principles of semi-bluffing and bluffing apply.

Example

You have T9o in the big blind and call an aggressive late-position raiser.

Your hand: T9o
Flop: J-7-3 rainbow

You have an inside straight draw. You should consider check-raising the original raiser with this semi-bluff to get her to fold hands such as A5 or KT. Check-raising with a semi-bluff works well on the Flop against aggressive late-position open-raisers because they are more likely to fold than calling stations and less likely to have great hands than rocks. (Rocks fold hands that aggressive players raise in late position. Hence a rock who raises is more likely than an aggressive player to have a great hand.)

Calling stations: calling stations can call you down with A-high and no pair; so the bluff value of the semi-bluff check-raise is minimal. If a semi-bluff has no bluff value, then it is no longer a good play.

Aggressive players: if you check-raise with both made hands and drawing hands against aggressive players, you have become more unpredictable to your opponents, which is good for you and bad for them. You should check-raise with T9o as well as QJo.

Rocks: rocks are more likely to have a strong starting hand; so they have more reason to stay in the hand. But if they were raising with AK or AQ, and have not hit a pair by the Turn, they may fold to a check-raise on the Flop and a bet on the Turn. Your semi-bluff check-raise can be valuable. Be wary if a rock raises you later in the hand.

Check-Raising in a Multiple-Player Pot

Check-raising can be useful in multiple-player pots, especially when your hand is best but is vulnerable to overcards. One bet from you in early position is not enough to get players with overcards to fold; however two bets may do the trick.

Example

You are in the big blind with pocket T's. Two players limp. An aggressive player on the button raises. You call, as do the two limpers. Four players see the Flop, which contains no card higher than a 9. If you bet, any players with overcards could correctly call with 9:1 odds and 6 outs. (They have pot odds to call; see the section on the DIPO method in Chapter 5 "Pot Odds.") However if you can count on the aggressive late-position player to bet when it is checked to her, then you have an opportunity to check-raise and make it 2 bets to the limpers. With overcards and 2 bets to them on the Flop, they face a negative EV call. If they fold with overcards, your strategy has worked. If they call, they are making a pot-odds mistake.

Be careful, though. This strategy can backfire in two ways: you can cost yourself a bet if everyone checks; and you can lose more chips by playing aggressively if the aggressive player has a higher pair or a set.

Check-Raising in a Heads-Up Pot

How often should you check-raise in a heads-up situation when you have the best hand? Here is a common Hold'em situation. Everyone folds to a late-position player, who raises. You are in the big blind and are the only player who calls. The Flop is a good one for you, and you think you have the best hand. You check with the intention of check-raising. If you are ahead and check, and the late-position player bets, you gain by check-raising because he puts in more chips to see the next card. However if he checks after you have checked, then he gets to see the next card for free. Compare the two scenarios to see how often the late-position player has to bet in order for your check-raise strategy in the big blind to have positive value.

Assumptions:

- The pot has 2.25 big bets.
- Two players see the Flop.
- You are in the big blind, have an 80% chance of winning the hand and are ahead on the Flop.
- There are no more bets on the Turn or River.
- Your opponent will not raise if you bet nor reraise if you raise.
- Your opponent will bet if you check and call if you bet or raise.

Action	*Computation*	*Result, EV*
Checking if LP checks	(80% x 2.25) + (20% x 0)	+1.80
Successful check-raise	(80% x 3.25) + (20% x -1)	+2.40
Betting out if the LP calls	(80% x 2.75) + (20% x -0.5)	+2.10

With these assumptions a big blind who bets out has an EV of +2.10 big bets. If you are able to check-raise, then your EV increases to +2.40. If the late-position player checks behind you, then the EV decreases to +1.80. Using these numbers, if you assume the late-position player bets exactly half the time after you check, then the EV of checking is the same as the EV of betting.

Action	*Computation*	*Result, EV*
Check if LP bets 50% of the time		
	(1.80 x 50%) + (2.40 x 50%)	+2.10

If the late-position player is expected to bet 60% of the time, then check-raising is the better option.

Action	*Computation*	*Result, EV*
Check if LP bets 60% of the time		
	(1.80 x 40%) + (2.40 x 60%)	+2.16

If the late-position player is expected to bet less than 50% of the time, then betting instead of checking is the better play. The EV equation using 40%:

Action	*Computation*	*Result, EV*
Check if LP bets 40% of the time	(1.80 x 60%) + (2.40 x 40%)	+2.04

If a player has raised pre-Flop and only you in the big blind call, the pre-Flop raiser is likely to bet after you check, regardless of the Flop. This is why it is correct strategy to go for the check-raise when you are the first to act in a raised heads-up pot and you think you have the best hand. If you believe the pre-Flop raiser is less likely to bet than check, then you should think about betting out.

This scenario comes up often in Hold'em, on the Flop as described here, and on the Turn or the River as well. When you think you are ahead, it is better to check-raise if you believe your opponent is more likely to bet than to check. Knowing how your opponent plays is crucial. If she is passive and a scare card that hits your hand comes on the Turn or River, you may have to bet because you cannot count on her betting after you check. However if she is aggressive, then you can be more confident that she will bet after you check.

Defending Against a Check-Raise

How to play against a check-raise depends on your opponent. If you are sure he will not check-raise with a semi-bluff draw, such as an inside straight draw, then estimate the number of outs you have.

Suppose you raise in late position with ATo and only the big blind calls.

Your hand: ATo
Flop: Q-9-3 rainbow

Your opponent checks. You bet. He check-raises. You are getting 7.25:1 odds (4.25 small bets before the Flop, and so far 3 more small bets on the Flop). If your opponent has a split pair of 9's (without an A or T kicker), then you have 6 outs, which is enough to continue and call to see the Turn. However if your opponent has A9 or a split pair of Q's, then you have 3 outs. If the Flop gave you two overcards to the board rather than one, you can expect more outs.

If you have a strong hand (such as AQ) and get check-raised, you can expect the check-raiser to bet again on the Turn; and you should wait until the Turn to raise him. Reraising on the Flop may lose you an extra small bet as he is likely to check on the Turn due to your show of strength. This effectively makes it a free-card raise for all the wrong reasons, since the option to get a free card on the Turn is worthless when you have the best hand.

If a player check-raises you on the Turn, and the Turn card is the second card of that suit to hit the board, there is a chance that he is making a semi-bluff check-raise. He may have picked up four cards to a flush and realize he has added 9 more outs to his hand. It is easier to see semi-bluff check-raises with a newly-formed flush draw than with a newly-formed straight draw. If you think the check-raiser is capable of semi-bluffing in this spot and you have a good hand, such as top pair with a good kicker, then call him. Not only is there a chance that he will not hit his draw if he was semi-bluffing with a draw, but if he has a pair, your top pair may be good.

Defending against a check-raise is more difficult if you have a worse hand, such as middle pair. In that case you should consider calling if a flush draw appears on the Turn. But after the third flush card comes, consider folding on the River. An opponent who was semi-bluffing with a flush draw now has a flush. An opponent who was not semi-bluffing with a flush draw probably has a better made hand than yours.

CHAPTER 11 SUMMARY OF STRATEGIES

Fancy Play Syndrome

Fancy Play Syndrome is a phrase coined by Mike Caro. Fancy play syndrome is the overuse or misuse of plays like semi-bluffs, free-card raises, check-raises and slowplays. These plays may seem advanced and often look cool when they work, but they are not always the best way to increase your expected value (EV) on a particular hand. If your opponent is a calling station, then semi-bluffing has little value since the bluff factor is not worth much against a calling station. Using a free-card raise against an overly aggressive opponent may not work if he decides to reraise you or bet out on the Turn if you did not hit your draw. A check-raise may not work against passive opponents who turn your check-raises into checks. Each of these plays has its merits, but only with the right opponents and the right situation. Players who learn about these strategies feel empowered by the knowledge, and sometimes feel they must put the strategies into play as often as they can. The purpose of these plays is to increase EV, not dazzle your opponents.

Table 9
Advantages and Disadvantages of Strategies

Strategy	*Advantage*	*Disadvantage*
Raise for Free Card	You reduce your losses and increase your wins.	If your opponent uses counter strategies, you could lose more bets.
Bluff	You steal a pot.	You may get called and lose an extra bet.
Semi-Bluff	Same as bluff, but with a chance to win a showdown.	Same as bluff.
Slowplay	Players who would have folded might call later.	You may miss a bet or give a free card.
Check-Raise	You get more money into pot. You force multiple players to fold.	You give a free card. If someone else has the best hand, you lose more.

Table 9 summarizes the advantages and disadvantages of various strategies. Table 10 shows which players you should use these strategies against.

Table 10
When to Use Fancy Plays

Strategy	*Best Against*	*Worst Against*
Raise for Free Card	Passive to Average	Aggressive
Bluffing	More situation-dependent than player-dependent.	Calling Station
Semi-Bluffs	More situation-dependent than player-dependent.	Calling Station
Slowplays	Aggressive	Calling station
Check-Raise	Aggressive	Passive

CHAPTER 12
STARTING HANDS

The first decision in Limit Hold'em is how to play the first two cards, the starting hand. The quality of a given starting hand is not static. Some hands may be good or bad in different situations, depending on the characteristics and actions of the other players as well as your position. This chapter explains what to look for when deciding what to do with your starting hand.

Number of Hands: 1,326 or 169

There are 1,326 different starting hands. This counts K♣T♥ and K♠T♦ as two separate hands. If you cared about the order in which you receive the two cards, then you would be interested in the number of permutations of starting hands, which is 52 x 51 = 2,652. In Hold'em you do not care about the order of the two cards. Since every combination is represented twice, the 2,652 permutations are divided by 2 to get 1,326 combinations of starting hands.

These 1,326 different starting hands can be separated into three main categories: pairs (example: 9♠9♥), suited hands (example: A♦5♦), and unsuited hands (example: Q♣5♠).

Pairs

There are 13 different pairs, from AA down to 22. There are six possible combinations for each pair. The combinations for AA are:

A♥A♦	A♦A♣	A♥A♣
A♦A♠	A♥A♠	A♣A♠

That means 78 (13 different pairs x 6 combinations each) out of the 1,326 different hands are pairs, which is 5.9% of all hands.

Suited hands

There are 312 different suited starting hands, 78 per suit. Examples are A♥K♥, A♥5♥ and Q♥J♥. Why 78? There are 13 cards per suit and you want two of them. The number of combinations of two out of thirteen is 13 x 12 / 2, or 78.

One way to understand this is to look at the number of suited combinations with each card. If you take the A♥ first: there can be 12 different suited hands with the A♥, ranging from A♥K♥ down to A♥2♥. With the K♥: there are also 12 different combinations, of which you have already counted A♥K♥. There are 11 additional different suited cards with the K♥. The Q♥ has 10 different new combinations; and so on until you get to the 3♥, which has one new combination, 3♥2♥. Added up (12+11+10+9+8+7+6+5+4+3+2+1), the total number is 78 different hands with each suit. There are four different suits; so there are 312 (78 x 4) different suited hands, or 23.5% of all hands.

Unsuited hands

There are 78 different hands of each combination of unsuited hands. But instead of four different suits, there are 12 different suit combinations. For example AK can come in 12 different unsuited ways:

A♥K♣	A♥K♠	A♥K♦
A♦K♣	A♦K♠	A♦K♥
A♣K♦	A♣K♠	A♣K♥
A♠K♣	A♠K♥	A♠K♦

There are 936 (78 x 12) different unsuited hands, or 70.6% of all hands.

Table 11
Frequencies of Starting Hands

Starting Hand	*Types*	*Combos*	*Total*	*Pct of Hands*
Pair	13	6	78	5.9%
Suited	78	4	312	23.5%
Unsuited	78	12	936	70.6%
Total	169		1,326	100.0%

Overall there are 78 combinations of pairs, 312 combinations of suited hands and 936 combinations of unsuited hands. These add up to 1,326 total different hands. Table 11 shows the breakdown.

In Hold'em you do not care about the particular suits until after the Flop. For example before the Flop A♣J♣ is the same as A♦J♦, and 9♦8♣ is the same as 9♠8♥. It is only after the Flop that 9♦8♣ and 9♠8♥ can diverge in strength. A total of 169 different starting hands can be dealt. This is reflected in the "Types" column in table 11.

Understanding the distribution of starting hands is useful in determining how rare or common a type of starting hand is, and in narrowing your guess about your opponent's hand down to a few quality hands. For example a tight pre-Flop player might raise from under the gun with six different hands: AA, KK, QQ, AKs, AKo and AQs. With all other hands, such a player is likely to fold or call. The chart below shows the possible raising hands. "Percentage" is the percentage of the time the raising player holds this hand.

Hand	*Combos*	*Percentage*
AA	6	15.8%
KK	6	15.8%
QQ	6	15.8%
AKs	4	10.5%
AKo	12	31.6%
AQs	4	10.5%
Total	38	100.0%

Since this particular player raises under the gun with only these hands, he raises under the gun 2.9% of the time (38/1326). If you have played against this player often, you know he seldom raises under the gun. After he does raise, you know to get out of his way unless you have one of the strongest hands yourself.

If you hold pocket J's, normally a strong starting hand, you know you are in a dangerous position against this specific player. Against AA, KK, QQ, your JJ is an underdog. Against AKs, AKo, and AQs, JJ is a slight favorite. Table 12 shows how often you should win if you were all-in before the Flop.

If you assume no other players are going to play and the blinds will fold, then calling this tight pre-Flop raiser is a losing play with a strong hand like JJ! If you have only 3 small bets left in your stack and are reraising to go all-in, then you are risking 3 small bets to try to win 4.5 small bets (3 from the pre-Flop raiser, 1 from the big blind and 0.5 from the small blind). You would need to win 40% of the time to break even. The table above shows that JJ wins 38.4% of the time on average. Playing JJ with these parameters is slightly below the break-even goal of 40%.

In practice JJ is a playable hand against most tight pre-Flop raisers. Tight players are likely to raise with more hands than the ones listed in the table 12. You have positional advantage if you are not all-in. Table

Table 12
JJ vs. AQ or Better

Opp.'s Hand	*Combos*	*Percentage*	*Win Pct*	*Equity*
AA	6	15.8%	19%	3.0%
KK	6	15.8%	19%	3.0%
QQ	6	15.8%	19%	3.0%
AKs	4	10.5%	54%	5.7%
AKo	12	31.6%	57%	18.0%
AQs	4	10.5%	54%	5.7%
Total	38	100.0%		38.4%

Note: For tables 12 through 17, "Percentage" is the percentage of the time the opponent holds the hand described. The numbers in the "Win Pct" columns are from twodimes.net. "Equity" is the third column times the fourth column.

Table 13
JJ vs. TT or Better

Opp.'s Hand	*Combos*	*Percentage*	*Win Pct*	*Equity*
AA	6	10.5%	19%	2.0%
KK	6	10.5%	19%	2.0%
QQ	6	10.5%	19%	2.0%
AKs	4	7.0%	54%	3.8%
AKo	12	21.1%	57%	12.0%
AQs	4	7.0%	54%	3.8%
AQo	12	21.1%	57%	12.0%
JJ	1	1.8%	half	0.9%
TT	6	10.5%	81%	8.5%
Total	57	100.0%		47.0%

Note: There is only one possible combination where your opponent has JJ because you have JJ as well. "Half" means your hand value comes from splitting the pot, not from winning it all.

13 adds AQo, JJ and TT as other hands with which a tight early-position player raises.

With these assumptions: the average winning percentage for JJ is higher, jumping from 38.4% to 47.0%; and JJ has a high enough winning percentage to be playable. The under-the-gun raiser is raising with 4.3% of his hands (57/1326) rather than 2.9%; and this makes a big difference to JJ.

The AQo Debate

AQo is an interesting starting hand. Normally it is a high-quality hand. Most players open-raise pre-Flop with it. In some situations it is a hand worthy of reraising. However in a situation similar to the one discussed in the previous section, the correct decision is to fold! John Feeney brought up this issue in his book *Inside the Poker Mind* (pp 33-34). After Feeney's book was published, this issue was hotly debated on Internet forums.

Table 14
AQo vs. TT or Better

Opp.'s Hand	*Combos*	*Percentage*	*Win Pct*	*Equity*
AA	3	6.7%	7%	0.5%
KK	6	13.3%	28%	3.7%
QQ	3	6.7%	30%	2.0%
AKs	3	6.7%	24%	1.6%
AKo	9	20.0%	26%	5.2%
AQs	2	4.4%	48%	2.1%
AQo	7	15.6%	half	7.8%
JJ	6	13.3%	43%	5.7%
TT	6	13.3%	43%	5.7%
Total	45	100.0%		34.4%

Assume the following:

An early-position player open-raises. You know she plays tight and raises with high-quality hands. You know she will raise with AA, KK, QQ, AKs, AKo, AQs, AQo, JJ and TT, as shown in table 14. (Feeney's book makes different assumptions on the open-raiser's possible hands.) Your target is to win at least 40% of the time on average against this player, the target for an all-in player. You do have positional advantage. There is also a chance another player behind you holds a strong hand. Using 40% as the target should get you close to the true break-even point.

Note: Because you have AQo, there are two other ways to make AQs and seven other ways to make AQo.

On average you expect to win 34.4% of the time. This does not meet the 40% threshold in the all-in situation. There is a chance AQo is playable at a level slightly below 40% because of positional advantage and possible poor post-Flop play by the opponent. However 34.4% is so much below 40% that playing AQo in this situation does not make sense.

But what if the same raiser was in middle position rather than early position? This position difference means that she will open-raise with more hands. Similarly you could keep the player in the same under-the-gun position and assume she will raise with more hands. In either case the key is that the player is willing to raise with hands that are worse than the hands listed above. Suppose the player adds five other hands to her

Table 15
AQo vs. KQs or Better

Opp.'s Hand	*Combos*	*Percentage*	*Win Pct*	*Equity*
AA	3	4.6%	7%	0.3%
KK	6	9.1%	28%	2.6%
QQ	3	4.6%	30%	1.4%
AKs	3	4.6%	24%	1.1%
AKo	9	13.6%	26%	3.6%
AQs	2	3.0%	48%	1.5%
AQo	7	10.6%	half	5.3%
JJ	6	9.1%	43%	3.9%
TT	6	9.1%	43%	3.9%
99	6	9.1%	44%	4.0%
88	6	9.1%	44%	4.0%
AJs	3	4.6%	69%	3.1%
ATs	3	4.6%	69%	3.1%
KQs	3	4.6%	70%	3.2%
Total	66	100.00%		41.0%

open-raising hands: 99, 88, AJs, ATs and KQs, as shown in table 15. Totals may appear off due to rounding.

You can beat your opponent's average hand 41.0% of the time, which barely meets the 40% threshold. This is clearly a better situation for AQo than the one in table 14.

Starting Hands Can Change in Value

Some hands can be played in some situations but not in others. The variables that affect your decision include your position, previous players' actions, and the characteristics of players who have yet to act. Another key variable is how well the hand plays in multiple-player pots. Is it a good drawing hand? You care about the expected value (EV) of the hand, not just the probability of winning. Having a high chance of winning a small pot is good. Having a small chance to win a large pot can also be good. Unsuited high cards are better hands in small pots against few players. Drawing cards (suited connectors, small pairs) are better hands in large pots with multiple players. Here are a few examples of hands that should be played differently in different situations.

AQo

As shown in the previous section, although AQo is usually a reraisable hand, you should throw it away if a tight pre-Flop player open-raises in an early position. If a tight pre-Flop player open-raised from middle or late position, then you can feel more comfortable reraising. If the early-position player who open-raised was not as tight as originally described: then he could be raising with worse hands, and you can correctly play AQo. The value of AQo depends on other players' actions.

ATo

In late position after no other player has come in yet, this is a fine hand for stealing the blinds. Even if either or both of the blinds call, ATo is likely to be the best hand. If the blinds do not call, then you are happy to win the pot right there. If there is a limper or two, ATo may be the best hand, depending on who the limpers are and what positions they are limping in from. However if there are several limpers, then ATo decreases in value, becoming a marginal hand. ATo is not a good drawing hand, and could be dominated by a player limping in with AQo or AJo. Against a raise and a couple of callers, ATo should be thrown away.

JTs

In early position some players feel JTs is a good enough hand to limp in with and hope other players limp in with them. They think their bet helps build the pot as it encourages other players to limp along. If other players call, then the player with JTs is in a multiple-player pot, a good situation for JTs. This is a sound strategy as long as it is reasonable to think the pot will be unraised and have multiple players, as it is in most low-limit games. But in an aggressive game, as most middle- and high-limit games are, limping with JTs is asking for trouble because it would not be a surprise if the hand is played heads-up post-Flop.

In late position JTs has enough value to open-raise to steal the blinds. However if there is a raise from a reasonable opponent in early or middle position and no other player has called, then throw this hand away as it does not perform well in a heads-up pot.

A7o vs. 76s

When the hand is down to heads-up, A7o is a better hand than 76s. First, A7o has the advantage of having the ultimate high card. Second, A7o dominates 76s. After a 7 hits the board, the kicker usually means the difference in the hand. However if there are many other players involved in the hand, then the value of A7o decreases dramatically relative to 76s.

In multiple-player pots, the advantages that A7o enjoys over 76s when heads-up vanish. A7o no longer has the high-card equity; nor is it assured of being the dominating hand. A7o is likely to be dominated by another hand with an A and a higher kicker. 76s, on the other hand, does not need to worry about being dominated in a multiple-player pot because it is looking to make a draw, not a pair. 76s and A7o swap relative strengths when the scenario changes from heads-up to multiple-player. With fewer players, A7o is the better hand. With more players, 76s is the better hand. This makes A7o a good open-raising hand from late position to steal the blinds. 76s is a good hand to play in a cheap multiple-player pot.

ATo vs. T9s

This match-up is similar to the previous one. When matched head-to-head, ATo is superior to T9s. However in the big blind against a tight early-position raiser, T9s is the better hand of the two. As shown earlier, AQo does not play well against a tight early-position player. The same

Table 16
ATo vs. TTs or Better

Opp.'s Hand	*Combos*	*Percentage*	*Win Pct*	*Equity*
AA	3	6.3%	8.7%	0.5%
KK	6	12.5%	29.2%	3.7%
QQ	6	12.5%	28.9%	3.6%
AKs	3	6.3%	25.0%	1.6%
AKo	9	18.8%	26.7%	5.0%
AQs	3	6.3%	25.2%	1.6%
AQo	9	18.8%	26.8%	5.0%
JJ	6	12.5%	28.7%	3.6%
TT	3	6.3%	30.7%	1.9%
Total	48	100%		26.5%

holds true for ATo in the big blind against a tight early-position raiser, though it costs 1 small bet to see the Flop. Being out of position in all future rounds makes ATo tough to play under these circumstances. On the other hand, T9s is a more playable hand since it is not dominated by most hands that a tight early-position player would raise. If other players call, T9s gains more equity than ATo because T9s has drawing qualities and is more likely to be independent from other callers' hands. Hands that dominate ATo (AK, AQ and AJ) are always played by most players. The same cannot be said for hands that dominate T9s.

Tables 16 and 17 compare ATo and T9s versus a tight early-position player. They show that T9s is a better hand in this situation. The difference is big enough that calling a raise with T9s is correct when calling with ATo is marginal.

In the big blind against a tight early-position raiser, you prefer suited connectors like T9s or 76s over two high cards like ATo or A9o. In this example above, T9s wins 31.4% on average, while ATo wins 26.5% on average.

Now change the position of the open-raiser. Instead of raising from early position, the tight player is open-raising from the button. In late position she will raise with many more hands. She may raise with hands such as A7, KT, Q9, and JT if everyone folds to her. Do you see what is happening here? Against these hands, ATo is a better hand than T9s, and is the dominating hand against some hands with which the button will

Table 17
T9s vs. TTs or Better

Opp.'s Hand	*Combos*	*Percentage*	*Win Pct*	*Equity*
AA	6	10.2%	22.8%	2.3%
KK	6	10.2%	21.6%	2.2%
QQ	6	10.2%	20.3%	2.1%
AKs	4	6.8%	38.7%	2.6%
AKo	12	20.3%	41.2%	8.3%
AQs	4	6.8%	38.6%	2.6%
AQo	12	20.3%	41.0%	8.4%
JJ	6	10.2%	18.9%	1.9%
TT	3	5.1%	17.7%	0.9%
Total	59	100%		31.4%

raise. On the other hand, T9s now has a greater chance of being dominated. Hands like KJ and QJ, with which a player will raise on the button but not in early position, are favorites over T9s but slight underdogs to ATo. ATo is a better hand than T9s against a raise from the button. The open-raiser's position affects the relative value of these starting hands.

Starting-Hand Actions

Tables 18 through 20, "Starting-Hand Actions," show the recommended action for different starting hands in different situations. Each situation is shown with three different positions: early, middle and late. You can adapt the strategies on these tables to your environment. They are not analogous to a blackjack basic strategy chart, where it is crucial to memorize the table. Instead the importance is in understanding the reasoning behind each situation. When you are at a poker table, you can use the same logic to make your decisions.

Most hands have four rows attached to them. For hands with one row, the same strategy should be used in all situations. The four rows cover the following situations:

1. No one has yet called.
2. There are limpers but no raises.
3. There is a raise and no other players are involved yet.
4. There is a raise and there are at least two other callers.

The hands are categorized three ways: pairs, suited cards and unsuited cards. Hands that are not included should be folded, with rare

Key to tables 18-20

Call w/2: Call with 2 or more limpers
FAT: Fold against tight raiser
RA1: Raise only against 1 limper
RA2: Raise against 2 or more limpers
RAL: Reraise against late position raiser
RAM: Reraise against mid/late position raiser
RAW Raise against 1 or 2 weak limpers
ROB: Raise on Button

Table 18
Starting-Hand Actions, Pairs

Hand	*Early*	*Middle*	*Late*
AA, KK, QQ	Reraise	Reraise	Reraise
JJ/TT	Raise; Limp	Raise	Raise
	Raise	Raise	Raise; Call
	Reraise	Reraise	Reraise
	N/A	Call	Call
99	Limp; Raise	Raise	Raise
	Call	Call; Raise	Raise; Call
	Fold	Reraise; Call; Fold	Reraise; Call
	N/A	Call	Call
88/77	Limp	Raise	Raise
	Call	Call	Raise; Call
	Fold	Call; Fold	RAM; fold against earlier raisers
	N/A	Fold; Call	Fold; Call
66/55	Fold; Limp	Fold	Raise
	Call	Call	Raise; Call
	Fold	Fold	RAL; fold against earlier raisers
	N/A	Fold; Call	Fold; Call
44/33/22	Fold	Fold	Raise
	Call	Call	Raise; Call
	Fold	Fold	Fold; Reraise
	N/A	Fold	Call w/2; Fold

exceptions. These tables assume a typical nine-handed game, with a distribution among your opponents of two good players, three decent players and three bad players. Adjust the actions if your poker table has more good players or more bad players. At a table with more tough and aggressive players, refrain from getting involved in pots with drawing hands unless you are positive it will be a multiple-player pot. At a table with more passive players, take more chances with drawing hands in early position since the pot is likely to be contested by multiple players.
(continued on page 172)

Table 19
Starting-Hand Actions, Suited Cards

Hand	*Early*	*Middle*	*Late*
AKs	Reraise	Reraise	Reraise
AQs	Raise	Raise	Raise
	Raise	Raise	Raise
	Call; Reraise	Call; Reraise	Reraise; Call
	N/A	Call	Call; Reraise
AJs	Raise; Limp	Raise	Raise
	Call; Raise	Raise; Call	Raise
	Call	Call; Reraise	Reraise; Call
	N/A	Call	Call
ATs	Limp	Raise	Raise
	Call	Call; Raise	Raise
	Fold	Fold	RAL; Fold
	N/A	Call; Fold	Call; Fold
A9s/A8s/A7s	Fold; Limp	Raise; Limp	Raise
	Call	Call	Call; Raise
	Fold	Fold	Fold; RAL
	N/A	Call; Fold	Call
A6s - A2s	Fold	Limp; Fold	Raise
	Fold	Call	Call
	Fold	Fold	Fold
	N/A	Fold	Fold; Call
KQs	Limp; Raise	Raise	Raise
	Call; Raise	Raise	Raise
	Fold; Call	Fold; Call	RAL; Call
	N/A	Call	Call
KJs	Limp	Raise; Limp	Raise
	Call	Call	Raise; Call
	Fold	Fold	Fold; RAL
	N/A	Fold	Fold

Table 19 continued

Hand	*Early*	*Middle*	*Late*
KTs	Fold	Fold	Raise
	Call; Fold	Call; Fold	Call
	Fold	Fold	Fold
	N/A	Fold	Fold
K9s - K6s	Fold	Fold	Raise
	Fold	Fold	Call; Fold
	Fold	Fold	Fold
	N/A	Fold	Fold
QJs	Limp	Raise; Limp	Raise
	Call	Call	Call; Raise
	Fold	Fold	Fold
	N/A	Call	Call
JTs	Limp	Limp; Raise	Raise
	Call	Call	Call; Raise
	Fold	Fold	Fold
	N/A	Call	Call
QTs/T9s	Fold; Limp	Limp; Fold	Raise
	Call	Call	Call
	Fold	Fold	Fold
	N/A	Fold	Call; Fold
98s/87s/76s	Fold	Fold	Fold
	Fold	Call	Call w/2
	Fold	Fold	Fold
	N/A	Fold	Fold
Q9s	Fold	Fold	Raise
	Fold	Fold	Call w/2
	Fold	Fold	Fold
	N/A	Fold	Fold
J9s/T8s	Fold	Fold	Fold
	Fold	Fold	Call w/2
	Fold	Fold	Fold
	N/A	Fold	Fold

Table 20
Starting-Hand Actions, Unsuited Cards

Cards	*Early*	*Middle*	*Late*
AKo	Reraise	Reraise	Reraise
AQo	Raise	Raise	Raise
	Raise; Call	Raise	RA2; Call w/2
	FAT; Reraise	FAT; Reraise	FAT; Reraise
	N/A	Call	Call
AJo	Limp	Raise	Raise
	Call	Call	Call; Raise
	Fold	Fold	Fold; RAL
	N/A	Fold; Call	Fold; Call
ATo	Fold	Raise	Raise
	Fold	Call	Call; RAW
	Fold	Fold	Fold; RAL.
	N/A	Fold	Fold
A9o	Fold	Fold; Raise	Raise
	Fold	Fold	RA1; Call w/2
	Fold	Fold	Fold
	N/A	Fold	Fold
A8o/A7o	Fold	Fold	Raise
	Fold	Fold	RA1; Call w/2
	Fold	Fold	Fold
	N/A	Fold	Fold
A6o - A2o	Fold	Fold	In the cutoff, raise with A6, A5; Fold with A4 - A2. ROB with A6 - A2.
	Fold	Fold	Fold
	Fold	Fold	Fold
	N/A	Fold	Fold

Table 20 continued

Cards	*Early*	*Middle*	*Late*
KQo	Limp; Fold	Raise	Raise
	Call	Call; Raise	Raise
	Fold	Fold	Fold; RAL
	N/A	Fold	Fold; Call in a loose game
KJo	Fold	Fold	Raise
	Fold	Call	Call
	Fold	Fold	Fold
	N/A	Fold	Fold
KTo - K8o	Fold	Fold	In the cutoff, Raise with KTo; Fold with K9o and K8o. ROB with KTo-K8o.
	Fold	Fold	Call with KTo; fold K9o and K8o
	Fold	Fold	Fold
	N/A	Fold	Fold
QJo	Fold	Fold	Raise
	Fold	Call; Fold	Call
	Fold	Fold	Fold
	N/A	Fold	Fold
QTo	Fold	Fold	ROB; otherwise fold.
	Fold	Fold	Call
	Fold	Fold	Fold
	N/A	Fold	Fold
JTo/T9o	Fold	Fold	ROB; otherwise fold.
	Fold	Fold	Call against many limpers.
	Fold	Fold	Fold
	N/A	Fold	Fold

Differentiate between passive and aggressive players who act before you and who act after you. You can see the actions of those who act before you; but you will not know the actions of the players after you until after you have acted.

If the players after you are loose, you can be looser and call with some drawing hands because you can count on loose players to limp after you limp and make it a multiple-player pot.

If the players after you are tight, you can be more aggressive with unsuited high cards (such as AJo and KQo), as you do not have to worry about them calling your raise and making it a multiple-player pot. (A call by any player may encourage other players to call as well.) It also means your drawing hands (such as JTs and T9s) have less value since you cannot count on tight players behind you to follow your limp by limping themselves.

The correct strategy for some hands falls into a gray area. With those hands, all the choices are listed, with my preferred action listed first. You must choose for yourself, based on your own style and how your opponents play. If you do not feel comfortable being the aggressor all the time, especially in early position, you may choose to limp instead of raising if the recommended action on the table is Raise/Limp. JJ is such a hand. If you do not feel like mixing it up against tricky players, you may decide to limp in early position (the second option listed for JJ) rather than raise.

Table 21 summarizes the percentage of hands to call, raise and fold in each position. Each section of table 21 has lines for the four different actions, as in tables 18 through 20, and also has a line for the average.

Note: The Average rows at the bottom of each section of table 21 reflect the average of the four different situations. They are not weighted for the probability of each situation occurring. In late position it is more common to be faced with a raise (the third and fourth situations) than in the other two situations. The average numbers in table 21 do not reflect this; but they provide a useful way to view the differences in the positions.

As you can see, the recommendation is to fold a vast majority of your starting hands. When you do play them, play them more often from late position. Raise more from late position than from early or middle position.

Table 21
Starting-Hand Actions, Percentages

	Action	*Early*	*Middle*	*Late*
Call	No other callers	4.7%	2.4%	0.0%
	Limper but no raises	9.0%	13.6%	16.0%
	One raise, no calls	0.6%	1.5%	0.0%
	One raise, 2+ calls	N/A	4.7%	6.9%
Average	Call	4.8%	5.6%	5.7%

	Action	*Early*	*Middle*	*Late*
Raise	No calls	5.0%	11.2%	24.9%
	Limper but no raises	4.7%	5.3%	10.4%
	One raise, no calls	3.5%	3.9%	8.3%
	One raise, 2+ calls	N/A	2.6%	2.6%
Average	Raise	4.4%	5.8%	11.6%

	Action	*Early*	*Middle*	*Late*
Fold	No calls	90.3%	86.4%	75.1%
	Limper but no raises	86.3%	81.1%	73.6%
	One raise, no calls	95.9%	94.6%	91.7%
	One raise, 2+ calls	N/A	92.7%	90.5%
Average	Fold	90.8%	88.7%	82.7%

Calling in late vs. middle position

You should play more hands in late position than in middle position. Table 21 shows that in late position, you should call or raise in 17.3% (5.7% + 11.6%) of all situations. In middle position you should call or raise in 11.4% (5.6% + 5.8%) of all situations. Raisable hands increase from 5.8% (middle position) to 11.6% (late position), while callable hands stay nearly the same at 5.6% and 5.7%. Two of the calling categories decrease to 0% in late position. In late position in the situations of "No other callers" and "One raise, no other players yet," either fold or raise; never call. There is a big jump in the situation of "No other callers" from raising with 11.2% of all hands in middle position to raising with 24.9% of all hands in late position. Hands such as K♦T♥ and Q♣J♥ are raisable hands from the button if no one else has come in, but should be mucked in middle position.

Sunk Cost and the Blinds

Many people think they need to defend their blinds all the time because they have already partially called and get to see a Flop at a 50% discount compared to other players. This is incorrect thinking. Think of the blinds you have put up as part of the pot, not as part of your stack. The chips you put up for the blinds are a sunk cost. You had to put them up regardless of the strength of your hand. You have equity in the pot, as do the other players. However if your starting hand is poor, there is no reason to put in good money after dead money.

Playing the Blinds

Playing the Big Blind: One raiser and no other callers

Whether to play your hand in the Big Blind when there is one raiser and no other callers depends on the characteristics and position of the raiser.

If the raiser is a solid player...

From early/middle position

Play your hand as cautiously as you would if you were acting in late position. The early/middle position solid player's raise signifies a strong hand which may dominate many of your possible high card hands. As mentioned earlier, T9s is better than ATo in a spot like this. The earlier the position of the raiser, the worse ATo becomes. You are offered higher pot odds to see the Flop, so it is worthwhile to call. Be quick to dump your hand if the Flop does not fit your hand.

From late position

The raiser likely is trying to steal the blinds. Now a high hand like ATo becomes more valuable because it has a higher chance of being the dominant hand. You can defend your big blind more often and you can also play back aggressively if the Flop fits your hand. This means often check-raising on the Flop with any pair and any draw.

If the raiser is an aggressive player...

From early position

Against an aggressive player you still have to play your hand cautiously. Most aggressive players know to adjust their aggressiveness based on their position. An aggressive player raising from early position usually has a quality hand.

From middle position

An aggressive player will open-raise with more hands in middle position, so high cards have more value in the big blind than against a solid player's middle position raise. This is similar to a solid player's open-raise from late position.

From late position

The aggressive raiser likely is trying to steal the blinds. A high hand like ATo is valuable because it has a good chance of being the dominant hand.

If the raiser is a passive player...

From early/middle position

Watch out. It is likely that the raiser has a strong hand and you should be careful. The only good thing is that most passive players are typically poor players, so they may lose more to you if you get lucky on the Flop. For example if you have ATo a poor player may call you through the River with QQ when the Flop comes A-K-x.

From late position

Passive players are less likely to try to steal the blinds. They are likely to have a stronger hand than other players when they are open-raising from late position. High hands are still good in the big blind, but not as good as against other players.

Playing the Big Blind: A raise with one or more callers

When you are in the big blind, and there is a raise with one or more callers, then you know the pot will be a multiple-player pot. Typically with two other players the pot will be offering you at least 5:1 to see the Flop. With four other players the pot will be offering you at least 9:1 to see the Flop. The exception is if an early position player limped with the intention of reraising when it gets back to him. With more players you can see the Flop with more hands, especially if you are confident no one will reraise behind you. You can be liberal with calling in these situations, much more so than you would in late position because you are getting much better pot odds. When the Flop comes you have to play carefully since you will be out of position in every round. Loose play to see the Flop does not require playing loosely after you have seen the Flop.

Playing the Small Blind

In a typical blind structure, the small blind is half the amount of the big blind. In some games the small blind puts up 2/3 the big blind; in those games the small blind can be more aggressive because calling or raising means risking fewer additional chips. The discussion assumes the small blind is half the big blind.

The Small Blind is in a worse position than the Big Blind. The Small Blind does not have the advantage of being the last to act in the pre-Flop round. In order to see the Flop, the Small Blind has to commit more chips than the Big Blind. These two factors mean that the Small Blind needs to play more conservatively than the Big Blind. The Small Blind needs a better quality hand to see the Flop. If the Small Blind has a playable hand, and it looks like the open-raiser is trying to steal the blinds, then reraising is usually a better option than calling. Calling by the Small Blind offers the Big Blind good pot odds to see the Flop. A reraise with a worthwhile hand by the Small Blind puts the Big Blind in a tougher position with worse pot odds; and it also puts a late position blind stealer on the defensive.

Stealing the Blinds

When you are in late position and everyone ahead of you has folded, your decision is between raising and folding. Do not call. Factors to consider when trying to steal the blinds:

1. How likely are you to have the best hand?

After everyone ahead of you has folded and you are in late position, the better hands are the high-card hands. As discussed earlier, this is the position where a high-card hand like ATo is better than a drawing hand like T9s.

2. How loose are the blinds?

It is great to have loose opponents, except that loose opponents do not let their blinds get stolen. Tighter players are more willing to give up and fold their blinds after you raise, so it is easier to steal their blinds. Looser players call more often. They give up so much edge after the Flop with poor play that you will not mind when they call pre-Flop. However if they are loose pre-Flop but play decently after the Flop, you will not be happy. Against loose players you should limit the hands that you use to try to steal the blinds.

3. How aggressive are the blinds?

If the blinds are aggressive, then they may play back at you if they think are you are trying to steal the blinds. In particular the small blind can benefit by reraising if doing so makes the big blind fold. If the blinds are aggressive, you may have to put in 3 bets to see the Flop when you try to steal the blinds. Against aggressive players, limit your blind-stealing hands.

4. How well do the blinds play post-Flop?

If the blinds play well post-Flop, then there is less value in trying to steal blinds. If they play poorly, then there is more value in trying to steal the blinds. If their pre-Flop call is correct, they will give up enough edge after the Flop that it is worthwhile to be involved in the hand against them.

5. How tight do the blinds play on the Flop?

If the blinds like to call raises before the Flop, but play tight on the Flop, then a blind-stealing raise is worthwhile. You do not mind them calling and seeing the Flop if they will fold often on the Flop.

6. How predictable are your opponents?

Predictable players are better to play against. If a predictable opponent reraises before the Flop or check-raises on the Flop, you can be assured that you are beaten. It is more difficult to play against unpredictable opponents. Try to steal the blinds of the predictable players more often than the blinds of the unpredictable players.

7. How often have you raised the blinds in the last few rounds?

If you have raised the blinds often in the last few rounds, whether those raises were legitimate raises or blind-stealing raises, then you should be more conservative when you are in the position to steal the blinds again. If your opponents think you are taking advantage by raising their blinds, they are more likely to call your raises.

Playing the Blinds: To Defend or Not to Defend

The blinds are often faced with a late-position player's open-raise. When you are in this position you must decide whether to defend your blind hand. Factors to consider after a late-position player raises in an apparent blind-stealing attempt:

1. How likely are you to have the best hand?

If you think you have the best hand, you should consider reraising. Specifically when you are in the small blind, a reraise has value when you think you have the best hand because it forces the big blind to put in 2 bets or fold. If you raise in the big blind, you are making it more expensive for the blind stealer (and possibly the small blind if he called). If you reraise from either blind and the blind stealer's hand is weak: she will call your raise due to pot odds, but may then meekly fold on the Flop after you bet out.

2. How often does your opponent attempt to steal the blinds with unwarranted hands?

If your opponent is constantly open-raising in late position, then loosen up and call with more hands. You also need to play more aggressively and raise back when you have decent hands with which you might not normally raise back. Reraise before the Flop or check-raise on the Flop against these blind stealers. You do not want anyone to push you around at the poker table. When you are in the blinds, other players are looking to push you around.

3. How well does your opponent play post-Flop?

An opponent who plays well after the Flop is more difficult to play against. In a blind position you are in a worse position than your opponent because you act first. A good post-Flop player is able to take advantage of his position; so be more selective.

Deceptive Pre-Flop Play

Varying your play

In games where you face the same solid opponents routinely, vary how you play starting hands to a small degree. In certain situations you do not have to adjust at all, such as after everyone has folded to you in late position. If your strategy is close to what is suggested in the "Starting Hands Actions" tables in this chapter, then you will be raising with about 25% of your hands in those situations. With that many different hands it is no longer necessary to vary your play for the purpose of fooling your opponents. When you are raising with 25% of your hands, the texture and quality of your hand is already unpredictable.

The time to vary your play is when the pot has yet to be raised and you have a drawing hand. If the pot has not been raised, it is less likely that anyone else has a premium hand. With a drawing hand you can make nice hands and may surprise your opponents. For example open-raising in middle position with a hand like Q♣J♣ or T♠9♠ once in a while is useful. But do not do it often. It is less worthwhile to do it from the early positions because there are so many more players who have yet to act. If one of the players behind you has a premium hand, then a raise in early position with a drawing hand is too costly to be offset by the value of varying your play to throw off other players' perceptions.

Pre-Flop in early position

Do not worry about giving away information by your pre-Flop play in early position. Since many players will act behind you, it is difficult to be deceptive without giving up much edge. There are many players you will need to fool one way or another. Those players who know what a raise from a tight early-position player means will fold; and you will not be able to extract value out of them. But in typical games there should be enough players who are willing to call a raise with dominated hands such as AJo and KQo that it is worthwhile to raise in early position with your best hands.

In tougher games where more players are willing to fold decent cards against a tight early-position raiser, you should sometimes limp in with a stronger hand. If there are many players who will fold AQo to your raise under the gun, then when you raise with AA, you gain nothing from them. But if you limp in intending to reraise, then you may trap a player with a hand that she would not play if she knew the real strength of your hand.

Common Mistakes Made With Starting Hands

Early position: suited connectors and middle to small pairs

A common mistake players make with suited connectors and middle to small pairs in early position is either always folding or always calling with these hands. Instead of using one fixed strategy, you should be more flexible and adjust to your environment. The decision to limp with these drawing hands should depend on how other players play and on the mood of the table.

If you can count on other players limping along with you and the mood at the table is happy-go-lucky, then you can be more confident that the pot will be contested by multiple players and not be raised. When this happens, you have the pot odds you need to limp in and see the Flop. In low-limit games such as \$2-\$4, \$3-\$6, and \$5-\$10, the atmosphere of the game and the general personalities of the players usually make a limp with a drawing hand correct. In those games you will be more confident you can get into a multiple-player pot.

A problem occurs when you are not sure if others will limp along after you limp. Size up the other players before you are faced with a drawing starting hand in early position. If you are at a fairly tough table with a few professional players, these drawing hands may be unplayable. If you cannot expect to get many other callers, then you will not be able to put yourself into position to get the pot odds that would make your limp correct.

Middle position: limping with non-drawing hands

After a few players have limped, it is a mistake to limp along in middle position without a drawing hand. If you are in middle position and other players have limped, you can limp along with drawing hands like 9♣8♣ and A♦5♦. But other hands that may be as strong or stronger in other situations do not play as well in multiple-player pots. Hands like A♣7♥ and K♠9♣ should be thrown away in this spot. These are good hands to raise in late-position blind-stealing attempts, but they have drawbacks in multiple-player pots. The problems include kickers and drawing problems. Other players may be limping with dominating hands like A♠9♦ or K♥J♥. Even if you make a straight with K♠9♣, someone might beat you with a better straight.

Late-position: calling raises with high cards

An earlier section of this chapter discussed playing AQo against a tight early-position raiser. The same concept applies to other hands in late position after a middle-position player raises. Often players indiscriminately call raises with high-card hands such as K♣Q♠ and A♦T♣. If the raiser is a reasonable player with reasonable raising standards and is raising from middle position, then typically you should fold these hands. Often a legitimate raiser dominates K♣Q♠ and A♦T♣ with hands like A♣K♠ and A♥Q♥. Calling a raise when there is a good chance you are either dominated or facing a big pair is not a pleasant way to play poker.

On the other hand if you are on the button and an aggressive player open-raises in the cutoff seat, you can consider reraising with K♣Q♠ and A♦T♣. The difference is that the player in the cutoff open-raises with a wide variety of hands. Merely calling a raise gives the blinds too much equity to call and see the Flop. It is better to reraise and play the hand heads-up, because it is likely that you have the better hand and unsuited high-card hands play better in heads-up situations.

General: not being careful with pre-Flop calling standards

It is easy to loosen up and add to the hands you play. If you often limp with T9s, it is easy to take a step back and also limp with similar hands, such as T8s and 98s. Once you have made that move, it becomes easy to limp in with hands that resemble 98s, such as 98o. This is dangerous. You have gone from limping with a borderline hand such as T9s to limping with an unwarranted hand such as 98o. This is one of the dangers of playing marginal or borderline hands. The hands themselves may not be dangerous. The danger lies in what they can represent when you get a hand that may look similar in quality but is not.

Different Types of Starting Hands

Below are comments on different type of starting hands. Under each type of hand the following questions are answered:

1. How many players is it best to play against with this hand?
2. How aggressive can you be pre-Flop?
3. How does this hand play on the Flop?

Big pairs (AA, QQ)

1. Big pairs play well against any number of players. With more players the chance of winning the hand decreases; but the increased size of the pot compensates for it. With KK and QQ against multiple players, you may worry after an overcard comes on the board making it likely that someone has made a bigger split pair.

2. These are the best hands and you should be aggressive. Try to get the most money you can into the pot. Some players limp in early position with AA because they do not want to scare off opponents. They are hoping someone else will raise so they can reraise.

3. Big pairs play well on the Flop if there are no overcards on the board.

Middle pairs (99, 77)

1. Middle pairs play best against either one opponent or several, rather than two. Against multiple players, middle pairs play the same way as low pairs. You need to hit a set to have the best hand. Against one opponent you are more likely to have the better hand. There is a smaller chance your opponent will hit a split pair (whereas two opponents would have four possible overcards combined).

2. You can be aggressive with middle pairs if playing heads-up. Against multiple players you are looking to hit a set on the Flop; so it is logical to get in as cheaply as possible. If you are last to act, a raise pre-Flop after many others have limped in could be worthwhile when you think there is a high chance it may buy you a free card on the Flop.

3. These hands play well in heads-up spots, especially if there are no overcards. They are playable against multiple players if you have hit a set, or have other reasons to stay in.

Low pairs (44, 22)

1. Several opponents are best if you have one of these hands, so that you will win a big pot if you hit a set. In heads-up hands it is likely you are facing two overcards, and low pairs have a small edge.

2. You cannot be aggressive with these hands. You are looking to hit a set on the Flop; so you should try to see the Flop as cheaply as possible.

3. On the Flop you will have either a great hand or a bad hand. If you hit a set, you can raise and be aggressive. If you do not hit a set, you should get out if any other player shows aggression.

High suited connectors (KQs, QJs)

1. High suited connectors play well in most pots. Against multiple players, high suited connectors have the qualities of a drawing hand. In heads-up situations they have high-card qualities.

2. Unless you are open-raising from late position, you should not be too aggressive with high suited connectors before the Flop. If you are in a multiple-player pot, you should see if you have a draw on the Flop. If you are heads-up against a raiser, you could be facing a hand with higher cards.

3. Many Flops are good with high suited connectors. If you have a draw on the Flop or hit a split top pair, you will be able to continue.

High suited one-gappers (AQs, KJs)

1. The gap between the cards hurts the drawing aspect of these hands. You are playing for the high-card factor more than the drawing factor. Although these hands play all right in multiple-player pots, it is better to play against few players when you have the highest cards of the bunch.

2. If there are few players, you can be aggressive with these hands. With AQs you can open-raise from any position and often reraise another player. With KJs you can open-raise from late position. If many players have limped in, AQs can be a raisable hand but KJs no longer is.

3. When you are heads-up, these hands usually play well on the Flop. Even if you do not hit a split pair, you may have the better high hand. Against multiple players you need a reason to continue, such as a draw or split top pair.

Middle suited connectors (T9s, 98s)

1. You are trying to hit a flush or a straight with these hands. They play well in multiple-player pots.

2. You should not invest many chips before you see the Flop. Try to get in as cheaply as possible. Fold if there is a raise. Avoid limping with these hands in tight and aggressive games.

3. Against multiple players you need to hit a strong hand such as two pair or a draw to continue. A split middle pair is usually not strong enough to stay against multiple players, although it would be in a heads-up hand.

Middle suited one-gappers (T8s, 97s)

1. These hands play well if you can get in cheaply and there are multiple players. The odds of making a straight are lower than with middle suited connectors. These are not good hands against few players. Most of the time these hands should be folded.

2. You cannot play aggressively pre-Flop with these hands.

3. These hands have the same quality as middle suited connectors; but they have a smaller chance of picking up a good draw.

High non-suited connectors (KQ, QJ)

1. These hands play best in heads-up situations where you are confident you have the high cards. High non-suited connectors play well in late position as an open-raiser. They do not play as well in multiple-player pots, though they can be playable in a multiple-player pot if you are sure you will not be raised pre-Flop.

2. Unless you are a late-position open-raiser, you cannot be aggressive pre-Flop with these hands.

3. In multiple-player pots these hands need to hit either a top split pair or a straight draw in order to be playable on the Flop. In heads-up pots where you are the late-position raiser, you can continue without a pair, hoping the other player will yield and fold.

A-middle suited (A9s, A8s)

1. These hands play best either heads-up or against several opponents (rather than just two). Heads-up they play well because you have the A with a middle kicker. If there is a raise, you should fold unless you believe it will be a multiple-player pot. Against multiple players these hands have greater value in the possibility of hitting the nut flush.

2. You can be aggressive as a middle- to late-position open-raiser, but not in multiple-player pots.

3. In multiple-player pots if you hit a split pair of A's, be careful since your kicker is mediocre. These are sometimes tough hands to play on the Flop and after for this reason.

A-small suited (A5s, A3s)

1. The high-card quality of the A is reduced with these hands because of the small kicker. These hands play best in multiple-player pots, as there is also straight potential. They play well in heads-up situations if you are a late-position open-raiser. If there is a raise, you should fold unless you believe it will be a multiple-player pot.

2. You cannot be aggressive with these hands pre-Flop, except when stealing the blinds. In multiple-player pots you can raise if you are in late position. Most of the time you should limp along and see the Flop.

3. Like A-middle suited hands, these hands may be tough to play if you hit a split pair of A's, since your kicker is small. Do not be afraid to fold if you hit an A, especially if other players show aggression.

CHAPTER 13
THE FLOP

The Flop is a critical point in Hold'em. On the Flop players get to see three cards, which is more at one time than in any other round in the game. Each player has now seen five-sevenths of the total cards, giving them enough information to know how to proceed from this point forward with some degree of certainty. Since the betting on the Flop is on the cheap side, many players use this round to pose and to jostle for position; so aggressive play is not as meaningful as it may be on the Turn or River.

Thinking on the Flop

There are three main steps to analyzing the Flop.

- Analyze what the Flop means for your hand.
- Analyze what the Flop may mean for other players' hands.
- Analyze what your opponents may think about your hand.

Step 1: Analyze what the Flop means for your hand

Pre-Flop drawing hands

If you started with a drawing hand pre-Flop, you need to see if the Flop keeps your draw alive.

Example

Your hand: 9♥8♥
Flop: A♣T♦3♦

The three Flop cards are unrelated to your hand, so it is usually best to give up. The only time to continue is if you have raised pre-Flop into a small field, and they check to you on the Flop. Then a bluff on the Flop may win the pot.

If you do pick up a draw on the Flop with your 9♥8♥, it is possible you should continue, depending on the strength of the betting. With a Flop of T♥7♥3♣ where you have a straight flush draw, you can stay around until the River to see if you catch your draw. However not all draws are worthwhile to continue with on the Flop. For example with the 9♥8♥ as your starting hand: if the Flop is Q♠T♦3♠, you should fold if there is a bet and a raise.

Pre-Flop big pair

If you started with a made hand, such as a big pocket pair, be aware of any overcards or pairs on the Flop. If there are overcards or a pair on the Flop, then any player needs only one card in hand to have a better hand than yours.

Example

Your hand: Q♣Q♥
Flop 1: A♥9♣3♣
Flop 2: J♣J♥3♠

In Flop 1 any player with an A has a better hand. In Flop 2 any player with a J has a better hand. They need one card in their starting hands to work with the Flop, while you are working with both of your cards. No cards higher than your pair and no pairs on the board are usually good signs; but be aware of flush draws and straight draws.

Example

Your hand: Q♣Q♥
Flop 3: J♦T♣3♦
Flop 4: J♥6♣3♦

Flop 3 is more dangerous for your big pair than Flop 4. Flop 3 has possible straight draws and flush draws. In Flop 4 draws are less likely

Table 22
Chance of Pocket Pairs Facing Overcards on Board

Pocket Pair	*Overcard*	*No Overcard*
AA	0%	100%
KK	22.6%	77.4%
QQ	41.4%	58.6%
JJ	57.0%	43.0%
TT	69.5%	30.5%
99	79.3%	20.7%
88	86.7%	13.3%
77	92.1%	7.9%
66	95.8%	4.2%
55	98.1%	1.9%

since it is a rainbow Flop with big gaps between the cards. Flop 4 is less threatening to a made hand.

When you have a big pocket pair, you normally worry about an overcard hitting the board. The only pocket pair that does not have to worry about overcards is AA. Table 22 shows the percentage of Flops that have at least one overcard to your pocket pair, and the percentage of Flops that have no overcards to your pocket pair.

Pre-Flop high cards

If you started with two big cards, catching a pair is usually a good sign, especially if it is the top split pair. If you did not catch a pair, you may still be ahead with your big cards. You could catch on the Turn or River. If you were the pre-Flop raiser, and only the blinds call, there is a good chance you have the best hand. But if other players were aggressive before the Flop and/or on the Flop, then your chances are dramatically lower. Even if you catch a pair on the Turn or River, another player may improve simultaneously. High cards without a pair after the Flop are tough to play. Consider the quality of your opponents and the texture of the situation more than your own hand.

Step 2: Analyze what the Flop may mean for other players' hands

Looking for possible draws

Whether or not you have a possible straight draw or flush draw, watch out for all possible draws. Flush draws are the easiest to see on the Flop, as two or three cards of the same suit mean there is a chance someone has a flush draw. Straight draws are tougher to see. If the Flop has cards with two or fewer gaps, then there is a chance that someone is holding an open-ended straight draw.

Examples of Flops that offer a possible open-ended straight draw:

Flop	*Hands with Open-Ended Straight Draws*
Q-J-3	KT, T9
Q-T-3	KJ, J9
Q-9-3	JT
Q-9-7	JT, T8, 86

If there is a three-gap with any two cards on the Flop, then there is a possible inside straight draw. These are less worrisome since they have few outs.

Playing against a big pair or high cards

An opponent who was aggressive pre-Flop usually has a pair or two big cards. Flops that contain an A are dangerous, as are Flops with a K or Q, to a lesser degree.

Example

Your hand: 87s
Flop: A-7-3

You have flopped a split pair of 7's, but your opponent's raise from middle position probably means you are an underdog. Your opponent is likely to have a pocket pair bigger than 7's or two high cards with one of them an A. Five is not enough outs to continue on the Flop unless you think you can bully a player to lay down a pocket pair due to fear of the A on the board.

A better Flop for your 87s is one with three low cards.

Flop: 7-3-2

The hands you are worried about are a bigger pocket pair than 7's, a set, or a split pair of 7's with a higher kicker. This Flop is less worrisome than one with an A, given your hand and position.

Step 3: Analyze what your opponents think about your hand

You were the pre-Flop raiser

If you raised pre-Flop: then other players usually put you on a pair or two big cards, and for the most part they are correct. The sharp players will also notice if the Flop comes without any big cards. If you have a big pair, this is good for you as they will be willing to give you more action.

Example

Your hand: AA
Flop 5: 8-3-2
Flop 6: A-3-2

Players without an A in their hands are more willing to continue with Flop 5 than with Flop 6. The A in Flop 6 will scare off any player except for someone who holds the last A, especially after you raised pre-Flop.

You called a raise pre-Flop from the blinds

If you called a raise from the blinds, then no one can pinpoint your hand well. Your opponents will usually bet if you check to them, assuming it is a small field. You should consider check-raising anytime the Flop fits your hand.

You Flop a set

When you Flop a middle or low set, it is tough for your opponents to see what you have made.

Example

Your hand: 88
Flop: A-T-8

Any player may think an A makes a strong hand, especially with a strong kicker. Your trip 8's are difficult for any opponent to read. With a disguised hand like this, and a possible strong hand for your opponent, you can play aggressively on the Flop. You know your aggressive play will not chase away a split pair of A's on the Turn. An opponent who does not have a split pair of A's is likely to give up without putting in another bet anyway.

Betting on the Flop

Betting with the probable best hand

If you think you have the best hand and no one has bet, you should bet on the Flop. You do not want anyone to see the Turn for free if it might cost you the pot. However you should not bet if you are planning to check-raise or slowplay.

Raising with the probable best hand

If you think you have the best hand and another player has bet on the Flop, choose between raising now or waiting until the Turn to raise. Factor the texture of the hand and the number of players into this decision.

If the pot is being contested heads-up or by three players, and you are not sure if the bettor will bet again on the Turn if you call the Flop, then consider raising on the Flop. If you cannot count on the Flop bettor to bet again on the Turn, then you should get your opponents to commit as many bets as possible now rather than risk it being checked to you on the Turn.

If you are confident the bettor will bet again on the Turn (assuming you call on the Flop), then you can feel more comfortable waiting until the Turn to raise. Since the bet size on the Turn is larger than on the Flop, this strategy has a good chance of getting your opponent to put more chips into the pot.

If the hand is played with multiple players, then your decision depends on when you act relative to the original Flop bettor. If you have a probable best hand that is vulnerable in a multiple-player pot (such as top pair with a good kicker), you should make it expensive for other players to see the Turn. If you act right after the bettor, then the other players are faced with 2 small bets to call (and a chance that the original bettor may raise). This is a good time to raise on the Flop, because it will force players with middle or bottom pair to fold. If it were 1 bet to them, they would have pot odds to call. Faced with making 2 bets, they are unlikely to have pot odds to call.

If a few players have already called the original bettor's bet before you have a chance to act, a raise by you will not convince those players who have already committed one small bet to fold for another small bet. All it will do is make the pot bigger on the Flop so they have more reason to call and draw on the Turn. If there are callers between the original bettor and you, you cannot expect any of them to fold to your raise. It is advisable to call and see the Turn before deciding what to do. With so many players it is likely there will be a bet on the Turn before the action gets to you. If your hand still seems strong after the Turn, then you have gained by being able to raise on the Turn when others were not expecting a raise. If your hand seems weaker after the Turn, then you can call or fold without having committed too many chips on the Flop.

Betting on the Flop without a pair

There are reasons to bet on the Flop even if the Flop is not favorable to you. If you have raised pre-Flop, then often the other players will check to you. If you have nothing and the other players also have nothing, a bet from you might win the pot right there. Betting with nothing is better when the number of opponents is small, so that there is a decent chance all of them will fold after you bet.

Your hand: AJ
Flop: K-3-2

With this Flop you should bet. It is tough for anyone who does not have a K, a pocket pair or a pair to call you. If you have the best hand, you prefer to take the pot now instead of giving free cards to your opponents.

Bluffing

Since the bet size on the Flop is a small bet, it is difficult to bluff players who have legitimate hands. The best time to bluff on the Flop is if you are a late-position open-raiser and the only callers are from the blinds. They are more likely to call and see the Flop, and then fold if the Flop does not fit their hands. Other players who are not in the blinds are tougher to bluff on the Flop because they started with hands that they purposely chose to play.

Raising for a free card

The Flop is the best time to raise for a free card. Do this in late position against opponents who check to you on the Turn after you raise on the Flop, thus allowing you to see a free card. You should also be aware of opponents who may be trying this, because you may want to reraise them on the Flop or bet into them on the Turn if it looks as though their draw did not hit. See Chapter 7 "Raising for Free Cards" for more on this strategy.

Check-raising

If you are in early position, a check-raise is a workable strategy. This strategy is best suited for the Flop because the pre-Flop raiser is more likely to bet on this round than during any other round. For more on check-raising, see Chapter 10 "Slowplaying and Check-Raising."

Playing AK on the Flop

AK is a great starting hand in Hold'em; but if the Flop does not fit, AK can turn into a poor hand. Without a pair on the Flop, AK turns into a drawing hand. If no one has a pair on the Flop, AK is a good hand due to its high cards. Scenarios for how to play AK on the Flop:

When to check with AK on the Flop

If there are several opponents and the Flop misses your AK, do not think you are obligated to bet. Many players think that since they raised pre-Flop they must bet on the Flop even if it misses them; but this is incorrect. If many players are seeing the Flop, checking with AK is better than betting because of the chance that someone has a pair or better. Although you have overcards, one or both of your overcards may be counterfeited if someone with a pair has an A or a K as his kicker.

Example

You are on the button in an eight-handed game, and two players have limped in front of you. You raise with A♣K♦. Both blinds call, as do the two limpers. Five players see the Flop.

Your hand: A♣K♦
Flop: Q♠9♠3♣

If everyone checks to you, it is all right to check along and see a free card on the Turn. With two relatively high cards (Q and 9) as well as two cards of the same suit on the Flop, there are many possibilities for other players. One of the players may have checked with plans to raise after someone else bets.

The best card that can come on the Turn for you is an A or a K; but they are dangerous if they simultaneously improve someone else's hand to two pair. If a K comes on the Turn, it will make a straight for a player holding JT, a hand that many players play. Checking in a spot like this is not weak; it is a smart play. You probably had the best hand pre-Flop, but not now that you have seen the Flop. You have a drawing hand, and could be drawing thin or dead.

When to bet with AK on the Flop without a pair

If the action is checked to you and you have only one or two opponents, then you should bet. You may have the best hand and be able to pick up the pot right there. If you do not have the best hand, it is possible you will catch the best hand on the Turn or River.

Example

You raised pre-Flop with AKo in late position and both blinds call.

Your hand: AKo
Flop: 8-6-3 rainbow

If the action is checked to you, you should bet and hope both opponents fold. If you get check-raised, you can call, because you have good enough pot odds and two overcards.

When you have AK with a Flop of K-8-8

This is a great Flop if none of your opponents has an 8 but one or more has a K. Any other player with a K is in danger of losing to your split pair of K's with the A kicker. There are two K's left in the deck, as well as two 8's. Since players are more likely to play a starting hand that contains a K than an 8, if a K-8-8 Flop helps, the player is more likely to have a split pair of K's than trip 8's. Bet this hand aggressively on the Flop until someone indicates possible possession of trip 8's.

When you have AK and the Flop is Q-J-x rainbow

When you have AK and the Flop comes with both a Q and a J, then a T gives you a straight; but the A and K may or may not be outs. For example you could be in a three-handed pot against a player with AQ and another with T9. An A would make two pair for the player with AQ, and a K would make a straight for the player with T9. With that setup your only out is the T for a straight. But if neither of your opponents has an A or K as the kicker to a split pair, then you have additional outs. Sometimes neither the A nor the K is an out, sometimes they both are, and sometimes only one of them is.

Kicker Issues

The kicker is important in many hands. Often both cards play for the winning hand. The card that is not paired can make the difference between winning and losing the hand. This is why AK is such a good hand when it makes a split pair: it is the best pair with the best kicker. A common match-up:

Your hand: A♣K♠
Your opponent's hand: A♥J♣

You both have an A, but you have the better kicker with your K. The only way for you to lose this hand is if your opponent hits a J, a straight, or a heart flush. Your hand of A♣K♠ is expected to win 74.4%[a] of the time against A♥J♣.

Example

There are three players, one of whom has a kicker problem against the other two players:

Player 1: A♣K♠
Player 2: A♥J♣
Player 3: K♣J♥

If a K comes on the Flop, Player 3 has a kicker problem against Player 1. If a J comes on the Flop, Player 3 has a kicker problem against Player 2. Player 3 has a 7.5%[a] chance to win a showdown with this setup.

Issues with the kicker become clear on the Flop. With AKo if the Flop comes with a K, the A is the kicker. If the Flop comes with an A, then the K is the kicker. Before the Flop you have no idea which card will become the kicker. Here is the same hand with two different Flops and kicker issues:

Your hand: A7o
Flop 1: 7–4-2
Flop 2: A-4-2

[a] Results from twodimes.net

With Flop 1 you have a split pair of 7's with the best kicker. With Flop 2 you have a split pair of A's with a weak kicker. If no one has a pocket pair, a set, or two pair, Flop 1 is preferable to Flop 2 with your hand. This issue is discussed further in the next section.

Pairing your low card is sometimes better than pairing your high card

If you do not have a high kicker, it is often preferable to pair your lower card rather than your higher card. For example with a hand like AT, it is often better if the Flop is T-high rather than A-high. This sounds counter-intuitive since a pair of A's is better than a pair of T's. However, Hold'em is a community-card game. It does not matter how good your hand is except as it compares to other players' hands. If you see an A-high board, AT can be beaten by these hands that players play almost all the time: AK, AQ, and AJ. However if you see a T-high board, AT cannot be beaten by another split pair of T's. When you have AT, a T-high board is preferable against players who are playing high cards (such as a solid player open-raising from middle position). An A-high board brings a greater chance that an opponent has a higher kicker than your T; but against players who play any starting hand with an A, this factor is not important.

Assume a solid player open-raises in middle position, and you think the raise represents a legitimate hand. (This is an important assumption. With different assumptions the conclusion might be different.) The player might have AK, AQ, AJ, AT, KK, QQ, JJ, TT, 99, 88, KQ, or KJs. Everyone folds to you in the big blind and you call with ATo. To illustrate this concept, compare AT against those possible hands with these two Flops:

Your hand: ATo
Flop 1: A-3-3
Flop 2: T-3-3

The opponent hands you care about are AK, AQ, AJ, KK, QQ, JJ and TT. The strength of these hands will vary between the two Flops. For example if your opponent has JJ, you prefer Flop 1 over Flop 2. But if your opponent has 88, then you have the best hand with both Flops.

With a Flop of A-3-3 the hands that beat your AT are AK, AQ and AJ. The hands your AT beats are KK, QQ, JJ and TT. Given that there is an A on the board and you hold AT in your hand, there are 24 ways your opponent could have an A with a better kicker than you have. (There is an A on the board and you have one in your hand. There are two A's left. Those two A's can combine to make AK, AQ and AJ in eight different ways each. That makes 24 possible ways your opponent could have a pair of A's with a better kicker.) There are 21 ways your opponent could have a lower pair. (There are six possible combinations each for KK, QQ and JJ, but three possible combinations for TT since you have a T.) AA, KQ or lower pairs are not important because a Flop of A-3-3 is as good (or bad in the case of AA) as a Flop of T-3-3. There are 21 ways for you to be ahead on the Flop, and 24 ways for you to be behind. Things may change on the Turn and River, but you are concerned about the Flop comparison.

The Flop is A-3-3 and your hand is AT.

Opp Hand	*Ways*	*Percentage*
AK	8	17.8%
AQ	8	17.8%
AJ	8	17.8%
Total that your AT is behind against (AK, AQ, AJ)	24	53.3%
KK	6	13.3%
QQ	6	13.3%
JJ	6	13.3%
TT	3	6.7%
Total that your AT is ahead against (KK, QQ, JJ, TT)	21	46.7%

Against this opponent in this situation, when you have AT with a Flop of A-3-3: your chance of being ahead is 46.7%, and your chance of being behind is 53.3%.

With a Flop of T-3-3 the opponent hands that beat you are the overpairs. KK, QQ, JJ and TT account for 19 possible combinations (six each for KK, QQ and JJ, and one for TT). The AK, AQ, AJ hands have 36 possible combinations. There are more possible combinations for these hands compared to the previous Flop because no A has flopped, which means there are three A's unaccounted for. Since your opponent would raise with AK, AQ and AJ as well as big pairs, not seeing an A on the Flop increases the probability that she has an A-high hand. Your opponent would raise with any of those hands; so the information on the Flop gives you information on her hand.

The Flop is T-3-3 and your hand is AT. The individual numbers do not add to the total due to rounding.

Opp Hand	*Ways*	*Percentage*
AK	12	21.8%
AQ	12	21.8%
AJ	12	21.8%
Total that your AT is ahead against (AK, AQ, AJ)	36	65.5%
KK	6	10.9%
QQ	6	10.9%
JJ	6	10.9%
TT	1	1.8%
Total that your AT is behind against (KK, QQ, JJ, TT)	19	34.5%

Against this opponent in this situation, when you have AT with a Flop of T-3-3: you are ahead 65.5% of the time and behind 34.5% of the time.

So against a solid opponent who open-raised in middle position, a Flop of T-3-3 is preferable to a Flop of A-3-3. If you knew the opponent's actual cards, you would know exactly which Flop to prefer. With logical deduction you can see that you are more likely to have the best hand with a Flop of T-3-3 than a Flop of A-3-3 against this particular opponent in this situation.

If the situation and opponent are changed, the conclusion could be different. If an opponent is playing an A with a worse kicker than your AT, then you will be thrilled with a Flop of A-3-3. He is likely to pay you off with his split pair of A's. This can happen if the raiser is open-raising from late position, trying to steal the blinds. With a Flop of T-3-3 he may fold his hand (with the exception of A3, which is not a good hand for you to play against) since he has only one overcard and no pair. Figure out what type of hand your opponent could have. Consider the way he plays, his position, and the current situation to determine whether you are happier with a Flop of A-3-3 or a Flop of T-3-3.

Other Flop Issues

When there is a three-flush on the Flop

When three cards of the same suit come on the Flop: many players hang around with one card of that suit, the loosest players hang around with any card of that suit, and more reasonable players hang around with a T or higher card of that suit. If you have a pair, you may be correct to bet until you see a fourth card of that suit, or you get raised (someone could already have a flush). If you have a hand like Q♠J♣ and the Flop is Q♣T♣3♣, you should play aggressively. The players with just the A♣ or the K♣ will stay in the hand. If someone has a pair of Q's with a better kicker, then you have outs. The hands you should be most scared of are K♣Q♥ and A♣Q♥, as those hands have a better kicker along with a better flush draw.

AA: Would you rather be up against a draw or nothing?

If you have pocket A's, you have the best starting hand in Hold'em. If you are up against only one opponent on the Flop, would you prefer her to have a flush draw or nothing? If she has nothing, she folds to your bet on the Flop. If she has a flush draw, she calls both the Flop and Turn. By the River if she has made her flush, she bets and you lose an additional bet.

<u>Example</u>

You have A♠A♦ and you open-raise in the cutoff position. The big blind, a loose, passive player, calls your raise with 3♣2♣. There are two players and 2.25 big bets in the pot. Compare the situation with two different Flops.

Your hand: A♠A♦
Your opponent's hand: 3♣2♣
Flop 1: K♦9♠8♦
Flop 2: K♣9♣8♦

With Flop 1 your opponent checks, and folds if you bet; so you win the pot (2.25 big bets) 100% of the time.

With Flop 2 your opponent calls until the River with his flush draw. If he has not hit the flush by the River, he folds. To make the calculations manageable, assume he folds unless he catches a flush. If he does not hit his flush, you win an additional 1.5 big bets (0.5 of a big bet on the Flop and 1 big bet on the Turn). If he does hit his flush, you lose 2.5 big bets (0.5 of a big bet on the Flop, 1 big bet on the Turn and 1 big bet on the River). With this setup: there are 45 unknown cards, and 9 cards give him the flush. By the River there is a 63.6% (36/45 x 35/44) chance that he will not make his flush and a 36.4% (9/45 + 36/45 x 9/44) chance that he will. Compare the expected value (EV) of the two different Flops:

Action	Computation	Result, EV
Flop 1 (opp has nothing and folds)	100% x 2.25	+2.25
Flop 2 (opp has flush draw and stays in)	(63.6% x 3.75) + (36.4% x -2.5)	+1.48

The EV of Flop 1 is higher: +2.25 compared to +1.48. You prefer to win the pot uncontested.

On the other hand if your opponent has a split pair instead of a flush draw, then you would rather he call on the Flop than have nothing and fold. With a split pair on the Flop he has 5 outs. It is easier to do the calculations if you assume that when he catches trips or two pair, he wins the hand. He has a 21.2% chance to win the hand; and your EV of him calling you down to the River is +2.43. The breakdown of the match-up:

Your hand: A♠A♦
Your opponent's hand: Q♣J♣
Flop 1: K♦8♠7♦
Flop 2: K♠Q♦2♥

Action	Computation	Result, EV
Flop 1 (opp has nothing and folds)	100% x 2.25	+2.25
Flop 2 (opp has split pair and stays in)	(78.8% x 3.75) + (21.2% x -2.5)	+2.43

With Flop 1 your opponent has nothing on the Flop and folds after you bet. With Flop 2: you have a higher EV; but there is the risk of getting beaten if your opponent catches a J for two pair or another Q for trips. But the risk of getting beaten with Flop 2 is worth the extra EV if your opponent will chase. The next time you lose on a bad beat like this, find solace in the fact that you prefer your opponent to have the chance to give you a bad beat if your EV is higher.

CHAPTER 14
THE TURN

Thinking on the Turn

The Turn is a crucial time in Hold'em. The bet size doubles and the pot is bigger. Draws that were possible on the Flop may have hit on the Turn. New possible draws may have developed. You should think about what you want to do on the Turn, and also about the impact that your decision on the Turn will have on the play of the River. Questions to ask yourself on the Turn:

1. Did any draws on the Flop get there on the Turn?

If there were two cards to a flush on the Flop and a third card of the same suit comes on the Turn, then someone could have a flush. You could be drawing dead already. The same can happen to straight draws. You should not automatically fold when there is a possible made draw on the Turn; but you should be aware of that possibility.

2. Did the Turn card provide any new possible draws?

If the Flop was a rainbow, and the Turn card is the same suit as one of the cards on the Flop, then a flush draw is possible. A player may have picked up 9 outs in addition to the other outs she had. Opponents can also pick up new straight draws on the Turn. Tricky, aggressive players can use this opportunity to semi-bluff if they picked up a draw.

3. Does the Turn card pair the board?

If the Turn card pairs the board, someone could have a full house; and then any flush draws or straight draws (except straight flush draws) are drawing dead.

If the Turn card pairs the top card on the Flop, then a split middle or bottom pair could be drawing dead against trips. A player with a pocket pair probably has 2 outs.

Example

Player 1: A3
Player 2: JT
Player 3: 55
Flop: A-J-2
Turn: A

Player 2 had 5 outs on the Flop, but is drawing dead after the Turn. Player 3 had 2 outs on the Flop, and has 2 outs on the Turn. If Player 3 had 33 instead of 55, he would have no outs.

If your opponent is on a draw (flush draw, straight draw or over-cards to the board), the board pairing on the Turn is good news because the opponent could not have made his draw.

Example

Your hand: T♦9♦
Flop: 9♠8♠3♣
Turn: 3♥

Only a hand that contains a 3 could have been trailing on the Flop and improve to better your hand. Against any hand without a 3, the status quo holds: if you were ahead on the Flop, you are still ahead. If you were behind on the Flop, you are still behind. Any draws are still drawing to beat your made hand of top pair. You can be comfortable that you are ahead against draws or lower pairs. Other cards that could come on the Turn and what they could signify:

7♦: Straights are made by JT, T6 and 65. There would be two pair for 87 and 97.

A, K, Q, J: Any of these overcards could make a higher pair for someone else.

Any ♠: A player on a spade flush draw has made it. A player with one spade has a flush draw and has added 9 outs.

Any ♣: A player with two clubs has a flush draw and has added 9 outs.

Many cards could have dangerous implications. The Turn pairing the board is likely to be good news for your vulnerable top pair.

4. Do you have only overcards on the Turn?

If you have overcards to the board on the Turn, the pot usually is not big enough to justify continuing with the hand if someone else is betting. If someone has a pair, at most you have 6 outs. If someone has two pair or better, you are drawing dead. If a player with a pair has a kicker that matches one of your cards, you have 3 outs. In order to call correctly with two overcards on the Turn against a player who has a pair, you need the expected pot size to be at least 7 big bets; but that is if you do in fact have 6 outs. Adjust for the possibility that you may have 3 outs and sometimes no outs at all.

On the positive side there are cases when you are ahead without a pair, such as when you have high cards and your opponent is on a draw without a pair. She could have as many as 15 outs (a flush draw when neither of her hole cards matches yours). If she doesn't hit one of her outs, then you win the hand. If you can identify these situations correctly, then you can call or raise a Turn bet with two overcards. Knowing your opponents and having the ability to read their hands both work to your advantage.

5. Are you drawing to a straight or a flush on the Turn?

Typically when you are drawing to a straight or a flush on the Turn, you want to see the River as cheaply as possible. If you are drawing to a flush, you have a 19.6% (9/46) chance of hitting it on the River. If your opponent cannot be bluffed out on the Turn or on the River, you should see the River as cheaply as possible. This applies to straight draws as well. If there is a chance your opponent will fold on the Turn or on the River even if you do not make your draw, then weigh that chance against the pot odds. This is not easy, and no book or calculation can give you the solution. Every situation is different. Use your player-reading skills to determine how to proceed.

6. Did an A come on the Turn?

Many players play any starting hand that contains an A, but not necessarily any hand that contains a K or Q. Some players go one step further and call a bet on the Flop to see if they can hit a pair of A's on the Turn. They are less apt to "take a card off" with a K or Q. Normally these players are calling stations in a regular game or normal players in a shorthanded game. (It could be correct strategy to play a particular hand this way in a shorthanded game when it is not correct strategy to play it this way in a full game.) If you are up against a player like this, be wary after an A comes on the Turn.

If an A does come on the Turn while you are in early position, and your opponent is an aggressive player who plays any hand that contains an A, then you may decide to check and let him bet. Aggressive players may be willing to bet whether or not they have an A because they think it is worth trying to buy the pot, especially after you have shown weakness with a check. If you are in last position against an aggressive player, and he checks to you after an A comes on the Turn (signifying that he does not have an A, or he would have bet): you can check back and try to induce him to bluff on the River. When you check on the Turn, it becomes clear to the aggressive player that you are afraid of the A. He may think he can win the pot with a bluff.

When there are several opponents and an A comes on the Turn, it is likely that at least one player has a split pair of A's.

7. Is there a change of pace by an opponent?

When a player' actions on the Turn are inconsistent with her actions on the Flop, the actions on the Turn better reflect the true strength of her hand. Many players start playing their hands straightforwardly on the Turn, since the bet size doubles. A check on the Turn by a player who raised in late position on the Flop means she probably was raising for a free card. An overcard on the Turn could mean she had top pair on the Flop, and is now scared that you picked up a higher split pair and are going to check-raise. If the board does not seem to improve anyone's hand (no overcards, no straight or flush possibilities, no pairing of the board), and a player who was meek on the Flop raises on the Turn, she could be slowplaying a strong hand.

Sophisticated players may double-cross solid players who understand this concept.

<u>Example</u>

A sophisticated player with a strong hand raises on the Flop in late position. If she thinks her opponent will fold if she bets again on the Turn, she can check to make it look as though she was raising for a free card on the Flop. This may induce the early-position player to put in another bet on the River that he would otherwise not have. Use this fancy play only against the right opponent in the right situation, because its pitfall is that you could be giving your opponent a free card.

Betting on the Turn

Part 1 If you believe you have the best hand

If you have a hand that you believe is the current best hand, you should usually bet on the Turn rather than try for a check-raise. Trying for a check-raise is more dangerous on the Turn because a free card has more value to players who are behind, since the bet size on the Turn has doubled. Many hands that had correct pot odds to call a small bet on the Flop do not have correct pot odds to call a big bet on the Turn (unless the hand improved on the Turn). Players who call on the Turn without correct pot odds are making a mistake. If you check and accidentally give your opponents a free card to see the River, then the mistake is yours.

In early position if you think a late-position player is on a draw and you have the best hand at the moment, you should bet instead of trying for a check-raise. You can bet out on the Turn if the late-position player raised on the Flop, as she may have been raising to get a free card on the Turn. In practice, though, you cannot be sure if she is drawing or has a made hand. In these spots, as in many other spots, knowing your opponents and reading hands will yield a big advantage.

When you are in late position and other players have checked, you should bet, even with a mediocre hand. Their checks signify that they have weaker hands than yours, although they could be setting a trap with a check-raise if they suspect you will bet when checked to. Unless you suspect a check-raise is coming, you should bet and give them a chance to fold before seeing the River.

Part 2 Betting for a free showdown

Sometimes you should bet on the Turn with the intention of checking on the River. This is similar to the strategy of raising for a free showdown, except that you are betting instead of raising. This strategy requires that you are last to act and that you have been the aggressor in the hand. If you raised pre-Flop and you bet on the Flop and on the Turn, you are clearly saying you have a strong hand. But if you are not sure you have the best hand, it is still a good idea to bet on the Turn. Your bet gives your opponent a chance to fold a hand that may have outs. If he folds, you take the pot. If he calls, you can decide to check on the River, assuming he checks to you.

Consider what would happen if you check on the Turn. If your opponent was planning to fold to a bet on the Turn, then you give him a free card. If he bets on the River, you will call. (You are not sure if you have the better hand, so you should call since you have a chance of winning.) If your opponent checks, you will bet on the River since he showed weakness. You win or lose the same amount with the bet made on the River rather than on the Turn, but you do not give your opponent a chance to fold; instead you let him see the River for free.

Example

You are in late position and you open-raise. A loose player in the big blind calls. The two of you see the Flop heads-up.

Your hand: AQo
Flop: K-7-6 rainbow

Your loose opponent checks and you bet. She calls.

Turn: 2

Your loose opponent checks on the Turn. Though you do not have a pair, you should bet again. Your loose opponent calls with any pair. If she does not have a pair, then you are ahead and you do not want her to see the River for free. If you check you show weakness, and she is likely to bet on the River if she has a pair; at which point you probably have to call since she may be bluffing. If you check, you still win the bet that you missed on the Turn. The difference is that you do not give your opponent an opportunity to fold without seeing the River. If your opponent is passive and loose: she may call with an inside straight draw on the Turn, but not bet on the River. Thus you lose the chance to pick up a bet from her since a passive player is probably not going to bluff on the River.

The key to this hand is that you want your opponent to make the mistake of folding hands like T9 and T8 on the Turn. With T9 or T8, she has 10 outs: 4 for the inside straight and 6 for a pair. The pot is small (4.25 big bets), but she has pot odds she needs to call. From her perspective, if she knows she has 10 outs, then this is the DIPO analysis she should be making:

DIPO with 10 Outs	*Computation*	*Result*
Good Number	10 x 4.25	42.5
Bad Number	46 - 10	36

The pot is offering your opponent good enough odds to call, but she does not know she has 10 outs. She may think she has 4 outs, or she may estimate she has 7 outs on average. A call might look to her like a bad pot-odds play.

DIPO with 7 Outs	*Computation*	*Result*
Good Number	7 x 4.25	29.75
Bad Number	46 - 7	39

If you bet your AQo and she folds an inside straight draw, she is making a mistake without realizing it. Your bet gives your opponent a chance to make an incorrect decision.

If she does call you on the Turn, you can check on the River. (If she calls you on the Turn with an inside straight draw, she is making this call when you have a pair and she has only 4 outs; so she will be making many mistakes in other hands.) If she is on a draw, she will not call on the River unless she made the draw or a pair. If she has a pair, she will call again. If you bet on the River, you put yourself in a situation where you lose 1 bet if she has the best hand and win nothing if you have the best hand.

There is one type of opponent to whom you should not worry about giving a free card: a habitual bluffer. If you can count on your opponent to bluff after you show a sign of weakness, then the high possibility of gaining his bluff bet may outweigh the negatives of possibly giving him a free card. Knowing your opponents is useful in identifying these situations.

Betting when everyone else is weak

If there are no raises pre-Flop and every player shows weakness on the Flop, then you should consider betting on the Turn, even with nothing.

Example

You are in the small blind. A weak player limps in. You call. The big blind checks.

Your hand: JT
Flop: K-8-6 rainbow

Everyone checks.

Turn: K

The K on the Turn pairs the board and gives you extra incentive to bet. Any player with a pair on the Flop would probably have bet. Since no one bet on the Flop, and the Turn paired the board, anyone who had nothing on the Flop has nothing on the Turn. Since you are in the small blind and were first to act on the Flop, it may look as though you were trying for a check-raise. A bet from you on the Turn, after a Flop without any bets, is consistent with that strategy. You will be given more credit for having a legitimate hand if you make that bet from early position than if you make it from late position.

Raising on the Turn for a Free Showdown

Example

You are in late position with A♣9♣. You open-raise pre-Flop and both blinds call.

Your hand: A♣9♣
Flop: A♦K♣8♥

Both blinds check to you and you bet with your pair of A's and middle kicker. The small blind check-raises and the big blind folds. You call.

Turn: 2♣

With two clubs on the board and two clubs in your hand, you have added a flush draw to your pair of A's. The small blind, a loose and aggressive player, bets. You think she may have a pair of A's with a weaker kicker than yours. Her check-raise on the Flop was consistent with that. Or she could have a hand that is better than yours, such as AJ, AT, A8, K8, 88. You want to get to the showdown because you may have the best hand. The 2♣ on the Turn has given you a flush draw, adding 9 outs. You can raise on the Turn with the intention of checking on the River if you do not improve. Your opponent will probably call with an A and a good kicker (AJ, AT) as she will be afraid you hold AK. But if she re-raises you on the Turn with a better hand, you have 9 outs; or 7 outs, worst-case.

Your opponent folding to your raise is good, since you win the pot right there and she does not get to see the River. One time to avoid this strategy is when your opponent is a habitual bluffer who will bet on the River with a worse hand if you call on the Turn.

If your opponent does not fold, then you want her to call the raise on the Turn and check on the River. If you do not improve, you plan to check and show down your pair of A's. If the flush comes on the River, you should bet. Typically your opponent will be surprised to see you with the backdoor flush and will mumble something about a bad beat, even if she was already beaten by your kicker. If you lose, you lose the same amount you would have lost if you had called the Turn and then called her bet on the River. If you win without making the flush, you win the same amount you would have anyway. If you win with the flush or with a 9 on the River for two pair, then you win an extra bet that you would not have won if you had checked on the Turn. The bet on the Turn gives you an option to win another bet on the River if you get lucky.

Getting Raised on the Turn

Getting raised on the Turn is not fun when you do not have a quality hand. It means someone either has a better hand already or is trying to make a move on you. If you are raised by a late-position player on the Turn, it could mean that your opponent:

- Has the better hand
- Is raising for a free showdown
- Is semi-bluffing with a worse hand, but has outs
- Is bluffing
- Has a worse hand without realizing it.

The analysis of your opponent's raise depends on his characteristics and personality. If he is a passive player: then a raise almost always means he has the better hand, and you should fold unless you have many outs to a better hand. If he is an aggressive, tricky player, then he could be in any of the five possible situations listed. Against the passive predictable player, the decision is easy; against the unpredictable player it is not. This is one of the reasons why it is better when the unpredictable players are to your right, where they usually have to act before you.

An early-position player who has check-raised is likely to have the better hand. She is committing herself to a raise, and also to a bet on the River. An early-position player does not have the advantages of being able to get a free showdown with a raise on the Turn.

Bad Turn and River Cards

If you have a vulnerable hand and think there is a chance your opponent is on a straight draw, there are cards that are disastrous for you even if they do not make the straight for your opponent. If you have middle pair, a player with a straight draw could have as many as 14 outs.

Example

A loose player limps in and you raise on the button with A♠9♠. Everyone else folds except the loose player, who calls.

Your hand: A♠9♠
Flop: Q♠9♣3♦

The loose player checks. You bet. He calls. Even a loose player is more likely to be calling with something than nothing. Perhaps he has a straight draw with KJ, KT, JT, J8, T8. He could have top pair or middle pair; but concentrate on the straight-draw possibility in this example.

Turn: J or T

If a J or T comes on the Turn, be careful. If the loose player has an inside straight draw with hands like KJ, J8 or T8, then a J or T either makes the straight for him or gives him a higher pair than yours. If he checks, it is worthwhile to bet again on the Turn if he is a passive player. If he raises, you can fold with confidence that you are beaten. But if he calls and checks on the River, you can check behind him. The Turn is a better time to make a bet than the River, because he may call to see the River with hands such as A3 or K9, whereas on the River he may not call if he has not improved.

The same situation can come up when the cards are lower, such as when the Flop is T♠7♣3♦. In that case a 8 or 9 is dangerous if you have a split pair of 7's or 3's. All players, including loose ones, are more likely to play higher cards; so an 8 or 9 on the Turn is less dangerous than a higher card.

Large Pots on the Turn

When you probably have the best hand in a large pot on the Turn, you should be betting and raising. This is the time to charge the draws as much as possible to see the River. If your opponents do not hit their draws on the River, they will not pay you off on the River. If they do hit, then you will be donating to them. Figure out the best way to extract bets out of them. If no one is betting, then your best option is to bet yourself. If a player to your right bets, then you can raise and make it 2 bets to the players behind you. When the pot is large, do not use fancy plays like check-raises or slowplays. If you try to check-raise, but no one bets, then you have given a free card to the other players.

CHAPTER 15
THE RIVER

The River Paradox

There are two common mistakes made on the River, and they run counter to each other. Trying too hard to avoid one mistake means making the other mistake. I call it the River Paradox. The two mistakes are:

- Folding the best hand
- Calling too often with other than the best hand.

Folding on the River when you have the best hand is a big mistake because pots are often substantial and it is difficult to make up for the loss after someone steals the pot from you. This mistake does not have to happen often to be costly. On the other hand calling on the River costs 1 big bet. Opportunities to call on the river occur often. When you do it frequently, the costs add up quickly. So you should not fold the best hand and should not call too often with other than the best hand. Trying to avoid one mistake increases the possibility of making the other mistake. If you fold all the time: you never make the mistake of calling with the worst hand, but you occasionally make the mistake of folding the best hand. If you call all the time: you never make the mistake of folding the best hand, but you make the mistake of calling too often with the worst hand. It is difficult to balance your play on the River to avoid both mistakes.

How do you solve the River Paradox? The solution is complex, and involves figuring out other players' tendencies, reading hands well and being prepared for situations before they happen. Each hand requires consideration of its specific details. All situations can be analyzed away from the table. This chapter gives you the tools to solve problems on the River.

On the River, heads-up play is more interesting than hands with multiple players. With three or more players the pot is usually large enough that players are correct to call with hands that have any chance of winning; so stealing the pot is difficult. On the River there is more strategy after the hand gets down to heads-up play.

Thinking on the River: Heads-Up

There are three variables to think about on the River after a hand gets down to heads-up play. They are discussed below, and shown in table 23.

- Are you the first to act or the last to act? (Shown in the column headings on the table.)
- What is the probability that you have the best hand? You have been thinking about this issue since the first two cards. The River is the culmination of this thought process. (Shown in the row headings in the table.)
- How does your opponent play? Is she passive or aggressive? Which does she do more often, value bet or check? Does she bluff?

Use these variables to come up with the best plan to maximize profits or minimize losses.

A note on the % chance that you have the best hand

Estimating your probability of having the best hand is difficult. Think critically about the development of the hand, and have a good idea of how your opponents play. There are different situations in which you might have the same probability of having the best hand. The permutations are not as static as this table suggests. For example there are two

Table 23
Heads-Up River Play

Chance of Having Better Hand	*You are First to Act & Opp is Aggressive*	*You are First to Act & Opp is Passive*	*You are Last to Act Against a Check*	*You are Last to Act Against a Bet*
0%	Check/Fold or Bluff	Check/Fold	Check or Bluff	Fold or Bluff
25%	Check/Call vs Sharp, Bet vs Loose	Check/Call	Check	Call
50%	Check/Call	Bet or Check/Call if opp on a draw	Check	Call
75%	Check/Call or Bet if it looks like a draw succeeded	Bet or Check/Call if opp on a draw	Bet	Raise/Call
100%	Bet/Check-Raise	Bet	Bet	Raise

different ways you can think you have a 50% chance of having the best hand.

One is when your opponent is on a draw, there are two possible draws, and only one draw hits. For instance with a possible straight draw and a possible flush draw on the board, a card comes that completes a possible straight draw but not a flush draw. You do not know if your opponent has a straight or a busted flush, so your estimate is still 50%.

You and your opponent can each think you have a 50% chance of winning when you both have mediocre made hands, such as top pair with a low kicker or middle pair with a good kicker. Act according to the situation instead of the probability. These issues are discussed below in the sections on "50% of having the best hand" and "75% of having the best hand."

0% chance of having the best hand: first to act

If you have no chance of having the best hand, then your decision is whether to bluff or to fold. Situations where you may be able to bluff successfully:

1. If you think your opponent also has a weak hand, a bet may win the pot. Signs that indicate your opponent has a weak hand:

a. A straightforward late-position player checked on the Turn.

b. There is a draw on the board as well as an A. You have been betting all along while your opponent has been calling. This may be a sign he is on a draw and is afraid of the A on the board. If the draw does not come on the River, and you do not have anything either, it may be a good time to bluff.

c. There is a draw on the Flop and your late-position opponent raises you. After a blank card comes on the Turn, you check and then she checks. This indicates she is on a draw and her raise on the Flop was for a free card on the Turn. Even if you have nothing, if another blank card comes on the River you should consider bluffing.

2. A scare card coming on the River may give you an opportunity to bluff. An overcard, especially an A, is a common scare card, as is a third flush card. If it appears to your opponent that you were drawing, one of these cards may help you bluff successfully. For example if you had AK and were drawing to a pair after the Flop came with two cards to a flush, you should consider betting on the River if the River card is the third flush card. Your opponent may think you were drawing for the flush and make the mistake of folding after you bet on the River. Make this bluff

only against an opponent who might fold. Do not bet into calling stations since they do not fold.

0% chance of having the best hand: last to act

An aggressive player may bet on the River when he is first to act because he does not want to miss a bet if he is ahead. Against a player who bets for value with a tiny edge, a raise as a bluff has a greater chance of succeeding. If he bets when he thinks he has a tiny edge, your raise may convince him that his original evaluation was wrong.

Against a passive player, who is less likely to bet for value, a raise works less often, because she is usually in the mode of checking and calling. When she does bet, there is a greater chance she has a legitimate hand.

25% chance of having the best hand: first to act

With a 25% chance of having the best hand, your decision to bet or check depends on the willingness of your opponent to bet or call when you have the best hand.

Against a hypothetical straightforward player

Start examining this issue by looking at a hypothetical opponent who always makes the correct decision if you bet. If he has a best hand, he calls. If not, he folds. If you check, he bets as either a value bet or a bluff. So he:

- Always calls a bet if he has the best hand
- Never calls a bet if he does not have the best hand
- Always bets if you check.

The chart below shows the results when you are first to act and you bet or check. For example after you bet with the worse hand, your opponent calls; thus you lose 1 big bet (-1).

Action	*Your Hand Best*	*Your Hand Not Best*
Bet	0	-1
Check with intent of calling	+1	-1

The strategy of checking with the intention of calling is better than betting against this opponent. If you bet, you win 0 if you have the best hand and lose a big bet if you do not have the best hand. If you check:

you win 1 big bet if you have the best hand (because he will bet), and lose 1 big bet if he has the best hand. If you have the best hand against this hypothetical opponent, you are better off checking with the intention of calling. If your opponent has the best hand: it does not matter whether you bet or check, so there is no advantage to betting.

Example

Your hand: A♣5♥
Board: K♣Q♣5♠4♥2♥

You think there is a 25% chance that your opponent has a busted flush draw or straight draw. If she does have a busted draw, then you have the best hand with the pair of 5's. You think there is a 75% chance she has a pair of 6's or better. If you bet: she folds if she has a busted draw, but calls if she has you beaten. If you check, your opponent bets. If she has a busted draw, your check has induced her to bluff. If she has a pair, then she bets for value. Since the pot is normally greater than 3 big bets, you have pot odds to call her with a 25% chance of having the best hand. Against an opponent you know will bluff with a busted draw (especially after you show weakness by checking to her on the River), a check with the intention to call is a better strategy than betting.

Against a passive calling station

Against a passive player who calls with bad hands, the analysis is different but the result is the same: checking is better than betting.

Example

Assume the pot contains 6 big bets and if you bet, your opponent calls. If you bet and have the best hand, you win 7 big bets. If you check, your passive opponent bets only if he is sure he has the best hand. He bets 25% of the time and checks 75% of the time. (If you knew this, then you would fold. For this example, assume you call.) The other 75% of the time he checks, whether or not he has the best hand.

Action	*Computation*	*Result*
Bet	(25% x 7) + (75% x -1)	+1.00
Check	(25% x 6) + (25% x -1) + (50% x 0)	+1.25

The expected value (EV) chart above shows that you should check when you have only a 25% chance of having the best hand and your opponent is passive. Often when he has the best hand he checks because he is too passive to bet. If you bet with only a 25% chance of having the best hand, you are in effect betting his hand for him.

Take a tangent here and compare this to the scenario of you having a 50% chance of having the best hand. You can see that the choice of checking or betting against the passive player depends on the probability that you have the best hand, and you should not be checking against passive players in all situations.

Action	*Computation*	*Result*
Bet	(50% x 7) + (50% x -1)	+3.00
Check	(50% x 6) + (25% x -1) + (25% x 0)	+2.75

When your probability of having the best hand increases to 50%, your EV is higher against a passive player when you bet than when you check. Against a passive player the point where the EV of betting and the EV of checking are equal occurs when you have a 37.5% chance of having the best hand. (The pot size is irrelevant. You can put in 100 for the pot size and get the same difference for the EV of betting and checking.) Figuring out the probability that you have the best hand is difficult. It takes skill in reading the other player's hand as well as experience in understanding different situations in Hold'em. But if you can do it well, you can make optimal decisions on the River.

Now go back to a 25% chance of having the best hand.

Against a loose, aggressive player

If your opponent is both loose and aggressive, you are likely to put in a bet on the River regardless of whether you bet or check. Her looseness means she will call your bet, while her aggressiveness means she will bet if you check.

Action	*Computation*	*Result*
You bet and opp calls	(25% x 7) + (75% x -1)	+1.00
You check and opp bets	(25% x 7) + (75% x -1)	+1.00

Some players are looser than they are aggressive and others are more aggressive than they are loose. So when should you bet or check against a loose, aggressive player? Bet if you think the chance that she will bet incorrectly is lower than the chance she will call incorrectly. Check if you think the chance that she will bet incorrectly is higher than the chance she will call incorrectly. In other words, bet against players who are looser than they are aggressive; and check against players who are more aggressive than they are loose.

This chart shows that you should bet against a player who is more loose than aggressive.

Action	*Computation*	*Result*
You bet and opp calls	(25% x 7) + (75% x -1)	+1.00
You check and opp bets 90% of the time	(15% x 7) + (10% x 6) + (75% x -1)	+0.90

This chart shows that you should check against a player who is more aggressive than loose.

Action	*Computation*	*Result*
You bet and opp calls 90% of the time	(15% x 7) + (10% x 6) + (75% x -1)	+0.90
You check and opp bets	(25% x 7) + (75% x -1)	+1.00

25% chance of having the best hand: last to act and your opponent checks

In this situation, with a 25% chance of having the best hand, you should check. An opponent with the best hand will usually call after you bet; but one with a worse hand will probably fold. You seldom gain a bet when you have the best hand, but often lose a bet when your opponent has the best hand. The only advantageous time to bet in this situation is when you can pull off a successful bluff. For a bluff to work, you must convince an opponent to fold a hand that is stronger than yours. If he folds a hand worse than yours, you gain nothing by betting.

25% chance of having the best hand: last to act and your opponent bets

If your opponent bets, you usually have pot odds to call (3 big bets in the pot will do). Although you lose a bet more often than you win the pot, the EV of calling is greater than the EV of folding when you have a 25% chance of having the best hand. The difficult part is making the correct evaluation that you do in fact have a 25% chance of having the best hand.

50% chance of having the best hand: first to act

Against a passive player who was not on a draw

Against a passive player who was not on a draw, you should bet when you have a 50% chance of having the best hand. She will often call your bets. If you check, she will bet only her best hands. Take a look at an EV equation. Your opponent is a passive player who plays straightforwardly. If you bet, she calls. Since you believe you have a 50% chance of winning and she calls, the EV for betting is zero. If you check, your opponent has the option of betting or checking. Like most passive players, she does not bet unless she is confident she has the best hand. Suppose she bets only 20% of the time, but during those times she has an 80% chance of having the best hand. The 80% of the time that she checks, she has a 42.5% chance of having the best hand. (On average, these numbers are consistent with your assumption that you have a 50% chance of having the best hand: 20% x 80% + 80% x 42.5% = 50%.) Assume there are 5 big bets in the pot. This is important because if there were no bets in the pot, then you could fold after she bets since if she bets she is more likely to have you beaten.

Action	*Computation*	*Result*
Bet	(50% x 6) + (50% x -1)	+2.50
Check	(20% x 80% x -1) + (20% x 20% x 6) + (80% x 42.5% x 0) + (80% x 57.5% x 5)	+2.38

The EV of betting is greater than the EV of checking (+2.50 versus +2.38). So when you think you have a 50% chance of having the best hand, you should bet against a passive player who was not drawing to a straight or flush.

Against a passive player who may be on a draw

Against a passive player who may be on a draw, check and call.

Example

Assume there were both straight draws and flush draws on the Turn, and you are not sure what your opponent was drawing to. One of the draws gets there on the River. You still do not know if you have the best hand; but your opponent knows. You may think you have a 50% chance of having the best hand; but he knows for certain whether he has the best hand. If he did not catch his draw, you should not bet since he will not call. The best plan is to check and hope that his bet is a bluff.

Action	*Your Hand Best*	*Your Hand Not Best*
Bet	0	-1
Check with intention of calling	+1	-1

Checking with the intention of calling is best because the EV is the same as or higher than the EV of betting.

Example

Your hand: A♣T♠
Flop: J♥T♥2♣
Turn: 3♠
River: 9♣

Your opponent raised on the Flop and checked on the Turn, which makes you think she is drawing for a straight or flush. The 9♣ completes a straight draw but not a flush draw. If your opponent has two hearts for a busted flush draw, then she will not call if you bet. But if she was on a straight draw with KQ, then if you bet she will raise you. If you check and she was on a busted flush draw, then she may bluff. You think your chance of having the best hand is close to 50%, but your opponent has more information than you do. She knows whether she has made her draw; so she knows whether she has a 0% or a 100% chance of having the best hand. So instead of betting, check with the intention of calling and hope her bet is a bluff.

In this EV chart, assume the passive opponent was on a draw. You do not know if she made her hand. Assume a 50% chance she made it and a 50% chance she missed. She knows whether she made it. Assume that if she did not make it she bluffs 20% of the time and mucks her hand 80% of the time.

Action	*Computation*	*Result*
Bet	(50% x 6) + (50% x -1)	+2.50
Check	(50% x 20% x 7) + (50% x 80% x 6) + (50% x -1)	+2.60

In this example you gain little by checking instead of betting: +0.10 big bets. Passive opponents seldom bluff, but may bluff once in a while. The key here is: if you bet, you cannot win any money because your opponent will fold if she has a losing hand. But if you check: you win either the same amount, or more if your opponent decides to bluff. If she never bluffs, then the EV of betting is the same as the EV of checking, assuming that you call after she bets. But if she never bluffs, then you will fold after she bets; so checking is still better than betting.

Against an aggressive player

Against an aggressive player who bluffs after you check (whether or not he was on a draw), you should check and let him bet. This EV chart shows the results against an aggressive opponent who bluffs 40% of the time with the worse hand after you check.

Action	*Computation*	*Result*
Bet	(50% x 6) + (50% x -1)	+2.50
Check	(50% x 40% x 7) + (50% x 60% x 6) + (50% x -1)	+2.70

Against an aggressive opponent who bets more often than he calls, you should check and call.

Summary

The key to betting or checking when you are first to act and have a 50% chance of having the best hand is knowing your opponents and the type of hands they are playing. You should bet against a passive opponent who is not on a draw. Check with the intention of calling against a passive opponent who was on a draw if you are not sure whether she made it. Also, check with the intention of calling against an aggressive opponent who has a hand with which she is willing to bluff, but with which she might not call a bet.

50% chance of having the best hand: last to act

Before an early-position player acts, you may think you have a 50% chance of having the best hand. The early-position player's action may or may not give you new information with which to adjust your estimate of that chance. An early-position player who is passive will usually check, though in the same place you might bet. That check is unlikely to give you any extra information. If you think there is a 50% chance that you have the best hand: you should lean toward checking because he may fold with his worst hands, but call when he has the best hand. For example if you bet: he may call 95% of the time (50% of the time when he has the best hand and 45% of the time when you have the best hand), and fold 5% of the time (when you have the best hand). A bet has negative value against a passive player.

A sharp, aggressive player's check may give you useful information. It may signify that she is weak (otherwise she would have bet, since aggressive players are afraid to miss a bet). She could be trying to induce you to bluff. If you are not sure of her intentions, lean toward checking here as well.

If you know your opponent's tendencies, then you can use that information to decide whether to check, bet with the intention of calling a check-raise, or bet with the intention of folding to a check-raise. For example against a loose, aggressive player who likes to bet: you should consider betting after he checks, as his check may have given you new information that suggests there is a greater chance that you have the best hand.

If your opponent bets, you should call if the bet has not changed your opinion about the probability that you have the best hand. A passive player's bet may signify you have only a 25% or lower chance of having the best hand. In that case, quickly assess this new information and move forward with the correct decision.

75% chance of having the best hand: first to act

Against a passive opponent

If you are heads-up against a passive opponent and you have a 75% chance of having the best hand, the correct strategy is to bet. You cannot count on the passive player to bet if you check. You should bet and hope she calls. But if you think she was probably on a draw and missed, you should check with the intention of calling. You cannot count on a player who missed a draw to call a bet, no matter how loose the player is; and you do not want to bet if by chance she caught her draw.

Against an aggressive opponent

If your opponent is aggressive, then you have more options. You can bet or you can check with the intention of calling or raising, depending on how loose the aggressive player is. If you are check-raising, you want him to call with a worse hand than yours. If you think he will bet but not call after you check-raise, then you might as well bet. Instead of taking the chance that he will check when you have the best hand, bet to make sure he pays you off.

An aggressive player can turn passive if he thinks you were on a draw and the draw came on the River. You should bet because if you check, he is less likely to bet.

For example suppose you have top pair with top kicker. The board contains two cards of the same suit and the River is a third card of that suit. If you are planning to call a bet anyway, you should bet yourself. Any hand that you can beat is unlikely to bet after you check, even a hand belonging to an aggressive player. An aggressive player may not bet top pair if he thinks there is a chance you were on a draw and made it on the River. (He will bet if he thinks you are a calling station.) But he may call thinking you are using the scare card to bluff.

Whether or not you have a drawing hand yourself, figure out if there is a possible draw on the board. Not only is it useful to be aware that your opponent may have a draw, but it is also helpful in assessing what your opponent thinks about your hand.

75% chance of having the best hand: last to act

If the action is checked to you, you should bet against any player. If a player has bet, you can consider calling or raising. If you decide to raise, have a backup plan in case you get reraised. A reraise from certain players can only mean they have the nuts. Before you raise, decide if you are willing to fold if you get reraised by one of these players. A sharp player may not call with a worse hand if you raise on the River; so a raise has little value. (You should throw in a bluff now and then against sharp players.)

100% chance of having the best hand: first to act

If you are 100% sure you have the best hand, then you are in a great spot. Against a passive player, you should bet since she will not. Against a aggressive player, you may decide to bet or try a check-raise. The reasons to check-raise against an aggressive player:

1. You are sure she will bet based on the play of the hand

Check-raise to get more money into the pot; though sometimes you should bet and let her raise so you can reraise. This depends on how aggressive this player is and what you think she holds. For example you may have a full house and think she hit a flush at the same time. In this situation, against an aggressive player, you should bet and give her a chance to raise you.

2. Check-raise for future value

You should successfully check-raise on the River with a bluff once in a while, so that if you try for a check-raise with the nuts, your opponent may remember and think you are bluffing. You still need to be confident she will bet if you check, or the lost bet on the River is not worth the possible future value.

3. Check-raise so she learns to not bet for value against you

Convince her that a check by you in first position does not necessarily mean you are weak. You do not want an aggressive player always to bet after you check. A check-raise makes her hesitate about betting.

100% chance of having the best hand: last to act

This is the easiest scenario. Bet, raise and reraise. Have fun!

Thinking on the River: Multiple-Player Pots

If there are three or more players on the River, you should play in a straightforward way. Bet if you think you have a high chance of having the best hand, or check if you are not that confident. Call if you have a reasonable chance, relative to the pot size, of having the best hand. When you consider bluffing, take into account the possibility that all players will fold, rather than just one player.

When not to raise with the best hand

In multiple-player pots it is not always best to raise even if you think you have the best hand. You may be able to win more by calling when there are calling stations at the table.

Example: When you have the nuts

There are three players in the hand and you are second to act. You have the nuts. The second player bets. You are sure that both players will fold if you raise; but the third player may call if you call. You do not gain anything by raising; but if you call, the third player may call too.

Example: When you probably have the best hand, but not the nuts

Assume you have a 60% chance of having the best hand, and you are the second player to act in a four-way pot. You think the first player has 40% chance of winning. Both the third player and the fourth player are calling stations with 0% chance of having the best hand. If you raise, both calling stations will fold. If you call, there is a 50% chance that exactly one of them will call and a 50% chance they will both fold. If the first player bets, you should not raise even though you are a favorite to win the hand.

Action	*Computation*	*Result*
Call	(60% x 50% x 7) + (60% x 50% x 6) + (40% x -1)	+3.50
Raise	(60% x 7) + (40% x -2)	+3.40

The EV of raising (+3.40) is lower than the EV of calling by 0.10 big bets. You should call when you are not confident that you have the best hand, and hope a third player (who has little to no chance of winning) calls also.

Large Pots on the River

When the pot is large, it does not take a high winning percentage for a bet or a raise to be correct. Say you are in a 10-big-bet pot with two other players. You estimate that you have a 15% chance of having the best hand. If you can steal the pot an additional 10% of the time without the best hand, then you increase your winning percentage from 15% to 25%. This chart compares the EV of calling and raising.

Action	*Computation*	*Result*
Call	(15% x 10) + (85% x -1)	+0.65
Raise	(25% x 10) + (75% x -2)	+1.00

Raising is worthwhile in a situation like this, but only if you have correctly estimated the likelihood that all the players will fold. Your raise has to make both players fold, which is more difficult than getting one player to fold. For example if both of your opponents will fold only 5% of the time when one of them has the best hand, then the chance you will win has only risen from 15% to 20%. The EV of raising against these opponents:

Action	*Computation*	*Result*
Raise	(20% x 10) + (80% x -2)	+0.40

If these opponents both fold 20% of the time (5% of the time incorrectly), then raising is inferior to calling. The EV equations show that knowing the players and how they play is crucial to your decision process. The equations by themselves do not provide an answer; user input is the key to the equations.

Why is it correct to call on the River with zero EV or slightly negative EV?

If you play against the same opponents all the time, there is value to calling a bet or raise on the River with zero or slightly negative EV. Your calls on the River reduce the chance that other players will bluff you on the River in future hands. Since being bluffed out is the biggest mistake you can make, there is value in giving up a small amount of edge to reduce the frequency of being bluffed; but do not take this concept too far. You should not call when the pot odds offer you 5:1 but you have only a 10% chance of winning.

Example

It is the River and your opponent has bet. You estimate you have a 25% chance of having the best hand. After your opponent's bet there are 3 big bets in the pot. Calling is a zero EV play. If you played this hand a thousand times, it wouldn't matter whether you always called or always folded.

If you are seen as a player who folds often on the River, other players notice and take advantage of you. Therefore if it seems close, or if you have only slightly the worst of it, lean toward calling rather than folding to reduce the future aggressiveness of other players against you on the River.

Last to act: using a check on the Turn to induce a bet or call on the River

If you are last to act, there are times when you should check on the Turn with a hand that you think is probably the best hand. If you think your opponent is so weak that he will not call a bet anyway, it may be best to check on the Turn in last position, hoping to induce a bluff from a weaker hand on the River. If it turns out you are behind, you avoid getting check-raised. If you check on the Turn and your opponent bets on the River, you lose 1 bet if you are behind, the same amount you would have lost had you bet on the Turn. If you are ahead, your opponent gets a free card after you check on the Turn, which means an opponent who is behind is seeing the River for free to get a shot at beating you. The lower the probability of a free card hurting you on the River, the better this play is.

Example

You have K♠7♠ on the button and you open-raise pre-Flop. Only the big blind calls your raise.

Your hand: K♠7♠
Flop: K♣8♠3♦

You bet and the big blind calls.

Turn: A♥

With the A on the Turn: if your opponent checks, you should check. It will be tough for him to call another bet unless he has an A or a K. If he has a lower pair, the presence of the A on the Turn means he is likely to fold to a bet by you on the Turn. In this situation: a worse hand will fold, but a better hand will call or check-raise. Your opponent may call with a K and a weak kicker, but your kicker is weak too. He will have a hard time calling with a middle pair of 8's since there are two scary cards on the board. If the A had not shown up on the Turn, he might have hoped you had AQ or something like that and kept calling you. But with the A on the Turn, he cannot use that justification to keep calling. After you check on the Turn: you hope he is convinced that his hand is best, and bets on the River. But if he checks on the River, he is more likely to call a bet by you on the River than he would have been if you had bet on the Turn.

CHAPTER 16 READING HANDS

Reading a hand is deducing the two hole cards that your opponent may hold, based on the board cards and the player's previous actions in the hand and in previous hands. The skill of reading hands is difficult to learn without experience at the poker table. Experience exposes you to different situations so you can be more comfortable analyzing them in the future. Experience alone does not do the trick. You must be able to think critically about each situation and know what is relevant.

Reading the Player

The foundation of reading a hand is understanding and reading the player. It is your job to read the player first to get an idea of how she thinks. After you have done that, you can read the situation; and the player's actions will make more sense. If you do a good job of reading players, you have a greater chance of narrowing down their hands accurately.

The same action by different players can have different meanings. For example a calling station who raises after a third flush card hits the board definitely has a flush. On the other hand if the raiser is an aggressive player who likes to semi-bluff, then it could mean he picked up a four-flush and is raising as a semi-bluff.

If you understand how a player plays, it is easier to identify the possible hands she could hold. If you don't know how a player plays, her hands are less predictable.

Reading early-position players

Early-position players who raise think they have strong starting hands. Different players have different ideas of what constitutes a strong starting hand in early position. Some think it is only AK, AQ and big pocket pairs. Others think it also includes AJ, AT and middle pocket pairs. And yet others think a raise is worthwhile with any two high cards or any pair. If a tight player raises pre-Flop in early position, you have a better idea of what his hand is. Use that knowledge to stay out of those pots unless you have one of the stronger starting hands yourself. If you are in middle position and a tight early-position player raises under the gun, then you should fold all but the best hands, even good hands like AQo. (This topic is covered in detail in Chapter 12 "Starting Hands.") But if the early-position raiser is an overly aggressive player, you can stay in with more hands and consider reraising with hands that you would fold against a tight raiser.

An early-position player limping in usually means she has a playable hand, but not one she thinks is strong enough to raise with. Some players limp with pocket A's and pocket K's with the intention of reraising. Some players play drawing hands (like A5s and JTs); other players don't. The longer you play against these players and the more you pay attention to the cards they show down, the more you are able to decipher the specific cards they are willing to play.

Reading late-position players

Late-position players play a wider variety of hands than early-position players do. They open-raise and limp (after others have already limped) with more hands than early- and middle-position players do.

If everyone has folded to a late-position player, then a raise from that player does not necessarily mean a strong hand. He could be trying to steal the blinds with a mediocre hand. This raise should not be feared nearly as much as a raise from the same player in early position. An opponent who plays tight in early position may open-raise with many hands in late position that he would not dream of playing in early position.

If there are a lot of limpers ahead of him: a late-position player can limp in with many hands that he would not play in early position, such as 87s or A2s, because in early position he is not sure the pot will have multiple players. With multiple players in the hand he is comfortable knowing the pot odds are high enough.

In almost all cases it is tougher to narrow down a late-position player's starting hand before the Flop because he plays more hands than he would in early or middle positions. However there is one situation in which it is relatively easy to pinpoint a late-position player's starting hand: when a solid late-position player reraises a solid early-position player's original raise. The solid late-position player knows the solid early-position raiser has a strong hand; so a reraise by the late-position player indicates he thinks he has a stronger hand.

Reading players based on their thoughts instead of your own

Different poker players play the same hands differently. A tight player might fold AQo to an early-position raiser if the raise came from a good player. An aggressive player might reraise with that hand, while an average player might call. Three different players take three different actions with the same hand in the same situation. How you would play the hand is not important. When you are reading their hands, take into account what your opponents are thinking since players act differently.

In *The Psychology of Poker*, Alan Schoonmaker discusses Subjective Rationality and Egoistic Fallacy (pp 48-50). Subjective Rationality is the idea that even if you think another player is making an irrational play, the play is rational to her. Imposing your own idea of rational thinking on other players makes them seem crazy; but when you try to think the way they think, you see the rationality behind their play. Egoistic Fallacy describes a player trying to read an opponent's hand based on how he would play the hand himself. For example he may raise with only the best hands; so when he sees another player raise, he assumes that the player must have one of the best hands. Players project their own poker styles on their opponents. When they should be thinking about what an opponent is doing, they are instead thinking about what they themselves would do in the same situation. Schoonmaker says these two concepts are closely related.

This is an interesting way to approach reading hands. Think about what other players are thinking and why they are doing what they are doing. Get into their heads and see why certain plays are rational to them. When you do that, you will have an easier time reading and evaluating their probable hands instead of projecting your own reasoning and principles on them.

Reading skills in low-limit games

Some players play poorly and are unreadable. It is difficult to figure out what they hold since they will play with any two cards and call bets on the Flop hoping for a miracle card on the Turn. Low-limit games have a higher percentage of these players than middle- or high-limit games, although you may find them in any game. The advantages of having these players in the game outweigh the disadvantage of the difficulty in reading their hands. Do not read them incorrectly. Their actions may help narrow down what they hold to a degree, but their hands are still going to fit into a wider range than those of other players.

Reading Hands on the Flop, the Turn and the River

Reading hands with big cards on the Flop

Big cards (A's, K's or Q's) hitting the Flop mean someone probably has a split pair. If you have an underpair (a pocket pair lower than any card on the Flop), you should not always give up; but if the action is heavy on the Flop, consider yourself to have only 2 outs. Possible draws on the Flop could give you more outs.

Example

Your hand: J♣J♦
Board #1: A♠8♣4♦

You bet and get raised. There are no legitimate draws on the Flop; so it is more likely someone has a split pair of A's. But if the board had a draw, then the raise would have a different meaning.

Board #2: A♠8♠4♦

With a possible flush draw on the Flop, a raiser could be drawing to a flush, especially if she acts last. You are likely to have more outs when you get raised with Board #2 than with Board #1. You get raised less often with Board #1 than with Board #2 because there are fewer reasons for another player to raise. When you do get raised with Board #1, you are more likely to be an underdog.

Reading hands with an A on the Turn

Players with AK, AQ or AJ are often willing to call a bet or a check-raise on the Flop even if they do not have a pair, hoping to hit a pair on the Turn. Since players are more likely to play hands with an A in them than hands with any other card, the A on the Turn is a scary card if you do not have an A yourself.

Suppose you are in the big blind with T9s and you are the lone caller against a middle-position player's pre-Flop raise. The Flop comes 9-high and you check-raise with top pair. If an A comes on the Turn, it becomes difficult to play this hand. The middle-position player has two ways to beat you. He could have a big pocket pair, in which case he was already ahead on the Flop. He could have two big cards with an A, which means he has top pair. He is likely to have one of these hands and be ahead on the Turn. The only types of hands you can hope to beat are middle pocket pairs lower than 9, or two big cards without an A (like KQ or KJ). Your position and your cards make this a tough decision. Should you check and call him down through the River? Should you bet and fold to a raise? Should you check and fold to a bet? Should you bet and call a raise? Should you check with the intention of calling a bet on the Turn but not on the River? There is no clear-cut solution unless you have a good idea of how the opponent plays. If he is predictable, then you are in a better position and could save some chips if you are behind. Against an unpredictable player, this is a tough spot to read a hand. A couple of strategies to consider:

1. Check on the Turn with the intention of calling a bet on the Turn and folding if he bets again on the River. Many players bluff on the Turn after you show weakness with the A on the board. Your call on the Turn indicates you are in it for the long haul. If the bettor was bluffing on the Turn, there is a good chance he will not fire another bluff on the River. If he was not bluffing, then he will not mind betting again.

2. Bet on the Turn with the intention of not putting another bet into the pot. Fold if he raises on the Turn. If he calls on the Turn, check with

the intention of folding on the River. If he takes the initiative by raising on the Turn or betting after you check on the River (remember, your bet on the Turn showed him that you were not worried about the A), it is a sign he thinks he has a winner. Your bet is also a sign that you are not weak. Players are less likely to bluff into those who show strength.

Reading a raise on the Turn

On the Turn the bet doubles. Many players with strong hands wait until the Turn to raise, especially if there is an indication that another player will keep betting.

Example of a raise from a hand that is probably legitimate

You are in late position and open-raise with Q9s. Everyone folds except an average player in the big blind, who calls.

Your hand: Q9s
Flop: K-9-3 rainbow

The big blind checks. You bet and she calls.

Turn: 3

The big blind checks. You bet and she check-raises. Coming from an average player, this usually indicates she has trip 3's or a split pair of K's. There is a small chance she has a split pair of 9's. Even if she does, you are playing only for a tie since your kicker does not play with the K and the pair of 3's on the board. Against tricky or sharp players in short-handed games, there is a higher chance you have the best hand. Against most players in full games, a raise on the Turn is a sign that you are beaten.

Reading the board on the River

On the River, players know whether there are flush, straight, or full house possibilities. Without three cards of the same suit on the board, there can be no flush. Without three different cards that are within a five-card range, there can be no straight. Without a pair on the board, there can be no full house or four-of-a-kind. The relative value of a hand is based on the possibilities that the board presents. Although a royal flush is the best poker hand, it is not usually possible in Hold'em. A three-of-a-kind could be the best hand, depending on the board. Other times a three-of-a-kind is not playable because there are other possibilities on the board and other players are playing strongly. Knowing this is important because it allows you to deal with the key aspects of the best possible hand given the board.

Reading Flushes and Flush Draws

By the River it is easy to see if a flush is possible. If there are three cards of the same suit on the board, then both of a player's hole cards must be of the same suit to give him a flush. If there are four cards of the same suit on the board, then a player with one of that suit has a flush. If all five cards on the board are of the same suit, then all players have a flush; the ranks of their flushes depend on any cards of the same suit in their hands.

If the starting cards are suited, there are three ways to arrive at a flush.

- All three cards on the Flop are the same suit as the two hole cards; the player has a flush on the Flop.
- Two cards on the Flop are the same suit as the two hole cards; the player needs another card of the same suit to come on either the Turn or the River.
- One card on the Flop is the same suit as the two hole cards; the player needs both the Turn card and the River card to be the same suit as well.

If a player's starting cards are suited, how often does she flop a flush? How often does she flop a flush draw with two cards of the same suit on the Flop? Table 24 shows frequencies with which three, two, one

Table 24
Chances of Suited Hole Cards Flopping Flush Cards

Suited on Flop	*Computation*	*Pct Flush*
3	11/50 x 10/49 x 9/48	0.8%
2	11/50 x 10/49 x 39/48 x 3	10.9%
1	11/50 x 39/49 x 38/48 x 3	41.6%
0	39/50 x 38/49 x 37/48	46.6%
Total		100.0%

and zero cards of the same suit come on the Flop when the hole cards are suited.

Totals starting with table 24 may not add to 100% due to rounding.

Starting with suited cards, a player hits a flush on the Flop less than 1% of the time. Most often the Flop has one or no cards of the same suit as the hole cards.

This does not mean that when all three cards on the board are of the same suit, someone has a flush less than 1% of the time. In fact when all three cards on the Flop are of the same suit, a random hand has a 3.8% (10/49 x 9/48) chance of having a flush. These numbers may seem contradictory, but they are not. In the first scenario, a player starts off knowing two of his cards are of the same suit; and he needs all three cards on the Flop to be of the same suit. In the second scenario, he starts off knowing that the Flop is all of the same suit; and he needs to calculate the chance that the two cards in any one hand will be that same suit. The difference is the starting point. In the first situation he knows two cards and needs three more. In the second situation he knows three cards and needs two more.

The most common way a player makes a flush is having two cards of the suit in hand and two more on the Flop. Then she can get her flush on either the Turn or the River by hitting a fifth card of her suit. Many players like to play suited cards for this reason. Suited cards are useful because they add another way of winning a hand. They are often overrated by players who will play any two suited cards no matter what their rank or the straight potential is.

A player raising in late position after there are two cards to a flush on the board could signify that the player is on a flush draw and is raising to get a free card on the Turn. If an opponent makes this play when you

Table 25
Chances of Four Suited on the Flop Making a Flush on the Turn or River

When	*Computation*	*Percentage*
Turn	9/47	19.1%
River	38/47 x 9/46	15.8%
Total flush	9/47 + (38/47 x 9/46)	35.0%
Never	38/47 x 37/46	65.0%

are in early position, you may want to think about betting on the Turn if you think your made hand is ahead at the moment. The free-card raise strategy is useful, as is the counter-strategy of betting into the raiser if a flush card does not come. This is discussed in greater detail in Chapter 7 "Raising for Free Cards."

If a player flops a flush draw with two cards of the same suit as his two hole cards, how often does he make the Flush on the Turn, the River or neither? The calculations are shown in table 25. These calculations also apply if his hand contains only one card of the flush and the other three are on the board.

The chance of the flush hitting on the River is reduced by the chance of the flush hitting on the Turn. (The chance of the flush *not* hitting on the Turn is 38/47.) If the flush already hit on the Turn, getting another flush card on the River is meaningless. If the Turn card does not make the flush, then there is a 19.6% chance that the flush will come on the River (9/46).

Another way a player makes a flush is by starting with two suited cards, flopping one card of the same suit, and then catching a runner-runner flush (catching a card of the same suit on both the Turn and the River). Catching a flush this way is almost an accident. The player would not be correct to draw to the runner-runner flush unless she had something else going for her, such as a split pair on the Flop. Not until the Turn should a player who catches a flush use it as a primary reason to stay in the hand.

If a player flops a runner-runner flush draw, how often does he have a four-flush on the Turn and how often does he make a flush on the River? The calculations are shown in table 26.

Table 26
Chance of Catching a Runner-Runner Flush

Action	*Computation*	*Percentage*
Pick up a flush draw on the Turn	10/47	21.3%
No flush draw on the Turn	37/47	78.7%
Catch the flush on the River	10/47 x 9/46	4.2%
Pick up a flush draw on the Turn but do not catch the flush on the River	10/47 x 37/46	17.1%

When there are four cards of the same suit on the board, it is easier for any player to have a flush. Any player who has the A of a suit of which three cards show on the Flop or Turn is likely to have good enough pot odds to see the hand to the River to try for the nut flush. A player with the K or the Q of that suit is drawing to a flush other than the nut flush. She might catch her draw and still lose.

By the River if the board doesn't have three cards of the same suit and you think your opponent was on a flush draw, you do not need to worry about a flush. This may allow you to bluff if your opponent had a flush draw while you do not have much of a hand yourself; or it may give you the idea to induce a bluff if you do not think your opponent will call if you bet.

Reading Straights and Straight Draws

Straights are tougher to read than flushes. After the River card is on the board, it is simple to determine if a flush is possible by looking for three or more cards of the same suit. Made straights are more difficult to spot. Most boards have straight possibilities, especially boards without a pair. It can be difficult to determine if someone has caught a straight. The sequence of the board and the actions of the player can help you determine the possibility that the player has a straight.

Board #1

Flop: K-J-5 rainbow
Turn: 9
River: 7

With Board #1, three different starting hands could make a straight: QT, T8, 86. Of these, QT is played most often. Since QT consists of two high cards, many players are willing to play it, especially if it is suited. Some players are more selective and play QT in only certain situations. Other players are not selective and play QT in any position. The less selective players may also play T8 and 86, but not as often. Even terrible players understand that high cards are better than low cards.

The texture and sequence of the board is important. It would be a surprise if someone with T8 or 86 called a bet after the above Flop. On the Turn T8 and 86 pick up an open-ended straight draw or an inside straight draw, respectively, and might continue to the River.

The same board, with the sequence of the cards altered:

Board #2

Flop: K-9-7 rainbow
Turn: J
River: 5

With a Flop of K-9-7, both T8 and 86 have open-ended straight draws. Players holding these hands will continue through the River since they have 8 outs to make a straight. If flush possibilities materialize or the board pairs up and there is strength in betting, the odds may change; but that does not concern most players. A player with QT is likely to stay in on the Flop since QT holds an inside straight draw along with two cards higher than a possible middle pair. The QT hand has only 4 outs (the J's) to make a straight, and can be bullied out of the hand more easily than T8 and 86, which have a total of 8 outs each to make the straight. Not everyone folds QT; but the better players fold it if the bet size is too big relative to the expected pot size.

The key difference between the two boards is the sequence of the cards. When a board develops as Board #2 did, it has a greater variety of straights that someone could turn over on the showdown than Board #1 has, though the boards are identical after the River. On Board #2, even with three K's you should not be too comfortable, given the development of the board. After the Turn or River, you may have to back off and just call if another player gets aggressive.

Here is another board with the same five cards as on Boards #1 and #2, but the sequence is changed again.

Board #3

Flop: J-7-5 rainbow
Turn: K
River: 9

It would be surprising to see someone turn over QT on the showdown. Compared to the previous two Flops, there are not as many reasons for a QT to call a bet after the Flop. QT might call, depending on the player, the betting on the Flop and how the other players play. A player with QT who sees the Turn usually sees the River since he has 8 outs to make the nut straight. With Board #3 if you hold a set of K's against a solid player, you need not be afraid of a straight and you can be confident you have the best hand.

When and when not to be afraid of a possible straight

Be aware of the texture of the Flop in order to see what possible cards could fill someone's straight draw. This does not mean that you should hit the brakes after one of these cards hits. Flops with two high cards can have someone chasing a straight draw, because players play high cards more often. Sometimes the texture of the hand and the sequence of the board tell you whether to be concerned about a possible straight. Here are two examples, one with little chance of a straight and the other with a good possibility of a straight.

Example 1: No need to fear a straight

You hold KK in middle position and raise. A solid player in the cutoff seat reraises you, making it 3 bets. The big blind, an average player, calls the 2 bets. You decide to call and see the Flop.

Flop: K-5-7 rainbow

The big blind checks, as do you. The solid player bets; the big blind folds and you check-raise. The solid player calls.

Turn: 9

You bet and the solid player calls.

River: J

There are no flush possibilities. You bet again. The solid player raises. What should you do? Given the sequence of betting, it should be obvious that you have the best hand. The only hand that can beat your trip K's is a straight. A player with 86 would have flopped a straight draw and a player with T8 and QT would have turned a straight draw; but it would be unusual for anyone to reraise pre-Flop with 86, T8 or QT, so you can safely rule out those hands. The most likely hands for your opponent are pocket J's, pocket 9's or pocket A's. With JJ she is worried that you have a K in your hand to make a split pair of K's. With 99 she may have been waiting to spring the raise on the River rather than on the Turn. Since you have top set, you should be comfortable knowing you have the best hand, and reraise the solid player. There is no need to worry about a straight beating your set in this example.

Example 2: Possibly up against a straight

You hold KK in middle position and raise. A solid player in the cutoff seat reraises you, making it 3 bets. An average player in the big blind calls the 2 bets. You call and a total of three players see the Flop.

Flop: K-J-5 rainbow

The big blind checks, as do you. The solid player bets. The big blind calls. You check-raise with your trip K's. Both players call your raise. (The difference in the action between Example 1 and Example 2 up to this point is that the big blind has called the Flop bet and raise.)

Turn: 7

The big blind checks. You bet. Both the solid player and the big blind call your bet.

River: 9

There are no flush possibilities. The average player in the big blind checks and you bet again. The solid player folds. The big blind check-raises. What should you do?

Given the sequence of betting, you should consider the possibility that the big blind has hit a straight with QT. He may have a hand that your trip K's can beat, such as a set of 5's, and have waited until the River to raise. He may have two pair, such as K9, that he hit on the River. Those are hands you can beat. The only hand you cannot beat is QT, which is the nut hand. Whether you reraise depends on how comfortable you feel about how the big blind played his hand, and your opinion about his actions.

The difference between the hands in the two examples is the sequence of the cards that hit the board. In the first example the big blind would not be in the hand past the Flop with a hand like QT. In the second example it is obvious that the big blind should be playing QT until the

Table 27
Flops with Straight Draws

Flop	*Starting Hands with Straight Draws*	*Total Hands*
K-Q-x	AJ, AT, JT, J9, T9	5
Q-J-x	AK, AT, KT, K9, T9, T8, 98	7
J-T-x	AK, AQ, KQ, K9, Q9, Q8, 98, 97, 87	9
T-9-x	KQ, KJ, QJ, Q8, J8, J7, 87, 86, 76	9

River, after seeing the Flop. In Example 1 you can be confident of having the best hand. In Example 2 you should be less confident.

Dangerous Flops for straight draws

Not all straight draws are built alike. Hands that are connected without any gaps, such as QJ and JT, are played more often than hands with one gap, such as QT and J9. Table 27 shows dangerous Flops that offer a higher chance that a player holds a straight draw: two relatively high cards that are connected with no gaps. Players could flop straight draws or two pair with these Flops.

In comparing the Flop J-T-x and Flop T-9-x, you can see that both Flops have the same number of two card hands with straight possibilities. More players will play the hands that correspond to J-T-x than the hands that correspond to T-9-x because the hands that correspond to J-T-x have higher cards.

Playing a pair of A's vs. a possible straight draw

Consider these two Flops and their possible starting hand combinations

Flop	*Starting Hands with Straight Draws*
A-6-5	98, 97, 87, 84, 74, 73, 43, 42, 32
A-9-8	QJ, QT, JT, J7, T7, T6, 76, 75, 65

Which Flop allows more players to continue with a straight draw? If you assume that every player sees every Flop with every hand, then they are equal. Both Flops have the same number of possible two card combinations that make a straight draw; but the hands that have a straight draw when the Flop is A-9-8 are played more often by all players. For example QJ is played more often than 98; and JT is played more often than 87. If you have AK, be more wary of the straight potential on a Flop of A-9-8 than a Flop of A-6-5.

Determine the position of the players remaining in the hand after the Flop. If an opponent in late position calls your middle-position raise, there is a better chance she has a straight draw with a Flop of A-9-8 than of A-6-5 (possibly with a hand like JT or QJ). While there is a better chance of the blinds having a straight draw with a Flop of A-9-8 than A-6-5, the blinds are less likely to fold small cards; so the blinds are more likely than a late-position cold-caller to have a straight draw when the Flop is A-6-5.

Double inside straight draws

Double inside straight draws (Doyle Brunson calls them "double belly busters" in *Super System*) are a tougher hand-Flop combination to recognize. These hands allow two different ranks of cards to fill up a straight draw. They are not like an open-ended straight draw, where you already have four consecutive cards and need one higher or one lower to complete the straight, such as JT (as the hole cards) with 9-8-x (on the board). A double inside straight draw also can be filled by two possible cards, but those cards are more difficult to identify. In order to have a double inside straight draw, you need three cards on the board to work for you.

Example

Your hand: J9o
Flop: K-T-7 rainbow

A Q or an 8 on the Turn or River will give you the straight. The double inside straight draw is deceptive. If a Q comes, an opponent may think you have caught a straight with AJ. But if an 8 comes, it is tough for anyone to put you on a made straight; so you get more action after an 8 comes.

Double inside straight draw hand-Flop combinations

There is no need to memorize these hand-Flop combinations. There are too many situations in Limit Hold'em to make memorizing everything practical. Just get into the habit of recognizing these types of hands and Flops so that when you do encounter them in a game, you do not have to start from scratch. Preparation is a key to winning at Hold'em; and this is one of the situations that calls for it.

The following chart shows double inside straight draw hand-Flop combinations where either inside straight card gives you the nut straight.

Hand	*Flop*	*Cards for Nut Straight*
QJ	A-T-8	K or 9
QT	A-J-8	K or 9

When you have a double inside straight draw with one-gap hole cards, only the low inside straight card makes you the nut straight for certain. The higher card gives you a nut straight only if the straight is A-high. Without the A, the higher card gives you a straight but gives another possible hand the nut straight. You are happy to see the card that makes the higher straight. You are happiest to see the card that fills the lower inside straight, since it is the nut straight.

Hand	*Flop*	*Card 1*	*Card 2*
J9	K-T-7	Q (AJ)	8
T8	Q-9-6	J (KT)	7
97	J-8-5	T (Q9)	6
86	T-7-4	9 (J8)	5
75	9-6-3	8 (T7)	4
64	8-5-2	7 (96)	3
53	7-4-A	6 (85)	2

Key:

Card 1 is the card that fills the higher, non-nut straight. The hand that has the nut straight with that Flop is shown in parentheses.

Card 2 is the card that fills the lower, nut straight.

Some starting hands with no gaps can flop double inside straight draws with two different Flops.

Hand	*Flop 1*	*Cards 1*	*Flop 2*	*Cards 2*
JT	K-9-7	Q, 8	A-Q-8	K, 9 (both make nut straights)
T9	Q-8-6	J, 7	K-J-7	Q (AT is nut), 8 (nut)
98	J-7-5	T, 6	Q-T-6	J (AK is nut), 7 (nut)
87	T-6-4	9, 5	J-9-5	T (KQ is nut, Q8 is also higher), 6 (nut)
76	9-5-3	8, 4	T-8-4	9 (QJ is nut, J7 is also higher), 5 (nut)
65	8-4-2	7, 3	9-7-3	8 (JT is nut, T6 is also higher), 4 (nut)
54	7-3-A	6, 2	8-6-2	7 (T9 is nut, 95 is also higher), 3 (nut)

Key:
Cards 1 are the cards that make nut straights with Flop 1.
Cards 2 are the cards that make straights with Flop 2.

These double inside straight draws are more confusing for other players to read. With a hand like J9 and a Flop of K-T-7, you can raise and bet aggressively since you have 8 different outs, which is similar to holding an open-ended straight draw such as 98 and QJ. Consider raising on the Flop for a free card on the Turn, a useful strategy against a player who understands raising for a free card. This opponent may be looking hard for the A or 9 (since it would fill an open-ended straight draw for QJ) if he thinks your raise on the Flop signified an attempt to get a free card on the Turn. If a Q or 8 hits on the Turn, he will be less aware that the card could give you a straight. It is easier for him to identify the straight draw by putting you on QJ (or on 98), since that offers a more visible KQJT straight draw. Without seeing your hole cards, it is tough for an opponent to see that a J9 offers a double inside straight draw with as much chance of catching the straight as QJ has. A Q might be a danger sign for him, since AJ is a playable hand. The Q might mean your free-card raise on the Flop was for a gutshot straight draw and an overcard (the A), which is a rarer move since you would have 7 outs (three A's which are overcards to the board, and four Q's for the straight) or fewer. The Q is deceptive for the straight, but the 8 is more deceptive.

The deceptive nature of these hands begs you to use them to your advantage. These situations allow you to bluff if an A or 9 hits the board against players who may think you were raising on the Flop to get a free card. The A and 9 allow you to put more pressure on your opponents. You cannot use those cards to bluff calling stations, who don't think about folding. Unlike better players, calling stations are concerned only about their own hands and are not concerned that you may have caught a straight. This shows both the importance of understanding how to read the board and the importance of knowing your opponents well enough that you understand how well they can read the board.

If there are two cards of the same suit on the Flop, your free-card raise is more dangerous to your opponents (provided they are not on a flush draw themselves). You have eight cards that make your straight, eight cards that are straight scare cards, and another seven cards that are flush scare cards (there are 11 flush cards, but four of them have already been counted as the possible straight cards). Of the 47 unknown cards, 23 of them either make your hand or put fear into your opponent. That is almost half of the possible cards. You have both the Turn and River to hit one of them. You can win the pot by hitting a straight, or by using a scare card to steal the pot.

Reading a danger card on the Turn

You are in the big blind with AT. A decent player raises in the cutoff seat and you call.

Flop: T-9-3 rainbow

You check-raise. You get reraised and you call. You think there is a chance the opponent is on a draw, with a hand like QJ or KQ. She could also have a higher pocket pair with AA, KK, QQ or JJ, or with a hand like QT or JT, she could have a pair of T's like you do but with a weaker kicker. She could have a set of T's or 9's or two pair with T9. Other hands that would be a nice draw for her are J8 and 87, both open-ended straight draws. You could be ahead or you could be behind.

Identify the most dangerous card that can come on the Turn: in this case, the Q or J. If you are ahead on the Flop, a Q or J can put you in the position where you will have to get lucky on the River to win the hand. If your opponent raised for a free card, she has either hit a straight or hit a pair higher than your T's. If she did not hit two pair or a straight, she could have picked up a straight draw, adding 8 outs to her hand. If the Q or J did not help your opponent, she was probably ahead already.

Reading a danger card on the River

You are on the button with AJ and you decide to reraise the cutoff's open-raise. Both blinds fold and the two of you see the Flop heads-up.

Flop: A-9-6 rainbow

He checks. You bet and he calls.

Turn: 8

He checks. You bet and he calls.

River: 7

He checks. What should you do? The decision to bet or check depends on what you think he will do with a big pocket pair such as KK, QQ, JJ. If he will not call another bet with those hands (because of the A on the board and your aggression), then you should consider checking. If he will call, then you can bet with more confidence. Since he raised pre-Flop and had no problem calling you on the Flop and Turn, there is a good chance he has an A. With a board like this, most hands with an A can beat you. Those with higher kickers are AK, AQ (although the fact he did not bet or raise on the Flop or Turn makes these hands less likely). Those that can make a straight with this board are AT and A5. Those that can make two pair with this board are A9, A8, A7 and A6. The only hands with an A that you can beat are A4, A3 and A2. So AJ in this case is a vulnerable hand against a player with an A.

Counter-Intuition

Most people play games with no community cards, like Draw Poker and Seven-Card Stud, before they play Hold'em. In those games every player would want a higher-ranking hand over a lower one. But this is not always the case in games where there are community cards, like Hold'em and Omaha. The following are situations in Hold'em where you should prefer a lower-ranking hand over a higher-ranking hand, since the lower-ranking hand is more likely to win.

When would you rather have a straight than a flush?

A flush is a higher-ranking hand than a straight, but it is not always preferable to have a flush. If you already have a nut straight, but also have a draw to a non-nut flush, it is better to finish with the lower-ranking nut hand rather than a higher-ranking hand that is not a nut hand. This is also an issue when you have both a straight draw and a flush draw, where the straight draw is a draw to the nuts while the flush draw is not.

Example 1

Your hand: 9♣8♣
Board: T♣7♦2♣6♠

You have the nut straight (T-9-8-7-6). If a third club comes on the River, your hand improves to a flush; but you no longer have the nut hand since you could lose to a higher flush.

Example 2

Your hand: 9♣8♣
Board: T♣7♦2♣2♠

You have both a straight draw and a flush draw. You would prefer to hit a J or a 6 for the nut straight rather than a club for a non-nut flush. Either hand would lose to a full house; but your straight would be the highest possible hand other than a full house.

When is trips better than a full house?

Sometimes your opponents have more outs when you have a full house than when you have trips.

Example 3

Your opponent: AK
Board: T-T-9-K

Which hand would you rather have?

Hand 1: 99
Hand 2: T8

With Hand 1 you have a full house: 9-9-9-T-T. With Hand 2 you have three-of-a-kind: T-T-T-K-9, using only one of your cards. In both cases you are ahead. What is important is not that a full house is a higher-ranking hand than three-of-a-kind, but that your opponent can come back and beat you on the River.

If you have Hand 1, your opponent (who has AK) can catch a K or a T to beat you. If she catches a T, she has a full house of T-T-T-K-K, beating your full house of T-T-T-9-9. It is a strange hand because you have two full houses, TTT99 and TT999; but, alas, that does not help.

There are two K's and two T's left in the deck, so your opponents has 4 outs.

If you have Hand 2, your opponent can catch a K to beat you; and a T gives you four-of-a-kind to beat her full house. If she catches a K: then you both make full houses on the River, and her full house is higher. There are two K's left in the deck, so she has only 2 outs.

It is always better to have two cards left in the deck to beat you than four cards. In this case you prefer a three-of-a-kind (Hand 2) over a full house (Hand 1), because you have a greater chance of winning.

When is QJ better than AK?

It is obvious that AK is a better starting hand than QJ. There are ragged Flops for which these two hands are equal in value, and times when you would rather have QJ than AK.

Example 4

You raise in late position. The big blind calls. The big blind is an average player who does his share of blind defending, but not with trash hands.

Flop: 7-5-2

You bet and get check-raised. Your opponent could have a pair with a 7 or a 5 in hand, or be check-raising with a straight draw such as 86 or 98. In any of those cases having QJ is as good as having AK. But when the check-raiser has a hand like A7 or A5, the QJ has a higher chance of winning since it has 6 outs while the AK has 3 outs. (Hitting a pair of A's would give two pair to your opponent). Players are more likely to defend their blind with hands like A7 and A5 (as well as K7 and K5) than with hands like Q7 and Q5. In a case like this, AK may be a weaker hand for you than QJ.

CHAPTER 17 SHORTHANDED LIMIT HOLD'EM

Introduction to Shorthanded Limit Hold'em

Shorthanded Hold'em games are hard to find in brick-and-mortar poker rooms. Shorthanded games are played at times at middle and low limits, but never with any regularity. Sometimes players will start a game shorthanded in the hope that it fills up; but if it stays shorthanded, they quickly move to another table or sit out, hoping for more players to arrive. Shorthanded games are more often found late at night or in the early hours of the morning, when many players leave to go home and the ones who still want to play are left with no choice but to play shorthanded. These are often good games, because the players still playing are usually the ones who are stuck and not playing their best game.

The Internet has changed the world in many ways. The Internet has brought online poker to players around the world; and it has brought more interest in shorthanded games. Many online poker rooms have tables set up specifically for shorthanded games, including six-player maximum tables, five-player maximum tables and heads-up tables.

Shorthanded games are different from full games. It takes a different skill set and attitude to beat shorthanded games. A proven winner in full games who does not adjust to the differences will not be a winner in shorthanded games. Shorthanded Hold'em may be right for you if any of these descriptions fits you:

- You can emotionally tolerate the wilder fluctuations in shorthanded games.
- You are willing to play more aggressively.
- You get bored waiting for hands in full games.
- You like action and would like to get involved in more pots while getting the best of it.
- You do not mind playing heads-up after the Flop often.
- Your strengths are reading hands and playing the players.

Shorthanded games are better suited to a loose, aggressive playing style. Loose, aggressive players get better results in shorthanded games by playing the same way they do in full games because their natural playing style is closer to the shorthanded game-winning formula. Tight, passive players have trouble in shorthanded games if they do not adapt. Playing tight and waiting for high-quality hands means giving up too much edge to aggressive players in shorthanded games.

Tables with Different Numbers of Players

Shorthanded Limit Hold'em is a different game from full ten-handed or nine-handed games. It looks like the same game, and the rules are the same; but there are many differences. Within the realm of shorthanded games there are distinctions between those that are semi-shorthanded (six-handed) and those that are extremely shorthanded (three-handed). The following are comments on the characteristics of games with different numbers of players.

Eight to ten players: full game

Most poker books assume that the game is played with a full complement of players. Some casinos have ten seats at the table, making a ten-player table a full table; while other casinos have only nine seats.

Seven players

There are two distinct types of seven-handed game; one plays more like a full game and the other plays more like a shorthanded game.

When a couple of players have left the table and the new players have not yet arrived at their seats, or when a couple of the players are taking a break from the game, a seven-handed game can play much like a full game. In these situations most players will not adjust much since there are still seven players and the table is likely to fill back up.

A permanent seven-handed game is one that has been played seven-handed for a while, and players are accustomed to it and have no expectation that the game will fill up anytime soon. The game will usually be slightly more aggressive than a full game.

Though some seven-handed games are more aggressive, most resemble a full game. Think of each hand as being part of a full nine-handed game where the first two players have already folded, thus leaving seven players in the game.

Six players

Many online poker sites have tables with only six seats. Some players play at these shorthanded tables exclusively. In this game the under-the-gun player should use close to the same strategy he would use in a full game. Later-position players can play more aggressively. The under-the-gun player needs to play fairly tight because of the increased aggression of the late-position players. Early-position players will get raised and/or reraised often. Multiple-player pots are not as common. In a game with six or fewer players, it is rarely correct to limp into the pot if no one else is in the pot yet. Any hand that is playable should be raisable if no other player has entered the pot. That's different from a full game, where more players mean more chance that others will limp in after you, making for a multiple-player pot. In a nine-handed game, limping into the pot in an early position with a hand such as JTs or 77 may convince others to limp also in the expectation of a big pot; but with only six players, this possibility is too slim for limping to be a viable strategy. You will not be happy if you get raised and have to play the pot heads-up (and in poor position) holding a drawing hand like JTs.

Five players

In a five-handed game, many players are ultra-aggressive. The under-the-gun position still needs to be selective. A hand like A8s is strong enough to raise all the time in this position. Some players will take this too far and raise under the gun with hands like K9o; and they will get punished, since they will often get reraised by players in later position with better hands.

Players on the cutoff and the button can be more liberal with the hands with which they open-raise. The button can arguably open-raise more often (when the opportunity is presented) in a five-handed game than in a three-handed game. In a three-handed game it is almost guaranteed that at least one of the blinds will call and see the Flop. In a five-handed game there is a slightly higher chance that the blinds will fold to a button open-raise. If they call the pre-Flop raise, they will fold more liberally on the Flop than they would in a three-handed game because the button raises often in three-handed games; so the blinds feel less threatened by it.

Four players

In a four-handed game the under-the-gun player is the same as the cutoff player. She should align herself more with cutoff strategy than with under-the-gun strategy, and should not think of herself as the player who is first to act, but instead focus on being the second-to-last to act. In a five-handed game the button needs to be somewhat selective in reraising the under-the-gun player's pre-Flop raise. In a four-handed game the button can reraise more hands, knowing that the under-the-gun player will open-raise with more hands when the game is four-handed.

The small blind should be aggressive and reraise when holding a legitimate hand. The small blind must force the big blind to fold (or call two bets), since the big blind has positional advantage. Many hands justify the big blind in calling one raise; but after there are two bets, he should be more selective. When there are two bets, at least one of the raisers has a legitimate hand; so the big blind needs a premium hand in order to continue.

Three players

There is only one non-blind hand in a three-handed game. The button must be aggressive because any chance that any of the blinds will fold increases her equity in the pot. If the blinds constantly call her, the button must throw away some hands. The keys to raising on the button: the likelihood that the blinds will call pre-Flop raises, and how the blinds will play post-Flop. If the big blind folds most hands, then this is a fantastic game for the button. Typically in a three-handed game the blinds call more often after the button raises than they do after the button open-raises in a five-handed game. In a three-handed game the blinds are constantly pounded with pre-Flop raises. Calling a raise in the blinds is automatic with any half-decent hand. Three-handed games online play fast, as there is no need to wait for a human dealer to shuffle the cards. If the online players are playing quickly and using the automatic buttons that the software provides, the game may seem more like a video game than poker.

In a three-handed game the small blind must be aggressive and re-raise with good hands. The small blind can three-bet with a larger range of hands than in a four-handed game after the cutoff player raises. That range of hands should stay the same as when the button in a four-handed game is the open-raiser. As in most cases, calling a lone raiser in the small blind position is a poor strategy because it gives the big blind, another player with position over the small blind, a cheap way to play the pot.

If the button is open-raising with many hands (typical of three-handed games), then the big blind should be calling with many hands. The big blind should also consider reraising often pre-Flop, depending on how the button plays on the Turn. The reason the big blind has to think all the way out to the Turn is due to the differences in how opponents will act on the Turn when they do not have anything. Against opponents who will keep betting until someone raises, it is better to call the pre-Flop raise and wait until the Turn to put in a check-raise with a good hand.

You should let the players who are ultra-aggressive hang themselves with their own aggressiveness. Do not stop them from playing aggressively too early in the hand. If you suspect these players will slow down and play more reasonably if you reraise pre-Flop or check-raise on the Flop, then you should not reveal the strength of your hand until the Turn, letting them do the betting for you instead. Against opponents who may slow down on the Turn when they do not have much, it is best to do the raising pre-Flop because you cannot count on these players to bet after you check to them on the Turn. Against opponents like these, it is best to get their money in early since they are less likely to put it in later. Understanding how your opponents play is always important, and more so with fewer players.

An interesting aspect of three-handed games as compared to games with more players is the different seat-selection strategy. It is usually good poker advice to have the aggressive players and the better players sitting on your right and acting before you act. However players who play well in shorthanded games will play correctly when in the small blind, and will usually reraise or fold in that position. A bad player will often call a raise while in the small blind, giving the big blind 5:1 odds to see the Flop (there are 5 small bets in the pot: 2 small bets from the button, 2 small bets from the small blind and 1 small bet posted by the big blind). The bad player in a three-handed game may also make the mistake of limping while on the button, which gives the small blind 5:1 odds to see the Flop. (There are 2.5 small bets in the pot. The small blind needs to put in 0.5 small bets.) So if the bad player sits to your right, you can benefit most from his mistakes when he is on the button and in the small blind. If he sits to your left, the player who will benefit most by the bad player's mistakes is the third player rather than you.

Tables 28 and 29 illustrate this concept. Assume you are in a three-handed game with one good player and one bad player. Table 28 applies when the bad player is sitting to your right. Table 29 applies when the bad player is sitting to your left.

Since you are part of the blinds/button dynamic in every single hand in a three-handed game, the advantage of having the bad player on your right is immense.

Table 28
Mistakes by Bad Player on Your Right

Your Position	*Bad Player*	*Mistake*	*Who Benefits*
Small blind	Button	Limps in too often on the button.	Small blind (you get 5:1 odds to see the Flop).
Big blind	Small blind	Calls raises by the button.	Big blind (you get 5:1 odds to see the Flop).
Button	Big blind	Calls raises by the button.	Nobody. Many players will call anyway.

Table 29
Mistakes by Bad Player on Your Left

Your Position	*Bad Player*	*Mistake*	*Who Benefits*
Small blind	Big blind	Calls raises by the button.	Nobody. Many players will call anyway.
Big blind	Button	Limps in too often on the button.	Small blind
Button	Small blind	Calls raises by the button.	Big blind

Most good players believe that they want other good players to sit to their right. While this is true in all other cases, a good player may not understand that it is not true when the game is exactly three-handed, and will often comply with your wishes by deliberately choosing to sit to your left if he considers you a good player. Typically players also care about position post-Flop, and want to act after the good players have already acted rather than before. However in three-handed games, many players will call with hands that they would not play in a full game. Hands are played on "cruise control," since it is difficult to get anyone who has a piece of the board to fold. Having position post-Flop is less meaningful in a three-handed game than in games with more players because the edge gained pre-Flop by having the good player to your immediate left is greater than the edge lost by having the good player to your left post-Flop.

Two players: heads-up

In a heads-up game, know where the small blind is located. There are online sites that will place the small blind on the button, first to act before the Flop and last to act after the Flop. Other sites will place the big blind on the button with the small blind in the other position, so that the small blind is the first to act in all rounds. There is a big difference between these two blind/button positions. If you are in the small blind and do not have the button, then you must act first on every round. The small blind with the button acts first only pre-Flop and after that has positional advantage in three other rounds. You can play more hands in games with the small blind on the button.

Playing the Players in Shorthanded Games

Understanding your opponents, knowing how they play and what they think, is a crucial element of Limit Hold'em full games, and even more important in shorthanded games. Even when you understand how your opponents play certain types of hands, in full games there are so many players that you cannot play too many hands without being reckless with your own bankroll. You cannot take advantage of the weaknesses of your opponents as often as you would like without getting run over by other players when they have legitimate hands. One of the fundamental guidelines of Limit Hold'em in full games is to be selective with starting hands.

In shorthanded games the relative strength of some hands changes. You can play a higher percentage of your hands. Hands play faster because dealers have to wait for fewer players to make decisions. You get more opportunities to butt heads with each of the other players. While you might have an advantage over a given player once or twice in an hour in a full game, you could have that advantage five or six times an hour in a shorthanded game.

Strategic Differences

Knowing pot odds is less useful in shorthanded games

Knowing if you have correct odds to continue with a hand is crucial in a full game, but less important in a shorthanded game. Usually you will have more outs than you expect in shorthanded games, though you may not know exactly what they are. For example if you have an open-ended straight draw, you are likely to have more outs than you would in full games because there is a higher chance that pairing one of your hole cards is an out. In general there are fewer opponents and they have lower-quality hands. Also since players bluff and semi-bluff more in shorthanded games, you have a better chance of being ahead and having more outs than non-outs. Thus it is less important to know your pot odds since there are fewer close decisions.

Giving free cards is less dangerous

It is less dangerous to give a free card in shorthanded games for three reasons:

- The pot is usually smaller than in a full game.
- Your opponent has less chance of drawing out, being more likely to have started out with a worse hand.
- Your show of weakness is more likely to induce your opponent to bluff due to the aggressive culture in shorthanded games.

Example

You raise pre-Flop and the big blind calls.

Your hand: KQo
Flop: K-8-3 rainbow

You bet and your opponent calls. Note that your bet is mandatory on the Flop because the bet on the Flop does not give any information to the other player. You raised pre-Flop; so she is expecting you to bet on the Flop no matter what you have. (This situation is discussed in the Monty Hall section of Chapter 20 "Extra Topics.") You would also bet with a hand like QT, hoping that she would fold on the Flop. It is the Turn that makes this hand interesting in a shorthanded game. If an A comes on the Turn and your opponent checks to you, you must decide whether to bet or check. The A is a scary card for both of you. If you bet on the Turn and she does not have an A or K, she will fold. Even with a split pair of 8's, she is likely to fold. Her thinking is that since you raised pre-Flop, you probably have an A, a K or a pocket pair between K's and 8's; so she is probably a major underdog. If she does not have a pair, you do not want her to fold, since you are giving her a free card if she is on a gutshot straight draw. Checking is a viable strategy. If she has an A: she will bet on the River, and you will call and lose; but this is better than possibly getting check-raised on the Turn. If she has only a split pair of 8's, she may bet on the River. If she checks and you bet, she is more likely to call on the River than she was to call on the Turn.

Check on the Turn against a better player and bet on the Turn against a calling station. Against a player who will fold a pair of 8's on the Turn after you bet, you should check. Against a player who will call with a pair of 8's, you should keep betting.

Shorthanded games vs. full games: When the action is folded to the cutoff

Many people compare shorthanded play to the times in full games after the action is folded to the late-position players. The two situations are different, although they may look similar. The difference is due to the mood of the table. In shorthanded games players play more aggressively, constantly raising, reraising, bluffing and semi-bluffing, and consequently calling down with hands that may look unwarranted. This aggressive atmosphere makes a raise or a semi-bluff appear less strong than would be the case in a full game.

Drawing hands

Drawing hands such as suited connectors are still playable in a shorthanded game; but they have less value since they play best in multiple-player pots. In a shorthanded game you can raise with these hands on the button or call one raise from the big blind; but these hands should not cold-call a raise from another player or to call raises in the small blind. Sometimes you will find yourself in a situation where you can play aggressively with drawing hands, and semi-bluff and/or raise with them.

Example

You are in a four-handed game and open-raise on the button with 9♥8♥ (the cutoff has folded). The small blind folds and the big blind calls.

Your hand: 9♥8♥
Flop: A♥6♠5♦

You have an inside straight draw and a runner-runner flush draw. You can also use the scare card on the board, the A, to your advantage. Most players will check to you; and you should bet. The A on the board will scare off players who do not have a pair or a draw. They will fold hands such as K3 and J8. On the other hand if they call, you still have a few outs. You can hit a 7 for an inside straight, or a 9 or an 8 for a pair that will beat any other split pair except a split pair of A's. How you continue with the hand on the Turn depends on how your opponent plays. If he is a decent player and you do not think he would call on the Flop with no pair, no draw, and no overcards to the board, then watch out. He may be letting you bet his hand for him. If he is a calling station who is loose and passive enough to call on the Flop with QJ, then bet again on the Turn and hope he folds. If your opponent raises you, telling you he has a pair, decide if your hand has any chance of winning. Some players will raise religiously with middle pair in a shorthanded game. With 98 you may have two overcards plus a gutshot straight draw for a possible total of 10 outs. It is worthwhile to continue with hand like that against a check-raise.

The main strength of a drawing hand in a "stealing" position is that there are many possibilities for continuing with the hand. You can appear to be strong and semi-bluff bet or raise. When you combine this strategy with the same aggressive play when you have a made hand, such as AK or a big pair, your opponents will be less confident about what to do against you after you raise. If they regularly call you on the Flop with hands like QT and a board of A-9-3, that is good for you too since you will be able to pound them and extract more from them when you do have a made hand.

Against an aggressive player: Calling instead of raising may be best, even with the best hand

If you think you might have the best hand, sometimes you should call instead of raise in a situation where you are not sure whether your opponent has a worse or better hand than you have. If her hand is worse than yours, you should avoid showing strength by raising her. Let her keep betting, hoping to get you to fold. If you raise when her hand is worse than yours she may fold, costing you the possibility of winning additional bets in later rounds. This passive strategy has risk: if she has a worse hand, she may be able to catch up and hit a 3- or 4-outer. This strategy works only against an aggressive player who will keep betting if you do not show strength. You cannot expect a calling station or an otherwise weak player to keep betting on future rounds with bad hands.

<u>Example</u>

You are in a five-handed game with A7o on the button. You open-raise. The small blind folds and an aggressive player in the big blind calls.

Your hand: A7o
Flop: A-9-8 rainbow

The aggressive player in the big blind checks and you bet. The aggressive player check-raises. You have to decide whether to reraise or call. If you reraise, you are telling him that you have a pair of A's (or something better). The aggressive player will check-raise with many hands, including a pair of A's, a straight draw, or a pair of 9's or 8's, knowing that if you do not have an A and you raised with two other high cards, such as KQ, KJ. It will be a tough decision for you to call both a Flop check-raise and a Turn bet.

You hope that your opponent has an A with a lower kicker. If you are sure he does, you can reraise on the Flop or raise on the Turn and win more than you would by calling him down. However if he has a better hand than yours, such as AK, AQ, AJ, AT or two pair, or if he is on a straight draw and catches it, you will lose more money by being aggressive. Showing aggression after you get check-raised may be putting yourself in a situation where you could lose more bets if you lose, and win fewer bets when you win. Compare the following two situations against an aggressive player:

Situation 1: Your opponent is on a straight draw. You call her check-raise on the Flop and you *raise* her on the Turn.

If she catches the straight, she will bet out on the River (because she is afraid you will check it down if she checks). If she does not catch the straight, she will check on the River and then fold to your bet. You have shown her that you have a made hand; so she will no longer consider bluffing on the River. So if you raise on the Turn and she catches on the River, then you will lose 3 bets (2 bets on the Turn and 1 bet on the River). If she does not catch on the River, then you will win 2 bets (2 on the Turn and none on the River).

Situation 2: Your opponent is on a straight draw. You call her check-raise on the Flop and you *call* her on the Turn.

If she catches the straight, she will bet on the River. If she does not, she will still bet on the River, thinking she has a chance of stealing the pot with another bet since you have not shown any aggression. So if you call on the Turn, you lose 2 bets (1 on the Turn and 1 on the River) if she catches her straight. If she does not catch a straight, then you win 2 bets (1 on the Turn and 1 on the River).

In Situation 1 you lose 3 bets when you lose and win 2 bets when you win. In Situation 2 you lose 2 bets when you lose and win 2 bets when you win. Because your opponent is aggressive, you can count on her to bluff on the River if she does not catch her hand.

Turn or River card pairs the top card on the board

Players are more likely to play aggressively in a shorthanded game when they have a piece of the Flop than in a full game. They will often raise on the Flop with hands that are worse than top pair, including middle pair, bottom pair, overcards, flush draws and straight draws. Players who are super-aggressive will continue betting with those hands through the River. If you have middle pair, you will have to call down your opponents more often in shorthanded games. Since you are likely to be ahead when you have middle pair, generally you should be happy when the Turn or the River pairs the top card. If you were ahead, you are still ahead after the top card on the board pairs.

Example

Your hand: AT
Flop: Q-T-3 rainbow

You bet and your late-position opponent raises. You know he is aggressive in shorthanded games; so you are sure he is as likely to raise with a split pair of Q's as with a split pair of T's. You are also sure he would be raising with bottom pair as well as a straight draw. This chart shows the type of hands he could have and the corresponding outs.

Type of Hand	*Estimated Outs for Opponent*
Top pair with a Q	40
Middle pair with a T	3
Bottom pair with a 3	5
Open-ended straight draw with KJ, J9	13 or 11
Inside straight draw with AJ, K9, J8	7

If he has a Q, you are drawing to 5 outs or fewer (there are two T's and three A's not accounted for). If he has any of the other hands, then you are the favorite. If you think he would raise with all of these hands, then you are likely to be the favorite with your AT.

Turn: Q

When the Q comes on the Turn and pairs the board, you can be confident that your hand is still best if you thought you were the favorite on the Flop. If your opponent has a worse hand than yours, the Q does not improve it. If he has a better hand, then you may be drawing dead (unless he has T3, as the second Q counterfeits his two pair). The chart above shows that against every type of hand, the relative strength of your hand has stayed the same. No hand that was behind you on the Flop could have improved past your hand, which is better because your opponent has only one more card to see if he can improve. You are happy to see the Turn pair the board. Compare that to a different card on the Turn, such as J or 9. With those cards you will not know if your opponent caught a second pair, trips or a straight. You could be ahead on the Flop but behind on the Turn.

Making all the betting round decisions on the Flop

If your opponent is steaming and you think there is a high probability that she is bluffing, the decision point for the whole hand may come on the Flop. You may need to decide whether to call or fold on the Turn and River as well as whether to call or fold on the Flop. Since she is on tilt, she is going to keep betting, hoping that you will fold. This will happen more often in shorthanded games, because players generally think they can bully their way through since there are fewer players who need to fold for them to win the pot. If the next card is a scare card, such as an A, that usually increases the chance that she will keep betting, since she wants to use it as a scare card against you. Against steamers you should not let a scare card frighten you into folding as often.

Also do not raise against a steamer, because you do not want to scare her off. A raise may force her to fold. If she has a strong hand, a raise will cost you more money. The trade-off of not raising is worth the risk of giving away a free card and having the steamer catch a pair to beat you.

Bigger wins and bigger losses in shorthanded games

All players play more hands in shorthanded games than in full games. They raise pre-Flop and defend blinds all the time. They may bet or raise with middle pair. They will semi-bluff with straight and flush draws more often. Because of the increased aggression of the other players, you can raise more often and play more aggressively, as well as calling down hands more often. All these factors mean that the good days will bring higher profits, while the bad days will bring worse losses. Be prepared for this in shorthanded play. It may be a good idea to play at a lower limit than you typically play in full games in order to keep your wins and losses at roughly the same amount. This may help with your sanity and keep you in the game.

Be careful when the table becomes full again

In a shorthanded game you will be playing more hands and more aggressively than you would in a full game. This is a good mentality to have in a shorthanded game, but not necessarily in a full game. A game will often start shorthanded, and slowly turn into a full game as more players sit down. Some players find it tough to adjust quickly in this situation, and keep thinking about raising aggressively and calling down potential bluffs. If they keep up that mentality after the game has turned into a full game, they will be in trouble.

Always keep in mind how many players are being dealt in the hand. Raising with KJo under the gun is fine in a four-handed game, but it is too aggressive in a seven-handed game. Change gears quickly after the table fills up and the game becomes full. The opposite applies too: when people start leaving and your game goes from full to shorthanded, adjust and adapt to the changing environment.

Shorthanded side games vs. shorthanded tournament situations

This book is written to cover Limit Hold'em side games, not tournaments. Shorthanded side games are not the same as shorthanded situations in tournaments. The all-in situations and prize structure in tournaments add dimensions. Players have fewer chips to battle with in tournaments than in ring games. There may be a huge disparity between fifth-place prize money and fourth-place prize money. This payout structure changes the expected value (EV) and thus the analysis and calculations. Do not think of these chapters on shorthanded play when you are in a shorthanded situation in a tournament. Shorthanded ring games and shorthanded tournaments are two different worlds.

CHAPTER 18 COMMON MISTAKES IN SHORTHANDED PLAY

Many players have misconceptions about shorthanded Hold'em games. Some players play the same way in shorthanded games as they do in full games; but the two are different. Although it is correct to play more hands in shorthanded games, many players will adjust too radically and play too many hands, especially in early position and in the small blind.

Mistake #1: Playing Too Many Hands in the Wrong Spots

Many players know they need to play more hands in shorthanded games. This is true; but the key is to play more hands, more aggressively, in the right spots. Below are some situations where some players are mistaken in believing that they can loosen up in shorthanded games. Hands in these spots should be played as they would in a full game.

1. Under the gun with KTo in a six-handed game

Some players believe they can raise here; but that is too loose and too aggressive. Many opponents will reraise with hands such as AJo, ATo, 77, KQo and KJs. KTo does not play well against those reraising hands. Open-raising with KTo in a later position is fine if there are fewer players left to act, but not under the gun in a six-handed game.

2. Calling a raise on the button with A3o

Calling raises is normally a bad strategy in shorthanded games, except in the big blind. Calling a raise with a hand like A3o is an especially poor decision. This hand will often be dominated by another hand with an A (with which many players will open-raise in shorthanded games). Also, if there are no A's in other players' hands and an A does come on the Flop, A3o will not get much action.

3. Calling a raise in the small blind with JTo

This is too loose. This play is discussed in detail under Mistake #11 in this chapter.

Mistake #2: Trying Too Hard to be Unpredictable

In any poker game you should be unpredictable to opponents. When there are nine or ten players at the table, sometimes this is tough to control. Playing unpredictably often means playing suboptimally, especially in early position. In shorthanded games there are more chances to be unpredictable and still play correctly. There are two specific positions where you must play predictably pre-Flop: under the gun and in the small blind.

Under the gun in a five-handed (or larger) game

You should play predictably in this situation. Two non-blind hands have yet to act; and there is a good chance at least one of them has a quality hand. In a shorthanded game when the blinds do play the hand, they will not be afraid to reraise. As in a full game, you should not raise too often from early position without a quality starting hand. Being unpredictable in this spot costs too much.

Small blind

After there is a raise, the small blind should either reraise or fold most of the time (see Mistake #11). The small blind is in too bad a position to be concerned with playing unpredictably. Playing too many hands from the worst position on the table costs more than unpredictability is worth.

Mistake #3: Being Too Predictable

Players who are not under the gun or in the small blind gain by playing unpredictably in shorthanded games. The big blind and the button gain the most.

Big blind

The big blind can call a raise with more hands in shorthanded games than in full games, and therefore is more unpredictable after the Flop. If there is only one raise and everyone else folds to the big blind, he can choose to reraise or call with many hands due to the 3.5 to 1 pot odds he is getting. He can mix it up with hands such as AK, AQ and pocket pairs.

Button

The button can raise with more hands in a shorthanded game since the action will be folded to her more often than in a full game. This is especially true when the small blind is playing correctly (either folding to the raise or reraising, thus driving out the big blind), and if the big blind is too passive after the Flop or folds too often pre-Flop. If the small blind is calling many raises, then the button should be more selective with his raising standards.

Early position

You should not be predictable post-Flop either. In the situation shown here, you can make the same play in early position with many different hands, thus making yourself less predictable to your opponents.

Flop: J♥7♠6♠

You should consider check-raising with:

- any hand with a J, such as JT, J8
- any hand with a 7, such as A7, 75
- any hand with a 6, such as K6, 65
- any straight draw, such as T8, 98
- any flush draw, such as K♠3♠.

Check-raising with any of these hands will make your play less predictable to opponents without giving up edge. If an opponent raised pre-Flop with a hand such as A5 or KT, she will have a tough time calling even though she may be ahead. If she does call on the Flop, she may fold to a bet on the Turn if she does not improve.

Mistake #4: Folding Too Often

In a full game a tight player who waits for the right hand often has an advantage. He is able to fold his mediocre blind hands to early-position raisers. He has the ability to throw away QQ when there is an A on board and a solid player bets. He can see when a player may have hit a flush draw and fold his top pair. All of these abilities are useful in a full game. They are useful in a shorthanded game as well, but the circumstances are not the same. Being able to adjust is the key. Sometimes the tighter players do not adjust correctly to shorthanded games. In a shorthanded game, medium to high pocket pairs should not be thrown away without a good reason. The presence of one or two overcards on the board is not enough reason to fold a pocket pair.

Example 1

You are in the big blind in a four-handed game.

Your hand: T8o

The button open-raises and the small blind folds. Do not automatically fold this hand as you might in a full game. You are probably behind; but if you play well post-Flop, you will have the pot odds you need to see the Flop. If you are up against a hand such as Q7 (which some players will raise with on the button in a shorthanded game), you are in a situation that is worth 3.5 to 1 to call. In a shorthanded game, players often feel they can raise with any two cards on the button; so seeing the Flop with T8o is not a mistake.

Example 2

You are under the gun and hold a pocket pair of J's in a five-handed game. You raise. An average player on the button calls, as does another player in the big blind. You think the player in the big blind is comfortable in a shorthanded game.

Your hand: J♦J♠
Flop: A♣T♠7♥

The big blind checks to you and you bet. The button folds and the big blind calls.

Turn: 3♥

The big blind checks and you bet. All of a sudden the big blind check-raises you. Do not automatically assume you are up against a split pair of A's and fold. In fact you could be up against a hand like J♥T♥ which picked up a flush draw along with the middle pair of T's. Many players do not have the creativity to make this play; but many do, especially in shorthanded games. Your decision to play on or to fold depends upon your opinion of the aggressiveness and the trickiness of your opponent. Keep in mind that play is more aggressive in a shorthanded game. There is more reason to call in this spot in a shorthanded game than in a full game.

Mistake #5: Being Too Passive in the Wrong Spots

A shorthanded game calls for more aggressive play because the average hand is not as strong as the average hand in a full game. Some hands get bumped up in relative value, and can be played more aggressively in a shorthanded game.

Reasons for playing aggressively:

<u>1. To get more money in the pot if you have a good hand so you can win more</u>

Since players are looser and more aggressive in a shorthanded game, many players have learned to call bets and raises with lesser hands. You should not be afraid to bet or raise when you have the best hand because your opponents are more likely to stick around in a shorthanded game. Avoid slowplaying, since other players will call and you will get paid off more often in a shorthanded game.

2. You have a good hand; but it is vulnerable

In this situation you prefer that your opponents fold. For example if you have top pair when the board is T-8-3, you may have the best hand; but it is vulnerable to overcards. Charge players with overcards a fee to see if they can draw out on you.

3. You need the other players to fear your raises so you have credibility when you are bluffing or semi-bluffing

Credibility is important because you will have more chances to bluff and semi-bluff in a shorthanded game. Make your opponents unable to deduce whether you have a made hand, because they may make mistakes when they are uncertain.

Example

You hold A3o on the button in a four-handed game. You open-raise and both blind hands call.

Your hand: A3o
Flop: A-7-6 rainbow

They both check and you bet. Both of them call.

Turn: 8

They both check again. Do not be afraid of a check-raise by one of the players; just keep betting. Do not allow a lone 5 or 9 to see the River for free. Although being up against a hand like 98 is not ideal (a pair of 8's with a straight draw gives your opponent 13 outs against your pair of A's), don't allow a hand like that to see the River without putting in a bet, and thus get "infinite" odds.

This situation is different from checking on the Turn with the intention of calling a bluff bet on the River. In this hand your opponent can have too many possible outs. The strategy of inducing bluffs is best used when your opponent has fewer outs and is likely to fold if you bet on the Turn. In those cases your check on the Turn is a ploy to lure her into betting a worse hand on the River by showing weakness on the Turn. But in this example most opponents with a straight draw will call. The looser players may call with inside straight draws (with a T or a 4) as well. Bet on the Turn since you are likely to get called by a worse hand.

Mistake #6: Being Too Aggressive in the Wrong Spots

Semi-bluffing is a powerful strategy when it is used at the proper time and against the right opponents. The proper time is when there is a scary board for the opponent, and the right opponents are players who will fold with a better hand after a player raises, at least once in a while. If there is no chance that the opponent will fold, then a semi-bluff is a poor strategy. It is correct to play aggressively in shorthanded games against normal players. Some players will not lay down a hand, being willing to call with A-high or bottom pair, no matter how scary the board. Against these calling stations, semi-bluffing or bluffing is a self-defeating strategy since they will not fold a hand better than yours. It is still worthwhile to be aggressive against calling stations, but only at times when you think you are ahead and are betting for value.

Mistake #7: Not Using the Option of Calling and Checking

Many decisions in poker boil down to raising or folding. Using these two extreme strategies is often correct. Calling and checking can be useful too. It becomes more useful in a shorthanded game when other players may be playing too aggressively. There will be situations where the best play is neither a fold nor a raise, but a check or a call. In these situations folding may be incorrect because you may have the best hand. Raising may be incorrect if you have the best hand. You should avoid driving out an opponent who will bet a worse hand into you on the next round.

Example

You hold KJ and open-raise in the cutoff in a five-handed game. The button folds. Both blinds call.

Your hand: KJ
Flop: A-K-4 rainbow

Both blinds check to you and you bet. The small blind folds and the big blind calls. Since the big blind called, she could have an A with a bad kicker, QJ or JT for an inside straight draw, or a K with a worse kicker than yours.

Turn: 6

The big blind checks. There are 4 big bets in the pot. If she is on a straight draw with a hand like QJ, then she has 4 outs. If you bet and she calls, you know that she is making a bad call since she does not have pot odds.

There are players who will automatically call with an inside straight draw without pot odds. Against those calling stations you should bet again to get their bets in. Other opponents are willing to fold a straight draw on the Turn since they know they do not have enough outs to make calling worthwhile. Against a player like that, it is correct to check on the Turn after his check. Let him think he can win the hand even if he does not hit his straight on the River. In showing weakness by checking on the Turn, you hint that you do not have a strong hand and that you may be willing to fold on the River if he bets. If you had bet on the Turn, he would have folded. Thus if he does not have an A and does not hit his straight, you have a good chance of inducing him to bluff on the River so you can win a bet that you would not have won had you bet on the Turn. You are giving him a free card. If there is a strong chance you will induce him to bluff by your check, it may be worthwhile given the relatively small pot.

Consider the situation when your opponent has an A with a good kicker or an even better hand. Or maybe her hand is A6 and she makes two pair on the Turn. After hitting her two pair, she no longer has to worry about her kicker problems. Maybe she flops two pair or a pair of A's with a decent kicker. In any of those cases after you raise pre-Flop and bet on the Flop, she knows there is a good chance that you will bet on the Turn. Many players with strong hands will wait until the Turn to check-raise. If your opponent has one of these hands you should not bet and get check-raised, because you would be forced to fold your own hand. Instead you should check and hope to get trip K's to give her a bad beat on the River.

In summary: if your opponent has little, your check may win an extra bet if he bluffs on the River; whereas if you bet on the Turn, he will fold. If your opponent is way ahead of you, then your check has given you a chance to catch up on the River. Compare this to betting against a better hand. You are likely to get check-raised on the Turn and be forced to fold without seeing the River. Checking should be part of your arsenal, used as a stealth weapon against solid players who can steal if they see weakness. Do not check against calling stations.

Mistake #8: Calling to the River with A-High on a Tough Board

Some players inexperienced at shorthanded poker take an A and play it through the River indiscriminately. There are occasions when this is the right play; but it is sometimes not correct. In shorthanded games, players see so many poor quality hands and A-high hands win that they automatically think they should call down to the River with any A without regard to the board or the actions of the other players. Below are a couple of examples where calling down with A-high is incorrect.

Example 1

Your hand: A6
Flop: K-Q-9
Turn: 8
River: 3

There is little reason to think a player who is betting here is bluffing. Trying to call her down on a bluff with a board like this will quickly dwindle your stack. In fact you should not have bothered to call on the Flop.

Example 2

You are in the big blind. There are two other players, the small blind and the button.

Your hand: A6
Flop: 3-4-5
Turn: K
River: J

The small blind checks to you on the River, and you check as well. The button bets. The small blind calls. This is a must-fold. You can only hope to win this hand in the unlikely event that the button made a bluff bet and at the same time the small blind called with a hand that cannot beat A6. You might have been able to beat a bluff from the button; but you definitely cannot beat the call from the small blind.

A couple of examples where calling down with A-high may be correct:

Example 3

Your hand: A6o
Flop: 3-4-5
Turn: T
River: 8

Your lone opponent is on the cutoff and raised pre-Flop. He is less likely to have a pair on a board with no high cards than on a board that contains high cards. It was correct for you to be in the hand on the Flop or the Turn since you had a straight draw and an A, although you could have chosen to put in a raise on the Flop or Turn. The main question is whether your opponent will try to make a value bet with AK or AQ on the River. If he holds a hand like KQ, K9, QJ, he may keep on betting, hoping you will fold an A. A call may be correct against an aggressive opponent. Alternatively a raise may be worthwhile in order to force a better A-high hand to fold.

Example 4

Your hand: A♠6♠
Flop: 9♠9♣5♠
Turn: T♦
River: T♥

There was a late-position pre-Flop raiser and you called in the big blind with A♠6♠. Deciding to call was not tough. You are beaten if your opponent has a 9, a T or a pair of J's or higher. You are tied if she has an A. You win the hand if she doesn't have any of those cards. You can beat a pair lower than 9's, such as 88 or 77. You will lose your fair share of hands in this situation. You will split the pot or win the pot outright often enough to make it worthwhile to call on the River against most opponents.

Mistake #9: Pre-Flop: Calling When You Should Be Folding or Raising

Habitually limping in the pre-Flop round in a shorthanded game is a strategy for losers. That is a strong statement; but it is true. Under the gun in a five-handed game, if you have a hand that you are not sure how to play, you should either fold or raise. There are not many hands you should limp with in early position in a full game; and that small number gets reduced to none in a shorthanded game. Hands that players in shorthanded games have trouble with: A3o, JTo and 87s. Players often limp in with these hands in early position, thinking: "I have seen other players raising with these hands and winning, so they're playable; but these cards are not great. I need to hit the Flop in order to keep playing them. The cards are too good to fold, but not good enough to raise with; so I'll call."

In early position both ATo and T9s are marginal hands in a full game. In a shorthanded game ATo turns into a raising hand while T9s turns into a folding hand.

T9s

Limping in early position with this drawing hand may be justifiable in a full game if you can legitimately expect others to call as well and make it a multiple-player pot. In a shorthanded game usually someone will raise behind or everyone will fold to the blinds. In either case the hand will be played with few players and you will not have correct pot odds to be playing. This hand is not strong enough for a raise. A call is incorrect because you cannot expect to get into a multiple-player pot. This hand should be folded.

ATo

ATo is not a great hand and can be dominated by AK, AQ and AJ; but it is strong enough to play when the game is six-handed or smaller because of its high-card quality. ATo is best played with as few players as possible since it is not a drawing hand. Raising is better than calling.

Mistake #10: Post-Flop: Calling Too Often

In shorthanded games you will often get raised, semi-bluffed, check-raised and bluffed. There are situations where it is right to call these opponents down: when you have the best hand and when you are making them aware that you will not easily fold and will call their semi-bluffs, so that they will think it is not worthwhile to semi-bluff against you. There are many situations where it is right to fold because the odds are too high against you both having the best hand at the moment and not falling behind in a future round. A couple of examples:

Example 1: When you should fold to a raise from a player in late position

You raised before the Flop from the cutoff in a five-handed game with A♠6♠. An average player cold-calls you on the button, as does the big blind.

Your hand: A♠6♠
Flop: K♣Q♦4♥

The big blind checks. You bet, hoping to win the pot. The button raises. The big blind calls. Deciding to fold is easy. It is fairly obvious that the possible hands for the two players are a pair of K's, a pair of Q's and a straight draw. Since two players are in, it is unlikely that both of them are on a draw. You will have to hit an A on the Turn to feel comfortable with your hand. An A will complete a straight for an opponent who has JT, which is a hand that many players will play. So when two players are in on the Flop, you should fold even though the pot is offering you 11:1 odds. The pot is not big enough to justify calling.

Example 2: When you should fold to a single bet on the Flop after getting reraised pre-Flop

You are the button and try to steal the blinds by open-raising with J♠9♠. A solid player in the small blind reraises. The big blind folds and you call to see the Flop.

Your hand: J♠9♠
Flop: A♣3♦3♠

The small blind bets out. It is time to fold, though you are getting 8:1 odds. You could be drawing dead. At best you are drawing to 6 outs, which is not enough to keep playing. Your opponent's raise indicates a pocket pair or a hand with an A; and you are a big underdog to either hand.

Example 3: When you should fold to a bet on the Flop when you were the raiser pre-Flop

You are in the cutoff holding K♠J♥, and you open-raise. Both blinds call.

Your hand: K♠J♥
Flop: A♣9♦9♣

The small blind bets. The big blind calls. You should fold. The best you can hope for is that they are both on club flush draws, which is unlikely. You are probably beaten by at least one opponent; and even if not you can still get outdrawn. With only one opponent in the hand, you could consider calling if he was prone to betting out on paired Flops as a bluff or betting out on a flush draw. With two opponents, a fold is correct.

Mistake #11: Frequently Calling Raises in the Small Blind

After a raise with no other callers, calling a raise in the small blind is a mistake. When there is one raiser, the small blind's decision is binary: reraise or fold. The first and main reason for this is the small blind's position relative to the big blind. If the small blind calls, she gives the big blind 5:1 pot odds to call. The big blind is correct to call with almost any hand. Calling puts the small blind in a horrible position for the rest of the hand, with two players behind her. To avoid this large disadvantage, the small blind should fold many hands, including hands like J9s, A2s and KTo. With playable hands she should reraise. Her reraise gives the big blind 7:2 pot odds to call, not nearly as attractive as 5:1.

The second reason for this binary decision is that a reraise makes the small blind look strong going into the Flop, which is useful if the button is stealing. A reraise pre-Flop by the small blind, followed by a bet on the Flop, will often force the button to fold if he doesn't hit the Flop.

You should not call raises often in the small blind with only one raiser and no other callers yet. If another player habitually calls in spots like this, you know you have an opponent who is giving away a lot of edge to the big blind. Try to move your seat to this player's left. (See the discussion on three players in Chapter 17 "Shorthanded Limit Hold'em" for more on this concept.) If more than one player in the game habitually calls raises in the small blind, then the game is better. It does not matter where you sit because you will be getting the best of it often.

Mistake #12: Not Adjusting to the Tempo and Mood of the Game

Different shorthanded games have different styles. Sometimes they play like a full game, with most of the players taking it easy and trying to play solidly, and no one trying to be a bully. The players may be used to full games, so as a group they are not as aggressive as players used to shorthanded games. At other times the game will play faster, with many raises and reraises. In these wilder games it is common to see half of the pre-Flop rounds being three-bet. Generally when the tempo of the game is faster and the mood is aggressive, the pots are bigger and semi-bluffing and raising are more useful strategies. A fold by any player adds equity for the remaining players.

In a game with a slower tempo and a more passive mood, a semi-bluff will need to work more often to have value since the pots will typically be smaller. When the tempo is slower, the correct strategy is generally to play more conservatively. (You can still selectively steal.) Great players can mold the tempo and the mood of the game in the direction they want it to go. For example if they want a faster tempo, they may try to trash-talk the players they think are susceptible to being manipulated, trying to get them on tilt; and all of a sudden the game becomes faster and more aggressive. Adjust to the tempo and the mood of the game; and try control and manipulate them.

Mistake #13: Playing Three-Handed Games Like Six-Handed Games

Shorthanded games come in different sizes. A six-handed game plays differently than a four-handed or three-handed game. There are more similarities between six-handed games and nine-handed games than between six-handed games and three-handed games. There a positional difference in three-handed games, since the under-the-gun player is also the button on the same hand. Every player is involved in every hand. Any weakness of any player is magnified if one of the other players is skilled enough to take advantage of it. Any player can win big due to good luck or lose big due to bad luck.

CHAPTER 19 ONLINE POKER

In general, online poker should be attacked the same way as poker in a brick-and-mortar casino. In order to play well and win, you have to adjust to the players and the circumstances. There are differences between the average online player and the average brick-and-mortar player. Those differences are small enough that minor adjustments should do the trick. This chapter specifically addresses the differences and uniqueness that online poker presents.

The question of the legality of online poker is unanswered in many states. Check on the legality of playing online poker before you play. Although this chapter is about online poker, I am not suggesting that it is legal nor am I suggesting that you play poker online. Make that decision for yourself.

Reasons to Play Internet Poker

There are many reasons for playing poker on the Internet:

1. You do not live close to a poker room

There are legal poker rooms all over America, but many people still live far from one. Online poker is a nice solution for the people who do not have a chance to play poker on a regular basis in brick-and-mortar card rooms.

2. You do not have to commute

Even players who live close to a poker room find it takes time to commute. It may take half an hour or more to get to the poker room. There is usually a waiting period before getting into a game. On the Internet there is no need to commute, and the wait for a seat is shorter. If you are physically challenged and find commuting difficult, playing poker online is an ideal solution. You can play comfortably at home, whereas you might not be comfortable in a casino environment.

3. There is no secondhand smoke

A few years ago California banned smoking in casinos, poker rooms, and other establishments. Several other poker rooms across the country have switched to nonsmoking poker rooms, examples being Bellagio in Las Vegas and Foxwoods in Connecticut. This is great for the players' lungs! Outside of California, many casinos with nonsmoking poker rooms allow smoking in other parts of the casino, and the smoke can creep into the poker room. Poker players sit at the table for long periods of time, so they may be susceptible to the harmful effects of secondhand smoke. Worse are the poker rooms that allow smoking. For players who are worried about secondhand smoke, online poker is a healthy alternative. On the other hand, smokers playing online poker are not affected by the smoking regulations or by other people complaining about secondhand smoke.

4. The rake may be lower online

Many online poker rooms take a lower rake per hand than their brick-and-mortar counterparts. They can do this because they deal more hands per hour and their costs are lower. This benefits players as they get to keep a bigger portion of the pots they win.

5. There is no tipping online

Tipping is controversial topic. In brick-and-mortar casinos a major part of a dealer's income comes from tips. Tips cut into the profits of winning players and increase losses for losing players. Online poker has no tipping; so winning players make more money and losing players can play longer.

6. You can play any time of day

Online poker rooms are "open" all the time. If there are players, there are games. Once an online poker room reaches a certain critical mass of players, it will have games at all times of day. Not every site has this feature since not all are that successful; but there are several that have achieved this critical mass. This is great for many people, including morning people, people who work at night and can play only during the day, and night owls who play in the wee hours of the morning

7. You can play for a short time if you prefer

When you make the effort to go to the local poker room, you probably feel you should stay there for a while. Nobody likes to drive half an hour to play a couple of minutes and then drive another half an hour to get home. But with online poker you can play just one round, which may take as little as one minute. You can play for five minutes and decide to leave. If you are waiting for something or someone, you can play for a short period of time, and log off when that something or someone is ready. This is a great option, although it does make for high turnover of players at online games as compared to brick-and-mortar games.

8. There are convenient ways to analyze your own play online

Most online poker sites have an option that lets you see your hand histories. This makes analyzing your own play easier than in a brick-and-mortar casino. Without hand histories, the only way to track your own hand-by-hand play is to write down every hand, which is not practical for most people. With the popularity of online poker, new software has been developed to help players analyze their game. It may be worthwhile to find out about these software programs to see if they can help you analyze your own game.

9. There are convenient ways to analyze the play of other players

Many sites have a feature that lets you write notes about each player. You have access to these notes the next time you are at the same table as that player. There is also software that lets you analyze other players' games. These programs can access only the hands that your opponents played when you were in the game, rather than every game they have played; but they still are useful.

10. More hands are dealt per hour online

More hands are dealt per hour online than in brick-and-mortar games. There is no need to wait for the dealer to shuffle, take in the mucked cards, collect the chips, make change, take the rake or time, get a rack fill, call for empty seats and settle player disputes. For the winning player, more hands per hour means a higher expected profit.

11. Shorthanded games are easy to find online

It is difficult to find shorthanded games in brick-and-mortar poker rooms. When they exist, they usually do not last long. Often these games break up, since most players do not like to play short; or the table fills up when other players come in. For those who like to play short, many online poker rooms maintain special tables, such as heads-up tables and tables where a maximum of five or six players can be seated.

12. You can play at more than one table simultaneously

One of the great advantages of playing online is the ability to play more than one game at the same time. In full games sometimes there is dead time as you watch the other players play out their hands. If you do not know the other players, this is a useful time to gather information about how they play. If you are well versed in their abilities and styles, it can be boring. In brick-and-mortar poker rooms, many people will take this time to chitchat with other players near them, get to know each other, discuss current events or eat a meal. Some players play poker primarily for the social aspects; they enjoy talking with friends while playing the game. Online poker is a different story. Many players know each other online, and can hold interesting conversations; but it is different from a brick-and-mortar casino. Once you get done with that stuff, you can get bored, especially if you are dealt junk hand after hand and are constantly folding. Some people like to play more than one table to deal with the boredom. Instead of getting distracted by non-poker issues, they choose to play two or more games and keep all of their attention on poker. There are advantages to this, but also disadvantages. Playing multiple tables simultaneously is discussed later in this chapter.

Getting Paid and Bonus Hunting

Since it is your own money at stake, it is your responsibility to make sure the poker site you play is trustworthy. Expect to get your withdrawal shortly after you ask for it. With the increase in the popularity of online poker in the last few years, many entrepreneurs are trying to capitalize on this expanding market. Some of these new sites may go under, taking players' money down with them. How would you get a few thousand dollars from an entity in one of the Caribbean Islands when you don't know the actual owners? That is one of the dangers of online poker; and it can be scary and frustrating.

Poker players should take a lesson from their sports bettor brethren. The offshore sports betting industry has been around longer than the online poker industry. Sports bettors have seen several big sports books go under due to mismanagement, insufficient capital and outright fraud. All sportsbooks need clients in order to make money. To find and retain players, new sportsbooks need to give players an incentive to give them a try. They entice players to join by offering deposit bonuses. This can lead to a business that seems to be built like a Ponzi scheme. An incentive might be an offer of a 25% cash bonus on a deposit, but with restrictions such as a five-times rollover and a one-month minimum before making a withdrawal. A five-times rollover means that players must bet their deposit amounts five times over before they are eligible to take withdrawals. On the surface this makes sense from the sportsbook's point of view, because it guarantees sufficient action from the player. The player is thrilled to get 25% of his deposit as a bonus for signing up and depositing, thinking that since he is going to play anyway. Why not get a bonus as an extra kick?

As the sportsbook signs up more players, it gets a reputation through sports gambling forums and word of mouth. With deposits from new players, the sportsbook has a steady stream of incoming cash, which means plenty of funds to pay anyone who requests a withdrawal. This leads to more confidence from players, especially those who have taken a withdrawal. They feel more confident about leaving the rest of their money in that book since they have already been paid once. It is logical to think that if a site paid you once, it is likely to pay you again in the future. However if the book does not do a good job managing its lines, it may start to lose to the sharp bettors. If the new deposits start to dry up at the same time, that could lead to the collapse of the Ponzi scheme. The book no longer has funds to pay everybody. Sooner or later the customers suffer. Yet players still think it is okay to give new sportsbooks a shot, because they believe in the "greater fool" theory. They believe they will be deft enough to get out before the impending doom hits. This is a dangerous game. It requires attention and calculation that most people cannot afford to take the time to give it.

Poker rooms operate differently from sportsbooks. Sportsbooks play against the customers, so sportsbooks bear more risk than do poker rooms. Aside from the possible legality issues, this is the biggest danger in the offshore sports betting industry. All the experienced sports bettors understand the danger since most of them have been affected by past collapses. The greed of bonus hunting leads to players losing their own deposits. This is a lesson to be learned for the upcoming years as more and more outfits try to take advantage of the online poker boom: it is more important to have your funds safe than to get a deposit bonus. What good is getting a bonus if there is a risk of not getting your own money out?

There are many reputable poker sites, but it is often difficult for players to identify which sites to trust with their funds. Research is recommended. Be more wary of start-ups unless you have a good reason to be comfortable. For example several high-quality sportsbooks that have been in business for many years and have impeccable reputations have recently created their own online poker rooms. These poker rooms will be safer than other start-ups that are not attached to any other known entity. If you are comfortable with the financial status of the online sportsbook, and it provides online poker as part of its business, then that may be a safer place for your money than a start-up online poker site with no link to an entity you trust.

In order to reduce the damage if one of these poker sites collapses financially, prepare ahead of time. Withdraw money constantly as your funds increase. Keep in mind a maximum dollar amount that you are comfortable leaving at the site; and if your balance ever goes above that number, consider making a withdrawal request.

Free Games Online

Online poker rooms and other Internet sites offer games that use fake or "play" money. These games are completely free: no risk, no reward. New players may be tempted to think of these games as a good practice field. Unfortunately they do not serve that purpose well at all. It is human nature to play differently when the play is free than when there is real money at stake. Players are not afraid to call any bets or raises, and are happy to bluff often. This is not what poker is about at all. The players in free games do not have anything to lose; and most people play accordingly. Poker is poker only when there is something at stake, where losing means losing something that has value to the player. Playing in free games to get an idea of the mechanics of the game is useful. Free games are not good practice for real-money play.

Pitfalls of Playing Online

There are more pitfalls to playing online. There are many possible distractions playing online poker that you do not have in a brick-and-mortar poker room, including surfing online, writing and reading email, watching television and reading a book. (If you are playing online poker as you read this, STOP. Either play the game or read the book. Don't do both at the same time!) If you are confident you know how your opponents play, it is possible you will lose little by focusing your attention elsewhere. However, they may be playing differently in this particular session. Maybe one of them is on tilt, having taken a few bad beats in a row. She may be playing more aggressively on hands that she normally would not play at all. If you know the players well, it is still beneficial to pay attention to the game. It is your own discipline or lack thereof that will determine whether the distractions cause you to lose your focus.

Many brick-and-mortar poker rooms allow players to read magazines or newspapers while sitting at the table. It may seem as though you are as likely to get distracted playing online as playing in a brick-and-mortar casino, if you can read at the table in both places. There is a big difference between the two. After a major occurrence in a brick-and-mortar casino, you will often hear the players talking about it. If you are reading, you can hear the commotion and lift your head to see what is happening. This does not happen in online poker rooms. The noise level will be the same whether or not there is a major bad beat or other interesting event happening.

Playing Multiple Games Simultaneously

Some players like to play more than one game at a time. On one hand, playing multiple games simultaneously may be good in that it forces you to focus completely on poker. On the other hand, one game can distract you from the other game. If you are involved in a hand in one game, you will not be able to examine the play of the hand in the other game as carefully as you normally do. You could miss important details about how the other players play.

The advantages of playing multiple games simultaneously are obvious for winning players. Although you may reduce your win rate at each table, your overall win rate could increase. If your win rate at each of these tables is more than half of your normal amount at one table, then you are making more money playing two tables simultaneously. If you are playing at three tables at the same time, then your win rate at each table has to be at least one-third of the win rate at one table. This is a good deal for those who can keep their win rate above those levels. Spending the same amount of time playing poker and making more money; who wouldn't want that? Losing players will lose their money at a faster rate too.

Another strategy for playing in multiple tables is to play at a lower limit at each table, making your total expectation roughly the same as it would be playing at one table with higher limits. This may allow you to get the same expectation out of multiple lower-limit tables while gaining the advantage of reducing variance. In other words you get the same reward for less risk through diversification.

In a full game a good player will not be involved in as many hands as the average player, so you will not often find yourself involved in two hands at the same time. You can devote most of your concentration to the table where you are involved in a hand. Some players do not lose much edge playing two full games simultaneously. Since their win rate would have to slip to less than half of their win rate at one table, it benefits them to play two full games at once. This is a big advantage that online poker rooms have over their brick-and-mortar counterparts, for both the players and the casinos. The poker rooms like it because they can collect more rake. Playing two tables may alleviate your boredom, and steer you away from doing other things that are harmful to your concentration, such as checking out Internet sites, listening to the radio, or writing a book. (That's a joke, folks.) Playing multiple tables may make you concentrate more on each individual table than you would if you were playing one table at a time and fooling around on the side.

The bottom line is that if you are a winning player, and do not lose too much edge from your normal win rate, playing at more than one table is a nice boost to your profitability and a nice reduction of risk.

There are disadvantages also. It is harder to concentrate on each table, so you may miss juicy pieces of information. Online poker players flit in and out of the table quickly. It is easy to miss changes in the table composition. If the loose table you thought you had fills up with tight players without you noticing, you may play some hands wrong.

Playing two or more shorthanded tables is tougher. You need to concentrate more on shorthanded games, since it is more important to have a good handle on how each player plays. A bad, loose player leaving the table and being replaced by a solid, tight player changes the characteristics and the composition of the whole table. One player in a shorthanded game makes up a higher percentage of the table than in a full game. You will be involved in hands more often in shorthanded games than at a full table. If you are playing two shorthanded games at the same time, you have a higher chance of being involved in hands at both tables simultaneously. Playing one shorthanded game and one full game simultaneously can also cause problems. You may find yourself being too aggressive in the full game and not aggressive enough in the shorthanded game.

Playing multiple games online will seem like playing a video game at times. For younger players who grew up in the video game age, this will enhance the experience of the game and make it more fun, although not necessarily more profitable. These players do not have a problem with the fast-changing screens or the action as they are used to it from their video game experience. It may be tougher for older players who are not used to video games to adjust.

Overall the advantages of playing two full games will outweigh those of playing one full game for most winning players. Losing players playing multiple games will lose their money at a faster rate. In shorthanded games it is prudent to stick to one game at a time, because you will need more concentration and you will be more likely to be involved in hands at both tables.

Stack Size and Pot Size Online

In online poker you can see how big the pot is and how many bets the other players have left in their stacks. In a brick-and-mortar poker room, reading stack sizes can be difficult. Even if they are not actively trying to hide their stacks, players often have both of their hands and arms on the table, as well as water bottles and other objects. This can affect how you play the hand. For example if you know your opponent has been losing and is down to just a couple of bets left, you may feel that he will play looser and more aggressively just to get all-in and end the pain. This happens frequently. These situations are easy to identify online but more difficult to notice in the brick-and-mortar casinos. If you do not notice he is close to going all-in, you may miss the fact that he is playing more aggressively than normal. Alternatively a player could have a large denomination chip along with his other chips, which might make it look as though he is short-stacked when in fact he is not.

It is also helpful to see the stack size when you expect a player to go all-in and you want to influence her bet. For example you are first to act in a three-player pot. You have a hand you think is strong but vulnerable to draws. You would be happy to have a player going all-in to your right. If you are first to act, you can check, hoping the second player also checks. After the short-stacked player bets and goes all-in, you can raise and make it more expensive for the second player to draw out. If the short-stacked player acts first and goes all-in, you can raise even if you are not sure that you have the all-in player beaten, since your raise will be in the side pot. In an online poker room you will have no problem seeing that the player has gone all-in; while in a brick-and-mortar casino you may not realize it immediately.

Seeing the pot size in exact dollar amounts is helpful when you have not been counting the pot size as this book recommends; but do not use it as a crutch if you play in real casinos as well. Counting the pot as the bets go into it is extremely useful to your play in a full brick-and-mortar game. You can make better decisions faster if you do not have to stop and take time to count the pot when you are at the decision point. With online poker you can allow the software to add up the pot size for you, and you can make decisions from that information. The danger is that you will get lazy and not count the pot as each hand is played in the brick-and-mortar poker room. You may find you have an advantage while playing poker online, but then see that you are not using all the tools available when playing in a brick-and-mortar poker room.

When you are playing multiple games simultaneously, it can be difficult to count the bets going into the pot. The ability to see the exact pot size at any time is useful.

Online Play is More Aggressive

The average online player plays differently than the average player in a brick-and-mortar casino. Online players seem to:

- raise more often
- bluff more often
- semi-bluff more often
- bet for value more often
- call more often.

In general it seems that the average online player plays more aggressively and expects other players to play more aggressively as well. Why is this? What is it about online play that results in more aggressive play? Here are some possible reasons:

1. There are more younger (20s and 30s) players online

Younger people are more apt to use the Internet than older people, which results in a higher percentage of younger poker players online than in brick-and-mortar casinos. It is also probably true that younger people on average are more aggressive and take more chances in life as well as in poker. They make the general play online more aggressive.

2. Ambiguity can foster aggression and suspicion

When players do not see each other face to face, it is easier for them to play aggressively against each other and to be more suspicious of each other. In brick-and-mortar casinos you can see all the players. Face-to-face interaction makes players less apt to bluff. Maybe they feel bluffing is not socially acceptable. Ambiguity also leads to suspicion. Players who do not know or see an opponent may become suspicious that the opponent is doing something underhanded, such as bluffing; so players are more apt to call in an online game.

3. The money feels less real online

In a brick-and-mortar casino, players have to buy their chips with cash. They hand the cashier or the dealer cash in exchange for casino chips. It is easier for players to take more chances with chips than they would with actual cash, as chips feel less like real money. Extrapolating this further, it is also easier for players to take more chances with cyber-cash than with chips or cash. However a player funds an online account, the money in that account feels less tangible than cash. Consequently players may be willing to take more chances when playing poker online; and this leads to more aggressive play.

Fluctuations are Higher

Online poker players experience higher fluctuations in their wins and losses than players in brick-and-mortar poker rooms do because:

- The average online poker player plays more aggressively than the average brick-and-mortar poker player. Aggressive play increases the volatility of the game.
- There are more shorthanded games online than in brick-and-mortar poker rooms. Shorthanded games have higher fluctuations than full table games because all the players are involved in more hands.
- In an online game more hands are dealt in the same time period. Since more hands are played per hour online, the results look more extreme.

To evaluate fluctuations, compare full-table games between online and brick-and-mortar rooms, measuring them in terms of the number of hands played. It does not make sense to use an hourly rate because online players play more hands per hour than brick-and-mortar players do.

To compare shorthanded online games to full-table brick-and-mortar games, adjust for two additional factors: shorthanded online games get dealt more hands per hour than full online games, and players play more aggressively and loosely in shorthanded games. Both factors will increase the fluctuations for all players.

When the extreme fluctuations are on the up side, meaning that you are winning, you don't complain. The sky is sunny; everyone is having a good time; and life is as it should be. It is when the extreme fluctuations are on the down side that you start to complain, wondering why you have such bad luck, cursing the computer, and wondering if there is a conspiracy against you. You start to wonder if other players are colluding. You think maybe someone has hacked into the software and your opponents can see all the cards or the future board. You wonder if maybe the site is rigged to make the poor players win and the good players lose. In times like these, be strong and do not give in to the urge to put all the blame on everything and everyone else. Maybe you were playing poorly

Technology is a wonderful thing; but you have to watch your back

I was sitting alone in an $10-$20 table in an online poker room that did not have much high-limit action. Normally the highest-limit game at this site was $5-$10 and it was rare for a $10-$20 game to get started. However, since this poker room was attached to an online sportsbook, there was a chance that someone would show up using funds from the sportsbook account. Usually these people are less experienced poker players checking out the poker room to gamble. I had the table up on my computer while watching an NCAA College basketball tournament game.

As luck would have it, a player sat down at the table. I was alerted by my computer beeping. I went to the computer to start playing. I recognized the player, and knew he played solidly. After a few hands it was clear that neither of us had an advantage over the other. It was not worth playing heads-up since the rake is relatively high in a heads-up game. In this game the button put up the small blind while the other player posts the big blind, thus giving the small blind a small advantage. That did not matter since the button rotated every hand.

He was the first to quit. After his hand on the button, he sat out of the game. Then an interesting thing happened: he quickly came back in. I had expected he would post the big blind, and I would get the button and the small blind. Instead the button moved back to his seat. He posted the small blind again. Since I had the "Auto Blind" option on, the computer posted my big blind automatically. Boy, was I mad! I had posted the big blind two hands in a row against the same opponent. I decided to leave the table after the hand. But then I thought maybe I could do same thing to get the button in consecutive hands. I

that day or had a string of bad luck, or a combination of the two. These fluctuations will happen in poker. They will happen with greater extremes in online poker. Some players even complain on Internet poker forums that they were cheated at certain sites. Instead of complaining, played the next hand with the button and the small blind. In the hand after that, I sat out and came back in, as my opponent had done previously. To my delight, it worked! The button came right back to me and the site prompted me to post the small blind, while my opponent posted the big blind for the second hand in a row. Apparently he did not realize what had happened, because I kept up the same routine and took the button for at least 20 straight hands. Finally he sat out. It had become clear to him what was going on. What shocked me was that this sharp player had not realized it earlier, maybe because he was also playing another game and not paying attention. I was laughing my head off at the situation since I was getting the advantage over him on every hand.

After I thought about it for a night, my conscience got the better of me and I felt ashamed of taking advantage of my opponent. I decided I would make it up to him if I ever saw him again. The next day I saw the same player at a different online poker site. He had the same screen name and was obviously the same player. I told him who I was and offered to give him the chunk of my winnings in the heads-up session that we had played. He was clearly upset, and he refused my offer. He threatened to go to the site and notify them about my transgressions. After that there was nothing more I could do, as he declined to let me to make it up to him. Oh well.

The moral of this story is that you should be alert and know the rules and the quirks of each individual site. Make sure you are aware of everything so you are not taken advantage of the way this poor fellow was.

take a break from poker. Clear your head. Come back when you are ready to play without anger or other negative emotions. Having a computer does not mean you have to play every day.

Deception is Less Useful

In online poker rooms where many people play, the turnover rate at each table will be high. This does not happen in brick-and-mortar casinos since it is tougher to get into another game. This difference in the turnover rate means you should use deception less when playing online. Deception can sometimes throw off observant players and regular opponents in a brick-and-mortar game. In most games, including brick-and-mortar games, players will not be that observant; but in tough games it may be worthwhile to use this strategy occasionally. However this strategy does not translate well to online poker and should be used less frequently. When the turnover rate is high, as it usually is online, your opponents will not know how you play nearly as accurately; so you have no need to deceive them.

Taking Advantage of Online Technology

Automatic buttons and online tells

The automatic buttons can be useful because you do not need to wait until the action gets to you to tell the computer what you want to do. If you click on an automatic button, your action of folding, checking, calling, betting or raising will appear to be instantaneous after the player in front of you acts. This can be a nice feature if you are playing in more than one game. A particularly good time to use it is when you have a starting hand that you know you will fold no matter what the action is in front of you. Clicking on the Fold button will tell the site to fold your hand once the action gets to you, allowing you to concentrate more on another game and not flit back and forth between the two games when it is your turn to act.

You can sometimes use the automatic buttons online to your advantage, determining the strength of another player's hand by the speed of his action. A player with a strong hand will often click on the Raise button to tell the site to raise no matter what happens. If someone raises instantaneously when it is his turn to act, it may be an indication that he indeed has a strong hand. This is an online tell. Each player is an individual and will have his own patterns. Be on the lookout for these patterns as they may become useful in a future hand. Also be aware that others may be looking at your play in this manner too.

Using four-color decks

If there is an option to use a four-color deck in the online site you are playing, take it. These decks have different colors for each suit, typically blue for diamonds and green for clubs. If you are playing more than one game at once, a four-color deck will help you notice flush possibilities.

Taking notes online

Many poker sites have a function that allows you to keep notes on your opponents. This is a useful tool. Every player should take advantage of it. Taking notes in live play is useful too; but it is not as necessary because the mind has an easier time forming opinions about players when there is facial recognition. If you have not played with a particular opponent for several months in a brick-and-mortar casino, you still stand a good chance of remembering roughly how the player plays. This is more difficult to pick up while playing poker online because there is no facial recognition. Most people find it easier to associate the qualities of a player with a face than with a name, so using the notes tool should help.

Suggestions for notes to take on your opponents:

- How loose or tight do they play pre-Flop?
- How loose or tight do they play after the Flop?
- How aggressive or passive are they?
- Will they bet when it seems like their edge is small or will they check?
- Do they check-raise often?
- Do they semi-bluff raise often or should their raises be respected?
- Do they often cold-call raises in shorthanded games?
- Do they three-bet from the small blind after a late-position player open-raises, or do they call?
- How often do they defend their blinds with hands that do not warrant it?

The answers to these questions are useful to know. If you have taken notes on a player, the next time you encounter her at the table you will be able to glance at your notes and have a better idea of how she plays.

Different Results at Different Sites

As discussed earlier in this chapter, fluctuations in online poker can be higher than in brick-and-mortar casinos. If you play at different online sites, you may be killing the game at one site while getting killed at another. You may start to think that the players at one site are generally better than the players at another site. Although there are differences in skill among the populations of players at different sites, the differences are probably not large. For the most part, the default opinion should be that the difference in profits and losses is a result of randomness and luck; you just had good luck at one site and bad luck at another. Due to online poker's large fluctuations, this can happen; but there still may be logical reasons for these differences in winnings other than plain luck. Here is a list of possible reasons.

1. The site you are winning at has worse players in general and the one you are losing at has better players. The difference in skill level may not be large, but it can still exist.
2. You are playing in shorthanded games at one site and in full games at another. Your playing style fits one better than the other.
3. You are being cheated at the site you are losing on.
4. There is a software glitch or quirk at the site that you are losing on and someone else has figured it out.

You can control reasons #1 and #2, and it does not take much effort and concentration to determine if either of them is the case. If you are indeed a good player, you should be able to identify the weaknesses of other players. Your opinion of the quality of the players at the different sites should be valid. If you notice that you are playing in shorthanded games at one site and in full games at another, then you should think about whether your game is more suited for one situation than the other. Maybe the aggressiveness and the fast play of the shorthanded games do not fit your style. Maybe the patience needed at a full table is something that you lack. You can control these issues. It is reasons #3 and #4 that you cannot control; they are discussed in the next section.

Cheating, Collusion and Glitches

It would be nice if everyone was honest and all games were on the up and up. Unfortunately where there is money, there are people trying to scam it. This is something that everyone should be aware of.

Cheating

Do not be concerned with outright cheating at poker online, either by other players or by the site operators. In a brick-and-mortar casino however, cheating may be a concern. A dealer may be in cahoots with some of the players; or a player may have marked cards in the deck. These particular issues are not concerns in the online atmosphere.

Collusion

Collusion is something that many poker players worry about. Other players could be seeing a friend's cards and using that information to take advantage of you. They could be playing side by side or exchanging information on their hands through the telephone or through an instant messenger. The best way to protect yourself from collusion is to play at a fair online site. Online sites have access to the hand histories of every player. A good management team can review those histories when there are complaints. If the play is obvious from the hands they review, they can catch those who collude. It may not be possible to catch everyone, so watch out for this possibility.

Software glitches

Is it possible for a site to have a software glitch that allows a smart computer programmer to re-engineer the system to give him inside information on the cards? Can he can figure out with precision what the Flop will bring? Does he have a way around the software so he can figure out his opponents' hole cards? These are scary questions. Although this may not be probable, it is not outside the realm of possibility. There is no proof to date that a person or a group is doing or has done this; but that does not mean it is not being done. This is a conspiracy theorist's dream (or nightmare, depending on how he looks at it). The truth is that many players are making money steadily online by playing the cards, the odds and the opponents. This fact alone should comfort everyone except the most ardent conspiracy theorists. Coincidentally these conspiracy theorists are usually not good poker players. You can determine for yourself if this is important.

Disconnections

Players can get disconnected from the game, sometimes because of a real disconnection from the Internet or sometimes because the player is trying to take advantage of the system. Most sites have an all-in rule that says disconnected players are considered all-in even when they still have chips on the table. Players who take advantage of the system will purposely disconnect hoping to see a free showdown. They do not want to invest any more money into the pot, so they do not want to call any bets or raises. However they still think there is a chance they can win. They purposely disconnect themselves so the system will treat them as all-in and they still have a chance to win the main pot. You can often tell when a player is messing around. For example if the board is K-9-A-T-7 and a player who got disconnected on the Flop reveals 43 during the showdown, it is obvious that the disconnection was accidental. However if the board shows K-9-A-T-Q and the disconnected player's hand is J9, then maybe she tried to take advantage of the system because she did not want to have to call on the Turn with an inside straight draw. Players who try this are a pain to the other players. Not only is it a form of cheating, but it slows down the game while the system waits the requisite time for the disconnected player to act when she is not there anymore.

Compared to brick-and-mortar poker rooms

Internet poker opens up new forms of cheating. It also eliminates other ways of cheating that are possible in brick-and-mortar poker rooms. Cheating in modern-day poker rooms is rare; but it can exist. Forms of cheating that are possible in a brick-and-mortar poker room but not online include marking cards, crooked dealers being in cahoots with other players, switching cards, holding out cards, front loading (seeing other players' cards as they are dealt), and sneaking a peek at another player's cards. Everyone likes to talk about the possibilities of getting cheated online, but no one seems to discuss the other forms of cheating that are eliminated by playing poker online.

CHAPTER 20
EXTRA TOPICS

The Monty Hall Problem

The popular Monty Hall Problem is confusing to many people. Often the confusion is caused by the person presenting the problem, who may phrase it incorrectly or fail to give all of the pertinent information. Here is an explanation as it applies to Hold'em.

The setup to the Monty Hall problem is that you are a contestant in a game show, and Monty Hall is the host. He will give you a product (like a blender or a toaster), but then offer you the choice to exchange the product. Usually the result of his offer is unclear and you make the decision with uncertainty. If you choose to make the deal, then you will have to play a game (it could be as simple as choosing between what is behind door number 1 or door number 2). If you get lucky, you wind up with a better product. If you don't get lucky, you wind up with nothing at all. What makes the show interesting is that the contestants are sometimes asked to make decisions that are tough and counterintuitive. The answer to the famous Monty Hall problem is counterintuitive.

In the problem there are three doors. Behind one of the doors is a brand new car; and behind the other two doors are goats. You the contestant do not know which objects are behind each door. Presumably you would rather win a new car than a goat. You choose a door; but the game is not over yet. Before Monty reveals what is behind your chosen door, he opens one of the other doors to reveal a goat. Then he says, "You may choose to switch to the other unopened door if you wish." If you switch, do you increase your chance of winning a car?

Often the answer to "How should I play this poker hand?" is: "It depends." That also is the answer to the Monty Hall problem as it is presented above. If the problem were presented slightly differently, the answer would be clearer. The key is whether you knew ahead of time that Monty Hall would always open a door with a goat behind it and offer to let you switch to the third door. This is important, and makes a big difference in the problem. Oftentimes the presenter of the problem does not make it clear whether this is true.

If you know in advance that Monty will always open up a door and show you a goat after you have already chosen a door, and then offer to let you switch doors, then the answer is yes, you should switch.

If you are not sure in advance whether Monty will offer to let you switch, then you do not know whether or not you should switch. Is he bluffing by offering to let you switch because he knows you have picked the car? Did he already plan to show you a goat behind one door and offer you the other door before you made the first choice? What is your opinion of Monty Hall as a person? Is he a nefarious man who wants you to get the goat? Or is he a generous man who wants to increase your chance of winning the car? What is your opinion of his intelligence? Is he smart enough to realize that if he always shows you a goat and offers to let you switch doors that he is increasing your chance of winning the car, or does he think that the choice does not matter?

Assume Monty knows what is behind each door and will always open a door with a goat and offer to let you switch to the third door that is not yet open. Monty will show you a door with a goat whether the door you have chosen has a car or a goat. One-third of the time the first door you chose will have a car behind it. Two-thirds of the time the car is behind one of the other doors. Since Monty will always open a door with a goat: if you switch, you will go from a 1/3 chance to a 2/3 chance of getting the car.

Many people confuse this issue and think the chances are 1/2 for both the door that you originally picked and the remaining door, since there are only two unopened doors left. They neglect the fact that if the car is behind one of the doors that you did not originally choose, then Monty will not open that door because he knows that the car is behind it; and he is not going to show you the car. Thus 2/3 of the time Monty has no choice but to open the one door that has the goat behind it (because 2/3 of the time you have picked the incorrect door, and the car is behind one of the other two doors). The other 1/3 of the time he can randomly decide which door he wants to open. Thus 2/3 of the time the door that Monty did not open will have the car behind it. The other 1/3 of the time there will be a goat behind the other door because you already picked the door with the car behind it. So if you knew that Monty Hall would, with 100% certainty, open up a door with a goat behind it and offer to let you switch doors, then by switching you will increase your chance of winning the car from 1/3 to 2/3, a significant improvement.

What happens if Monty Hall sometimes does not offer you the choice of switching? What if sometimes Monty will just open the door that you chose? If that is the case, then when he does offer to allow you to switch doors, he may be trying to bait you into switching to a door without the car behind it. Maybe Monty does not want you to win the car and will offer to let you switch doors only if you chose the door with the car behind it. In order to think you are going from a 1/3 chance to a 2/3 chance of getting the car, you have to be confident that he will ask if you want to switch no matter what door you choose, and that he does not have a nefarious reason for asking you if you want to switch. This is important information and pertinent to the problem. Many people who present the problem fail to make this fact crystal clear. The problem is difficult to understand; and the omission of this fact makes it more confusing.

Applying the Monty Hall problem to Limit Hold'em

The Monty Hall problem can apply to Limit Hold'em also. With certain opponents and certain situations, you will be 100% certain that your opponent will bet. If you know that, then the quality of his hand has no bearing on his bet. You may need to readjust your assessment of the value of your own holdings based on the Flop. The key is that you cannot adjust your assessment of your opponent's holdings based on the new information, since he would have acted identically no matter what the Flop was. This situation presents itself more often in shorthanded games than in full games. As in the Monty Hall problem where you knew Monty would show you a door with a goat behind it regardless of the door you picked, in the Hold'em situation you are sure your opponent will bet regardless of the Flop. You know that the chance you originally picked the correct door is 1/3; and it is still 1/3 after Monty opens one of the doors for you. In Hold'em you have the information on the strength of your own hand. The information you have about the strength of your opponent's hand does not change with his bet.

Example

In a four-handed game you are in the big blind and the player on the button open-raises. For the purposes of this example, your cards are not pertinent. The player on the button is a super-aggressive raiser when she is on the button in this game; and you are sure that she will raise with many hands. The small blind folds and you decide to call.

Flop: 9♣9♥2♦

You check. Your opponent bets.

This is the point where you know that your opponent will bet 100% of the time, regardless of the strength of her hand, especially on a Flop like this. Assume she is an aggressive player, and you have played short-handed with her before. You are 100% certain she will bet on the Flop. So her bet gives you absolutely no new information about her possible holdings. Your estimate of her hand should stay the same as before the Flop. Similarly in the Monty Hall problem your estimate of the chance that you had originally picked the door with the car behind it stays the same after Monty Hall shows you the goat behind one of the other doors and asks if you want to switch, because you knew he would show you a goat regardless of the door you picked.

All-In Situations

When one of the players is out of chips in the middle of a hand, he is considered all-in. He gets to see the rest of the hand played out through the River. If there is only one other player left in the hand, then the dealer deals out the rest of the hand and then asks the winner to reveal his hand. If there are two or more other players still in the hand, then a side pot is created. The player who is all-in cannot win the side pot; he can win only the main pot. The other players can win both the side pot and the main pot.

When betting, consider whether someone is all-in or is close to going all-in. Sometimes a player who is close to all-in is frustrated because she is in the midst of a losing session. If she raises, she may be raising to get all-in and end the betting. Understand the type of player who might do this so that you do not misinterpret her aggressiveness as anything other than a desire to commit her chips out of frustration.

Playing against a player who is almost all-in

Be aware when one of the players at the table is almost all-in. He will often play more aggressively, especially when there are already many players in the pot. He wants to get maximum value for his money and he figures that going all-in early after other players are already committed to seeing the Flop will accomplish this. As an example, consider a case where several players have already limped in, and a player in late position or in the blinds raises and goes all-in. Because he is going all-in, he may be raising with a hand with which he would not normally raise, using the logic that since he is going to go all-in soon anyway, it is better to do it now to get maximum value. His raise may not mean as much in this situation as it normally would. Even if you think he has a legitimate raising hand, he will not be able to pressure you further on future rounds.

Even if you do not believe a lone opponent who is almost all-in is playing differently, you still need to know that he is almost all-in. The expected pot size will be different, which may affect your pot-odds calculations and your decisions. Think your way through the hand since different situations may come up. The following is an example of what happens when you wind up heads-up against a player who is almost all-in and you flop a great hand.

Example

You raise pre-Flop with AK in a $20-$40 Limit Hold'em game. The only caller is the big blind, who started the hand with only $65. After putting in her big blind and calling your bet, she has $25 left.

Your hand: AKo
Flop: K-9-7 rainbow

She checks. Normally you should bet; but betting may not be correct when your opponent is almost all-in, because you want to increase the chance that she will put in all her chips. Giving her free cards is not dangerous since there are no overcards to your hand. Almost any hand she could have that would benefit from getting a free card is one that would have made her call on the Flop anyway, and almost always on the Turn as well. It may be better to wait until the Turn to bet.

Assume she has T9, and has a pair of 9's on the Flop. If you bet on the Flop, she will call or raise and be all-in. If you check, you will get her to put her chips in on the Turn anyway regardless of what card comes. (The only card that might deter her from calling is an A, in which case you should wait until the River to bet.) If she has a draw with QT, she will probably call, with or without correct pot odds, whether you bet on the Flop or the Turn. If you catch a bad beat and a J comes on the Turn or River, you can comfort yourself knowing that she would have gone all-in on the Flop if you had bet anyway. In this scenario it makes no difference if you bet on the Flop or wait for the Turn to bet.

It is a different story if she holds hands like A3 or J8, which she is likely to fold if you bet on the Flop. If you check on the Flop, she may bet on the Turn hoping to buy the pot even if she does not catch a pair. If she is more conservative, she may not bet without a pair; but she will bet if she catches a pair. Since you have a pair of K's with the A kicker, worry only about your opponent catching runner-runner trips or two pair. The trade-off between that unlikely event and getting your opponent to risk her remaining chips when she is a major underdog should make you lean toward checking on the Flop when you have a dominant hand.

Players who are almost all-in are unlikely to fold after they have bet or raised

It is difficult to bluff a player who has bet and whose remaining stack is a bet or less. Good cards or bad cards, this player might throw in the rest of his chips after someone raises.

In order to take advantage of this: bet with all marginal hands into a player who is close to going all-in, and forgo semi-bluffing or bluffing. If it is down to you and the player who is almost all-in: do not be afraid to raise him all-in with top pair and weak kicker or middle pair, but do not raise him all-in if you have an inside-straight draw.

A situation where you should have no fear of making the extra raise to put him all-in:

Your hand: T9o
Flop: K-T-8 rainbow

Your opponent raised in late position. You called in the big blind. You check to him. He bets and has only 1 more small bet left. Though you have middle pair, you should feel comfortable raising and making him go all-in. If you do check-raise here on the Flop, many opponents will throw in their last chips with a hand like A7.

Here is an example of a situation where you can semi-bluff against normal players, but should think twice about doing that against a player who is almost all-in:

Your hand: 98o
Flop: J-7-3 rainbow

If your opponent has bet, you should not semi-bluff raise because the value of bluffing is low. The player who is almost all-in is more likely to call with a hand like A4 or KT than she would normally be. The value of the bluff portion of the semi-bluff is nonexistent when a player is all-in or almost all-in and has already committed a bet.

How an all-in player protects the pot from a bluffer

When one of the players is all-in and there are at least two other players in the hand, a side pot is created. The other players in the hand can win both the side pot and the main pot. The all-in player can win only the part of the pot to which he contributed. If the main pot is relatively big compared to the side pot, the all-in player protects the other players from bluffing against each other. If a bluff is successful in getting the third player to fold, the bluffer has to show down her cards against the all-in player to win the main pot. If the bluffer cannot beat the all-in player, then there is no value in getting the third player out. The objective of bluffing is to win the pot with a weaker hand by getting the opponent to fold a stronger hand. Since the all-in player cannot fold, a bluff cannot work against him. Thus a successful bluff in this situation will not benefit the bluffer nearly as much. She will win the side pot after the third player folds; but she still must show down her hand against the all-in player in order to win the main pot. If the side pot is bigger than the main pot (and this can happen if the all-in player goes all-in in the early stages of the hand), then a bluff can be worthwhile.

Example

You hold a busted flush draw or a busted straight draw on the River:

Your hand: 87o
Board: 6-5-T-Q-K rainbow

You believe the opponent who is not all-in (the third player) holds a weak hand like a split pair of 6's. Since the Turn and the River were both overcards to the Flop, you believe there is a good chance the third player will fold if you bet. If the all-in player went all-in on the Turn, and there is no side pot created yet, then there is no reason for you to bet because it is almost inconceivable that you could win the main pot. The all-in player will have your hand beaten unless she miraculously has a hand like 43. The pot is said to be a "protected pot" because there is no benefit in bluffing.

As a less extreme case, say you have A5 with the same board; then you have a split pair of 5's. The all-in player went all-in on the Turn. You and a third player are still in on the River; and he bets to start the side pot. You had hoped he was on a busted straight draw. If he understands that the pot is protected, then he probably has a legitimate hand and you should fold.

Getting Counterfeited

One of the worst feelings in Hold'em is having a made hand counterfeited. Counterfeited means that you already have a made hand using both of your hole cards, but the Turn or River gives someone the same hand or better. Every time this happens to me, I weep inside. Here are several ways to get counterfeited:

1. Two pair getting counterfeited by a higher pair on the board

Your hand: 65
Flop: T-6-5
Turn: Q
River: Q

Tournament last-hand surprise

When I was new to casino poker, I bought into a Hold'em tournament in Reno, Nevada, in a casino that I had never been to before. I had seen the tournament schedule in Card Player magazine and thought it would be fun to play. The tournament started at 11 AM on a weekday, and cost $10. That buy-in was right for me at that time. After almost an hour I was doing well, with a decent chip position. All of a sudden the dealer said, "This is it" as he dealt the cards. The first player shoved all his chips in; and the next two players called, going all-in themselves. I was amazed; they all put in their chips so fast that I thought I was dreaming. I looked down and saw 72o and folded. The player to my left immediately put his chips all-in and said to me, "What are you doing?" I was puzzled. I thought I should have been the one asking that question.

As it turned out, this was not a regular tournament. It was supposed to last an hour, at which time the player with the most chips won. I was shocked and upset after I found out. I'd thought I had a good chance of winning based on my chip position; but mostly I was upset at myself for not knowing the exact rules before I sat down. It made me disappointed and grumpy for the next few hours. So let my mistake be a lesson to you!

You flopped two pair (6's and 5's). After the Q's show up on the Turn and the River, your five-card poker hand is Q-Q-6-6-T and the 5 in your hand is useless. A player with a pocket pair of 7's or higher has a better hand. A player with a T, or with a 6 (with a J or greater), has a better two pair than your two pair. A player with a Q that wasn't paired on the Flop has trips.

2. Pocket pair getting counterfeited by two higher pair on the board

Your hand: 22
Flop: 5-4-4
Turn: 3
River: 3

On the Flop you have two pair, 4's and 2's. By the River you are playing the board, so you have the worst possible hand because a player with any other card either has a better two pair, a straight or a higher kicker than a 5.

3. Flush using both your hole cards is counterfeited after a fourth flush card hits the board

Your hand: 3♣2♣
Flop: A♣8♣7♣
Turn: 4♣

You flopped a flush using both of your hole cards. With the fourth club on the Turn, anyone else with one club has a higher flush. It doesn't seem fair that they can use one card to make their hand when you can use two cards; but this is Hold'em, not Omaha.

4. Straight using both your hole cards is in danger after a fourth straight card hits the board

Your hand: 76
Flop: T-9-8
Turn: J

You flopped a straight using both of your hole cards. The Turn makes four to a straight on the board. Any player with a 7 has the same hand you have; and any player with a Q has a better hand.

Playing at Home and on the Road

Home-casino advantage

In sports the home team has a net advantage if the talent levels of the two teams are equal. There are two main reasons for this advantage. The first is that the home team members are used to their environment and are sleeping in their own beds. The visitors are travel weary and are sleeping in hotels that may not have all the comforts of home. The second reason is the home crowd will cheer for the home team and support them, which is a nice emotional boost to the home-team players. At the same time the crowd will scream and swear at the opposing team, which is not enjoyable for the visitors.

Similarly in poker, local players enjoy a home-casino advantage. When you live in the surrounding area and enjoy this advantage, you can go to your own home after playing. You visit the local poker room on a regular basis, so you are comfortable with the environment. You know the dealers, either by face or by name. You know the floor people and you know the wait staff. You know the specific rules of your poker room, which are not universal. For a professional poker player the environment is almost like a comfortable office.

Most importantly, when you enjoy a home-casino advantage, you know a higher percentage of the other players and their tendencies. If you are a skilled, observant player, when you approach your seat at a new table you already know the characteristics of many of the other players and how they play different hands. In a smaller poker room or after you have played in the room for a relatively long time, you can identify the characteristics of your opponents in finer detail than the stereotypes described in this book. You know that a raise from "Joe" can only mean he has the nuts; whereas a raise from "Bob" can mean a bluff or semi-bluff. It usually takes many hands to get to know how others play; so it is a nice advantage to know the players before sitting down. It also allows you to concentrate more on the one or two players who are unknown to you.

The less observant player enjoys the home-casino advantage to a certain extent. Even the worst players often have a decent idea of who the good players are and who the bad players are. And yet, although they can make this identification, many of them cannot recognize that they themselves are bad players! That is truly amazing. The important point here is that all players have a home-casino advantage; whether or not they use it to the fullest is a matter of skill and concentration.

A road game

When you travel, you need more time to identify the skill level of other players, since most of them will be strangers. You must be more observant on the road than when you are playing in your home poker room. You must watch the other players carefully and gather enough information so you can act appropriately in a hand against them. This makes it all the tougher on the road since the surroundings are not nearly as comfortable as they are in your home poker room. You don't know the dealers, the floor people, or the wait staff. You aren't entirely sure where the rest rooms are located. After a few hours you get situated, and everything becomes more comfortable; but it takes time. Recognize this when you are playing on the road, and make the necessary adjustments. Try to get plenty of sleep, and avoid being tired from the traveling.

Players often travel to casinos where major tournaments are being held, such as Las Vegas, Atlantic City, Los Angeles, Biloxi and Connecticut. Many players in the major tournaments also play in the side games. These tournaments attract players from across the country, and also entice players who live nearby who may not play as often. Confirm hotel-room availability when these tournaments are happening; rooms often are sold out.

Once right before the World Series of Poker I was playing at my local card room, and asked a professional poker player (who played $20-$40 Limit Hold'em) if he was going to Las Vegas for the World Series of Poker. He said he had no plans to go and was not interested, and that he would lose his home-casino advantage since he would not know any of the players in Las Vegas. In his local poker rooms he knew all the players and had studied them for some time. Without this knowledge, he felt his win rate would be significantly lower. There also are the added costs of travel expenses, hotel rooms and meals.

Tells, Feels and Vibes

There are three different kinds of players when it comes to tells: the clueless, the liar and the vault. Clueless players will let you know exactly what they are thinking by their actions. Liars try to lie to you and fool you with their actions. Vaults try to keep it quiet and act the same no matter what.

The poker player that everyone wants as an opponent is the clueless. The clueless is not aware that people are observing him; and he acts the way he feels. If his hand is bad, he will shake his head in disbelief. If his hand is good, all of a sudden he will be at full attention to see when it is his turn to act so he can raise. This player is mostly found in low-limit games, and would not last long in middle- or high-limit games as his bankroll would quickly shrivel. The clueless player should stay at home and play poker online, since his physical actions often give him away and playing online would negate this disadvantage. If he acts this way when playing poker, though, he is likely to have other leaks in his game and will probably lose his money sooner or later at online poker as well.

The liar shows strength when she is weak and weakness when she is strong. Aside from her physical actions, the liar likes to check-raise and slowplay, another way of feigning weakness when she is actually strong. The liar also likes to bluff and semi-bluff, feigning strength when she is actually weak. She shows these attributes through her physical actions by throwing her chips into the pot strongly when she has a weak hand and betting meekly when she has a strong hand.

The vault tries to act the exact same way no matter how strong his hand is. It is difficult to tell if he is bluffing or has the nuts because his facial expression and body language are always the same.

Like the vault, you should aspire to give few signals to the good players. Against bad players you can lie to fool them. Against better players who may understand the "strong means weak" and "weak means strong" strategy, it may be better to switch it around and act to your correct strength, letting them fool themselves. For the most part it is better to keep the same demeanor and not let subconscious actions and reactions reveal the strength of your hand.

Tells are great if you can spot one. Often there are no tells or a tell is difficult to spot. Even without tells, you can still get a feel or a vibe from your opponents. Sometimes an opponent you know well does something that just feels wrong. If you have experience playing against her, you probably have a decent feel or vibe for her game. If something is off-kilter, you may be able to sense it. You cannot learn this skill by reading a book. Rather you learn it through experience playing the game and playing against the specific opponent, which is one of the reasons that studying your opponents is crucial. This feel or vibe can mean something only if you know the normal behavior of your opponents.

Mental Topics

Treating each session as part of one big session

Poker is not like sports when it comes to winning and losing. In sports, winning or losing is all that is important; the margin of victory does not matter. Whether a football team wins by 5 touchdowns or by a safety, the team has earned one win. In poker, winning or losing is important; but the size of the win or loss is more important. If you play five times in one week and have three winning sessions and two losing sessions, that does not say much about your results in that week. You could still have lost money.

You should think of every session as part of one long session that you play throughout your life. It is sometimes difficult to think that way after the cards have run cold and it seems as though you are taking bad beat after bad beat. If you don't think in terms of one long session, you will be tempted to try to get back to even during a losing session, which may lead to playing too many hands, calling too many raises and bluffing in unwarranted spots. A football team that is behind can take more risk and play with desperation in order to get back to even, because all the players care about is winning or losing. Such a strategy would be disastrous for a poker player.

Oftentimes players at the table will say that they are "stuck," meaning they are losing. Thinking you are stuck can give you a negative attitude. You might start to play more aggressively at the wrong times to try to get back to even. Do not worry about trying to get back to even for the night, the week or the trip. Concentrate on playing each hand correctly and think of your wins and losses as a whole for your entire life if you are a long-term winner. If you are a winning player, this will also make the inevitable losing streaks easier to handle psychologically. If you have not shown as much success in the past, think of today as the first day of the rest of your Hold'em life.

Emotions at the table

For many players, playing poker is an emotional experience. After you win, there is a feeling of elation and a natural high. You feel on top of the world, like an Olympic champion. This is great, but the opposite is also possible. After the inevitable losing session happens, some players feel depressed. Poker can be an emotional roller coaster. It is how you handle the downside that can differentiate a winning player from a losing player.

How a losing player handles a losing session

1. Go on tilt

A player on tilt plays more hands than he knows he should, and plays them aggressively. There are different levels of tilt. A player going on tilt is more obvious at the blackjack table or at other casino games. You've probably seen it; and you may have experienced it too. After losing, a player gets the idea to bet big to try to get even in one hand. At the blackjack table, without the advantage of counting, a player who had been betting $25 per hand suddenly puts out a $200 bet on the next hand. This is not a good idea at the poker table, and may cause the player to play hands that have negative expectation. It may mean calling raises too liberally in the big blind, open-raising with J5s in the cutoff, or calling pre-Flop with ATo against an early-position raise from a good player.

Control your emotions. Do not let a losing session cause you to play poorly.

2. Get upset at the dealer

Some players blame all their problems on the dealer, calling the dealer names, throwing cards hard into the muck or throwing them at the dealer. It can be ugly; and it is something you should refrain from. The dealers are just trying to make a living. For the most part, angry players who get upset at the dealer are not accusing the dealer of cheating, but rather of treating them poorly by not putting the right card on the board. This is a ridiculous accusation; but in the heat of the battle it may be difficult for some players to control themselves. All players must control their own emotions, and also be willing to protect the dealer, which may mean standing up to other players or calling a floor person over. No one likes to play when there are angry players at the table.

3. Get upset at a bad player who is on a lucky streak

Worse than blaming the dealer is a player who gets a bad beat raging on the player who gave her the bad beat. The good player starts telling the bad player how bad a player he is, and how lucky he was. This is horrible for the game. Good players should want the bad players to stay in the game as long as possible. No good player wants a bad player to be educated at the table; and that is what happens when a good player demeans a bad player. Take a mean-spirited good player aside and let her know how you feel in a non-confrontational way, with statements such as "Hey, I know he gave you a horrible beat; but you know he'll give it back to you in the long run. Don't chase him away, please!"

How a winning player should handle a losing session

1. Analyze what went wrong

Think about the session. Maybe you lost due to random bad luck, or maybe you lost because you made mistakes. Think about what happened to see if there are mistakes you can correct in future sessions.

2. Learn from your mistakes

Players learn the most when they lose. After a winning session it is easy to walk away happy and complacent, thinking that everything went as planned. With all the positive thoughts, it is difficult to think back to see what mistakes you made at the table that day. It is after a losing session that your mind starts to think about the mistakes you made. This is a great exercise, because you will learn not to make the same mistakes in the future. Winning players use their losing sessions as stepping stones to future winning sessions by learning from their own mistakes instead of getting mired in their own sorrow.

3. Learn to appreciate the volatility of the game

Limit Hold'em is a volatile game. A good player might expect to make $30 per hour in a $20-$40 game, but in any given hour should not be surprised to win or lose $400. On the worst days a string of six bad hours at $20-$40 can mean a $2,000 loss. Winning players see more good days than bad; but bad days are inevitable.

If Limit Hold'em were a game of only skill and no luck, then it would be more like chess. In chess, grandmasters have no opportunity to win money from novices and bad players. Weak chess players are not willing to bet on themselves against a grandmaster because they know they have no chance to win. In poker everyone has a chance to win in the short run, but not everyone has a chance to win in the long run. The short run is easy to see: it is what you bring to the cashier's cage to cash out at the end of the session, and it's the thing that keeps bad players playing. But the long run is difficult for many to see, especially the bad players. Without this luck factor and without bad players having their share of winning sessions, poker would not be profitable for anybody, and there would not be any opportunities for the winning players. The good players learn to appreciate the volatility of the game. They chalk up a losing session as "one of those days," and move on to the next day.

Observing the play of the game when out of a hand

It is easy to pay attention to things outside of the game after you have already folded your hand. There are often many distractions. Many poker rooms have television sets within easy view of the seated players. When there is a sports event on television, it is tempting to pay attention to it instead of the poker game, especially if you have a wager on the event. It is also easy to read the current edition of Card Player Magazine, Poker Digest or a newspaper while waiting for the next hand. With cell phones so common these days, making a phone call can seem like a useful way to fill the time between hands. This is clearly not a good idea at a poker game, but people do it.

When you pay attention to something away from the table, you can miss the play of the hand and possibly the emotional state of the players. If one of the players gets dealt two bad beats in a row, that may change the way she plays from that point forward. If you are not paying attention to the hand, you may miss it. It can be just as difficult to concentrate in online poker, since at home there may be more distractions, including talking to other people and surfing the Internet.

Eavesdropping at the table

Society generally looks down on people who eavesdrop. People want their business and conversations to be private. Most people are taught as children to avoid eavesdropping and to respect the privacy of others. But at the poker table, conversations are fair game; and you should use them to your advantage. You can gather useful information by listening to two other players having a conversation. When they start talking about how they play, what they folded, their opinions of other players, and other information that pertains to poker, you should be listening carefully. Keep your eyes open and watch what other players are doing. Keep your ears open to hear if the other players are giving you clues about their own play, or that of other players.

Book knowledge vs. execution and experience

Learning poker by reading good books is a great exercise. If you are reading the right books, you will be able to help your own game. Good books will give you new ideas that you may not have thought about, and may also clarify your own ideas. However reading cannot replace actual experience and may not improve your execution of a hand. You will know how to play a hand correctly after thinking about it for a few minutes; but you still need to execute correctly under pressure. Two things are needed in order to execute the correct play: you must be able to identify a profitable situation for the play, and you must put your strategy into action without giving your intentions away. The game of poker goes fast, so you will have to identify the correct situations quickly. Thinking about specific situations and reading up on the ones that this book has covered will help you get to that point more quickly, but nothing replaces experience. You still have to go out there and play, and execute the correct plays. That is easier said than done for some people.

When is it time to leave?

A lot of players think about leaving a game when they are up big, but stay longer when they are down big. This phenomenon is common in home games. The losers are the ones who want to keep playing while the winners are the ones who claim they need to rush home for various reasons.

A friend named Dean Potashner used to talk about this phenomenon, saying it should be the exact opposite. He said that the players who are winning are playing their best game, in control of the game and feared at the table. The players who are losing may be on tilt, are often out of control and have a tougher time bluffing successfully. So it should be the winners who want to stay longer because they can expect to win more than usual. The losers should leave since they are probably playing worse than usual. If you are a good player and can control your emotions after losing, you should be playing if you still think you have positive expectation. Players often cannot tell when their emotions are getting the best of them. After the negative emotions hit, they are not usually thinking rationally; they are focused on trying to get back to even.

If you have taken a few bad beats recently, you may find yourself paralyzed and unable to bet or raise when you normally would. The recent bad beats may have clouded your mind and judgment. If this is the case, it is probably better to leave or at least take a long walk to shake the bad beats off. Come back and play when you can play at your best. On the other hand, the next time you are winning and feel the urge to run with the money, think again. Is the game still juicy? Are you playing well? If so, consider staying and playing longer. Try to complement this with reducing your hours after losing, when you may not be playing your best game.

APPENDIX A
RULES

The Rules and Mechanics of Limit Hold'Em

This book assumes that you are not a complete novice at playing Limit Hold'em. For completeness the rules of the game and some poker terminology are included in this appendix. Table 30 shows the ranking of poker hands, along with sample hands.

How a Hand is Made

Every player is dealt two cards face down; those cards are called hole cards or the starting hand. During the play of the hand, five cards are dealt face up in the middle of the table. These five cards are community cards, and are collectively called the board. Mentally take your two hole cards and combine them with the five cards on the board, making a five-card poker hand. You can use both cards from your hand and three from the board, or one from your hand and four from the board, or none from your hand and all five on the board. The purpose is to make the best poker hand possible from the combination of your starting hand and the board. The chart below shows a few examples. The bold cards in the

Table 30
Ranking of Poker Hands

Rank	*Example*
Royal Flush	A♠-K♠-Q♠-J♠-T♠
Straight Flush	K♣-Q♣-J♣-T♣-9♣
Four of a kind	J♣-J♦-J♥-J♠-x
Full House	J♣-J♦-J♥-3♣-3♠
Flush	K♦-J♦-T♦-3♦-2♦
Straight	9♥-8♣-7♠-6♥-5♠
Three of a kind	T♣-T♦-T♥-x-x
Two pair	T♣-T♦-9♣-9♦-x
One Pair	8♥-8♠-x-x-x
High Card	A♣-K♣-Q♦-9♣-8♦

"Final Poker Hand" column are the cards shown in the "Starting Hand" column that are used to compose the poker hand.

Starting Hand	*Board*	*Final Poker Hand*
J♠T♠	A♣-Q♠-J♣-4♣-3♠	**J♠**-J♣-A♣-Q♠-**T♠**
J♠T♠	A♣-Q♠-9♣-8♣-8♣	Q♠-**J♠-T♠**-9♣-8♣
J♠T♠	A♣-A♥-A♠-K♣-J♦	A♣-A♥-A♠-J♦-**J♠**
J♠T♠	8♣-7♠-6♦-5♠-4♣	8♣-7♠-6♦-5♠-4♣

The Cards

There are four rounds of card distribution and betting in Hold'em: pre-Flop, the Flop, the Turn and the River. After the cards are dealt on each round, there is a round of betting.

Pre-Flop

Each player is dealt two cards face down. These cards are used only in the hand of the individual to whom they were dealt. There is a round of betting after these two cards are dealt.

The Flop

Three cards are dealt face up in the middle of the table. This is called the Flop. These are community cards that all players can use in their hands, and are collectively called the board. After the Flop there is another round of betting. The term "the Flop" can refer to the three cards or to the betting round. It can be used as a verb too, as in "I flopped a great hand."

The Turn

A fourth card is dealt face up in the middle of the table. This fourth card is called the Turn and is part of the board. After the Turn card is dealt, there is another round of betting. The term "the Turn" can refer to the card itself or to the betting round.

The River

A fifth and final card is dealt face up in the middle of the table. This fifth card is called the River and is part of the board as well. After the River card is dealt, there is one final round of betting. The term "the River" can refer to the last card itself or to the betting round.

The Showdown

After the betting round on the River, all players who are still in the hand expose their cards. Each player's full poker hand consists of the best five-card poker hand possible from the combination of the two hole cards and the five cards on the board. The highest five-card poker hand wins the pot. If there is a tie, then the pot is split among the players who tied for the best hand.

The Betting

Before any cards are dealt, three things happen. One player gets the dealer "button." That player is the de facto dealer in the hand, though casino provides an employee to deal the cards. In home games the position of dealer usually rotates from player to player, and an actual button is not necessary.

The action starts to the left of the button and goes around clockwise. The player to the immediate left of the button is called the small blind. She is required to put up half of a small bet; so she is already partially in the hand. If the game is $10-$20 Hold'em, the small blind puts up $5. If the game is $20-$40 Hold'em, the small blind puts up $10. The player to the left of the small blind is called the big blind. The big blind must post 1 small bet. If the game is $20-$40, the big blind puts up $20. The money put in by the two blinds works similar to the combination of an ante and the bring-in in Seven-Card Stud, except that in Hold'em only two players put up the "ante" rather than all the players putting up an equal amount.

The term "blinds" is used because the players are in the hand before they see their cards. The action is clockwise. The dealer deals one card to each of the players, starting with the small blind. He then deals another card to each of the players in the same fashion. After both cards are dealt, the pre-Flop stage starts.

Since the blinds have already bet, they are considered to be already active in the hand. The action starts with the player to the left of the big blind, called the under-the-gun player. She can choose to fold, call or raise. If she calls, she must put in a small bet. To raise, she must put in 2 small bets. Calling in the pre-Flop round is referred to as limping. After the under-the-gun player has acted, the player to her left acts. He has the same options, except that if the under-the-gun player has raised, then he can fold, call the raise or reraise. The action continues until it gets back to the small blind, who is already in for half of a small bet. She has the same options as the other players, except that she needs to put in less money to call or raise since she already has half of a small bet in the pot. After the small blind acts, the big blind acts. If no one has raised, the big blind has the option to raise or check and see the Flop. This is the only time that a player may raise himself. Once the action has gone around to the player who sits to the right of the last player to raise, or if no one raises and the big blind checks, then the dealer can deal the Flop.

In the Flop round the action starts with the player to the immediate left of the dealer. If the small blind is still in the hand, then she acts first. If the small blind folded in the pre-Flop round and the big blind is still in, then he acts first on the Flop. The first player to act has the choice of betting 1 small bet or checking. In most casinos, players are allowed to check-raise. That means checking; and if someone else bets, the checker has the option of raising when the action gets back to him. (In some home games, check-raising is not allowed.) If the first player bets, then the second player has the option to call, raise or fold. Since this is a limit game, a raise is 1 additional small bet in the pre-Flop and Flop rounds. The action continues until the player to the right of the last player to bet or raise has acted.

Table 31
Player Positions

Position	*Number of Players at Table* 7	8	9	10
Blinds	1, 2	1, 2	1, 2	1, 2
Early Position (including under-the-gun)	3, 4	3, 4	3, 4, 5	3, 4, 5
Middle Position	5	5, 6	6, 7	6, 7, (8)
Late Position (including cutoff and button)	6, 7	7, 8	8, 9	(8), 9, 10

On the Turn the bet size doubles to 1 big bet. In a $10-$20 game a big bet is $20. The bet size on the River is 1 big bet as well. The betting procedure on the Turn and River is the same as on the Flop. After the betting round on the River is over, the players still in the hand expose their hands to see who has the best hand. Losing players often do not expose their hands. Once they see that their hands are beaten, they muck their cards face down to avoid exposing their cards to other players.

The Positions

The players at the table are identified by their positions relative to the button, as shown in table 31. The numbers refer to the position of the player: 1 means the player is first to act, 2 means second to act, etc.

The small blind and big blind are to the immediate left of the button, and are labeled 1 and 2 in table 31.

The player to the left of the big blind is called the under-the-gun player, and is labeled 3 in table 31.

Normally there are nine or ten seats available at a Hold'em table. If the game is full, then the first three players to act after the blinds are considered to be in early position. The next two players are in middle position. The last three players are in late position.

The player to the immediate right of the small blind is in last position, but is also called the dealer or the button.

The player to the immediate right of the button is called the cutoff, and is in late position as well.

Table 31 identifies positions for games with seven to ten players. Games with six or fewer players are generally considered shorthanded, and are discussed in Chapters 17 and 18.

After the end of a hand, the button rotates to the left; and the player who was the small blind becomes the button in the next hand. The player on the button gets to see the other players act before he has to act, so he has a positional advantage. The blinds are disadvantageous positions because the players must put money into the pot before seeing their cards. The button rotates, moving the advantageous and disadvantageous positions around the table.

The Nut Hand

The best possible hand in a poker game is referred to as the nut hand. In Draw Poker and other games without exposed cards, the nut hand is the Royal Flush, the best possible hand in poker. In Hold'em after all the cards are out, the nut hand can be as low as three-of-a-kind. For example with a board of A-K-9-8-3, the best possible hand is AA for three A's. Knowing what the nut hand is and what your hand is in relation to that is key in Hold'em. There are situations where you have a three-of-a-kind and you are willing to bet and keep raising because you know no other player can beat your hand. When all five board cards have been dealt: if you have the best three-of-a-kind and there is no possibility for a higher hand, you have the nut hand. For that to be true, there can be no pairs on the board (a pair on the board makes a full house or a four-of-a-kind possible), no flush possibilities (three cards of the same suit on the board make a flush possible), and no straight possibilities (three cards within five cards of each other on the board make a straight possible). But if the board offers something like a pair or three cards to a flush, then the same three-of-a-kind will not give you as much comfort since potentially stronger hands are possible. The strength of any particular hand is its strength relative to the board.

Once they have become experienced, Hold'em players do not consciously think about these issues. These considerations are so ingrained in their thinking that there is no need to specifically note what the nut hand is. Think of it as the difference between a novice driver and an experienced one. The experienced driver does not think about what she

Some Hold'em boards and their nut hands:

Hand #	*Board*	*Nut Hand*
1	A♠-J♥-T♠-J♠-A ♥	K♠Q♠
2	J♦-9♦-8♣-7♣-6♦	A♦ and any other ♦
3	Q♣-J♣-4♥-3♦-8♥	T9
4	A♥-J♥-6♥-4♥-4♠	44
5	A♦-A♥-K♥-K♦-4♣	A♠A♣, AK
6	Q♠-J♠-7♥-6♥-2♣	QQ
7	K♣-J♣-T♥-Q♠-9♦	any A
8	8♥-7♥-6♥-A♦-A♠	T♥9♥, 9♥5♥
9	A♠-K♦-Q♦-J♥-T♥	any hand
10	J♥-8♣-T♥-3♦-7♦	Q9

Notes on the above hands:

Hand 2. Having the A♦ with any other diamond will give you the nut flush; it does not matter if the other diamond is K♦ or 2♦.

Hand 3. Since there are no flushes possible with this board, the suits of the T and 9 are irrelevant.

Hand 5. AA is the best hand. AK cannot be beaten, though it can be tied by the other AK. If you hold AK, no other player can end up with four A's or four K's.

Hand 7. Any A makes the highest straight possible; the other card is irrelevant.

Hand 8. T♥9♥ gives you the best straight flush; but if you have 9♥5♥, no one can else can have a straight flush.

Hand 9. Every player in the hand has the nut straight by playing the board.

needs to do to make a left turn. She simply does it; whereas the beginner needs to think about turning on the turn signal and seeing if there is a traffic light or a stop sign, and then remember to watch for other vehicles and for people using the crosswalk. If you are a beginning Hold'em player, make sure you can figure out what the nut hands are in each of the situations in the chart above before you proceed.

The Nut Draw

Knowing the nut hand is important, and so is knowing what the nut draws are. A nut draw is a hand that needs only one card to become the nut hand. Since a nut draw needs one more card, it is usually referred to on the Flop or on the Turn. For example if you have A♠J♠ with two spades on the board on the Flop, you have the nut flush draw since no one can make a higher flush without the A♠, although a straight flush may still be possible. A hand such as K♠T♠ that has a flush draw could be seen as the second nut draw. If the A♠ hits the board, K♠T♠ turns into the nut flush.

One of the reasons that JT is a popular starting hand is that if both hole cards are used to make a straight, it will be the nut straight. That is the lowest two card combination you can make that statement about. The possible straights that JT could make are: AKQ(JT), KQ(JT)9, Q(JT)98, (JT)987. To make this nut straight the nut hand, there can be no pairs on the board and fewer than three cards of any one suit. Although other hands like AK will also make the nut straight whenever it takes two cards to make the straight, AK has fewer ways than JT to make a straight. AK can make a straight only after three specific cards are on the board: QJT. But strange things can also happen to JT to make it not the nut straight. For instance when the player no longer needs both the J and the T in hand to make a straight, and there are four cards to a straight on the board, such as Q-J-9-8-3, then KT makes a better straight (K-Q-J-T-9) than JT's straight (Q-J-T-9-8).

APPENDIX B OTHER SOURCES FOR LIMIT HOLD'EM INFORMATION

There are many good gambling and poker books on the market and many good websites as well. I recommend the following ones for Limit Texas Hold'em:

Internet Sites

TwoPlusTwo.com

This site is run by Two Plus Two Publishing: Mason Malmuth, David Sklansky, Ray Zee and Lynne Loomis. It is a great place to discuss poker strategy and exchange other poker information. It is probably the best site of its kind on the Internet.

UnitedPokerForum.com

This is a nice poker forum. There are forums for strategy, tournament poker and other topics.

RecPoker.com

RecPoker.com is a web-based portal to the Usenet newsgroup rec.gambling.poker. It is not moderated, so anyone can post messages. There are positives and negatives associated with this. Sometimes the newsgroup can be frustrating, as there are many useless posts; but there are enough interesting discussions to make it worth checking if you are interested in poker.

TwoDimes.net

This site allows you to run poker simulations. Some of the results in this book came from simulations run on TwoDimes.net.

Magazines

Card Player Magazine

This magazine is often offered for free at card rooms around the country. It has many interesting articles and news stories, and is a great resource for poker. Its website, Cardplayer.com, offers current and archived articles as well as tournament results.

Poker Player Magazine

This publication is offered for free at many card rooms. It is a useful resource for poker news and contains interesting articles.

Books

There are many poker books in print; and there will be more because poker is popular. I have listed a few books that I recommend for Limit Hold'em.

Caro's Book of Poker Tells: *The Psychology and Body Language of Poker* by Mike Caro

This book on tells in poker is the best of its kind. It has many illustrations and examples showing what certain actions can mean. Many of the tells are subtle movements and behavior. It's a great study on human nature, and an interesting read.

Hold'em Poker for Advanced Players by David Sklansky and Mason Malmuth

Almost any book written by either of these authors is worth reading. This one deservedly is the most popular Hold'em book. It is intended for middle-limit players, but anyone who wants to think about the game should read it. These authors coined the phrases "semi-bluff" and "implied pot odds." They are pioneers in the field. They also operate TwoPlusTwo.com (mentioned above), an Internet forum for poker discussions.

Inside the Poker Mind by John Feeney, Ph.D.

This is one of my favorite poker books. It is not for beginners; it is filled with interesting but advanced topics in Hold'em. This is a good book to any reader who is looking to read more advanced material.

Internet Texas Hold'em: Winning Strategies from an Internet Pro by Matthew Hilger

This book is well written and well organized. I recommend it to beginners, whether they play online or in brick-and-mortar casinos.

Middle Limit Holdem Poker by Bob Ciaffone and Jim Brier; *Improve Your Poker* by Bob Ciaffone

Middle Limit Holdem Poker analyses more than 400 hands that were played in poker rooms. This book is best for those players whose weakness is being too loose. Ciaffone and Brier give reasons why folding is often the best option when most players decide to keep playing. *Improve Your Poker* was written several years earlier, and covers poker in general instead of Hold'em specifically.

Hold'em's Odds Book by Mike Petriv

This is a good book for poker probabilities and odds. Petriv shows all the math that is needed to figure out combinations and other issues. This is a useful book for those who want to brush up on probabilities and poker math with regard to hands (as opposed to bankroll issues and standard deviations).

Poker Essays, and Poker Essays Volumes II and III by Mason Malmuth

These are three distinct books, all of which have interesting essays on poker. Malmuth is a thinking poker player, and discusses Hold'em, Seven-Card Stud and general poker issues. These are books for Hold'em players who want to continue to expand their minds and think more about the game.

The Psychology of Poker by Alan N. Schoonmaker, Ph.D.

This book deals with the different types of poker-playing personalities. The author, a psychologist, discusses reasons why people play poker and explains their motives. The book describes the four main types of players: loose-aggressive, loose-passive, tight-passive and tight-aggressive, and explains what to consider when playing against these type of players.

Real Poker II: The Play of Hands by Roy Cooke

This book is a compilation of Roy Cooke's excellent articles in Card Player magazine.

The Theory of Poker by David Sklansky

This is another great book by Sklansky. Although it is not focused solely on Hold'em, this book should enlighten anyone who is interested in poker. A must-read for all poker players.

APPENDIX C PROBABILITY AND ODDS CONVERSION

Probability of Independent Events

To calculate the probability of two independent events, multiply the probabilities that each event will happen.

Example

Assume:

- The probability that the New York Yankees will beat the Boston Red Sox is 60%.
- The probability that the New England Patriots will beat the New York Giants is 70%.
- These two events are independent, meaning neither event has an influence on the other event. Nothing can occur in one event to change the probability of the other event.

The probability that both the Yankees and the Patriots will win is 42% (60% x 70%).

The probability that both the Yankees and the Giants will win is 18% (60% x 30%).

The probability that both the Red Sox and the Patriots will win is 28% (40% x 70%).

The probability that both the Red Sox and the Giants will win is 12% (40% x 30%).

The sum of the probabilities of all possible combinations is 100% (42% + 18% + 28% + 12% = 100%).

The sum of the probabilities of all possible combinations that involve a particular occurrence is equal to the probability of that occurrence. Yankees + Patriots = 42%. Yankees + Giants = 18%. The probability of the Yankees winning is 60% (42% + 18%).

The probability that neither the Yankees nor the Patriots will win is the same as the probability that both the Red Sox and the Giants will win.

The probability that the Yankees and the Patriots will not both win is 100% minus the probability that they will both win (100% - 42% = 58%). It is also the sum of all the other probabilities (18% + 28% + 12% = 58%).

The probability of at least one of the two, the Yankees or the Patriots, winning is 100% minus the probability that neither team wins, which is equal to the probability that both the Red Sox and the Giants win (12%).

The probability of exactly one of the two, the Yankees or the Patriots, winning is the sum of the probability that both the Yankees and the Giants win and the probability that both the Red Sox and the Patriots win (18% + 28% = 46%).

The probability of all three New York teams winning is the multiplication of all three probabilities, because the results are independent. If the probability that the New York Knicks will beat the Boston Celtics is 50%, then the probability of all three New York teams winning is 60% x 30% x 50% = 9%.

Probability of Related Events

When the occurrence of one event changes the probability of the second event, the same method can be used with a slight adjustment. Take the probability of the first event and multiply it with the adjusted probability of the second event (given that the first event occurred). This method can be used when a sample is taken out of a population with no replacement.

If there are five red and five blue gumballs in a gumball machine, your first assessment is that your first gumball has a 50% chance of being red or blue. But once you know the color of the first gumball, you can adjust the probability of the second gumball's color because the composition of the population has changed. For example if the first gumball was red, there are four red gumballs and five blue gumballs left. With this new information the probability that the second gumball will be blue (given that the first one was red) is 5/9. The probability that the first two gumballs will be red is 5/10 x 4/9 = 20/90 or 22.2%

In Hold'em this method can be used to calculate the probability of a runner-runner flush. If there are ten hearts left in a deck with 47 unknown cards, then the probability of getting a heart on the first card is 10/47. Given that the first card is already a heart, then the probability that the second card is a heart is 9/46, since there are 9 hearts in the 46 unknown cards remaining. You can also calculate the other possible two card combinations. The full chart:

First Card	*Probability*	*Second Card*	*Probability*	*Cumulative*
Heart	10/47	Heart	9/46	10/47 x 9/46 = 4.2%
Heart	10/47	Non-Heart	37/46	10/47 x 37/46 = 17.1%
Non-Heart	37/47	Heart	10/46	37/47 x 10/46 = 17.1%
Non-Heart	37/47	Non-Heart	36/46	37/47 x 36/46 = 61.6%
Total				100.0%

Probability of Dependent Events

Calculating the probability of events that are related to each other is more complicated. It involves using correlations and is beyond the scope of this book.

Probability of an Event Occurring with Two Chances

To calculate the probability of an event occurring with two chances, it is easier to work backwards. First calculate the probability that the event will not occur with two chances; then subtract that probability from 100%. For example the probability of flipping at least one head with two flips is 100% minus the probability of flipping two tails. The probability of flipping two tails is 25% (50% x 50%); so the probability of flipping at least one head with two flips is 75% (100% - 25%).

In Hold'em this method can be used to calculate the probability of catching a draw on the Turn or the River, as is shown in table 32.

Example

You have two spades and there are two spades on the board. There are 47 unknown cards and 9 of them are spades. The probability you will not get a spade on either the Turn or the River is the probability that you will not get a spade on the Turn times the probability that you will not get a spade on the River. Of the unknown cards, 38 are not spades. The probability of not getting a spade on the Turn is 38/47. Once you do not get a spade on the Turn, then the probability of not getting a spade on the River is 37/46. Thus the probability that neither card will be a spade is 38/47 x 37/46 = 65%. The probability that you will get at least one spade is 100% - 65% = 35%.

Table 33 shows the probability of completing a draw on the River. In both table 32 and table 33, "SB Odds" means "sportsbook odds."

Table 32
Odds of Completing a Draw on the Turn or River

Flop: 47 unknown cards

Outs	*Pct*	*Odds*	*SB Odds*	*Outs*	*Pct*	*Odds*	*SB Odds*
1	4.3%	22.50:1	+2250	11	41.7%	1.40:1	+140
2	8.4%	10.88:1	+1088	12	45.0%	1.22:1	+122
3	12.5%	7.01:1	+701	13	48.1%	1.08:1	+108
4	16.5%	5.07:1	+507	14	51.2%	1:1.05	-105
5	20.4%	3.91:1	+391	15	54.1%	1:1.18	-118
6	24.1%	3.14:1	+314	16	57.0%	1:1.32	-132
7	27.8%	2.59:1	+259	17	59.8%	1:1.49	-149
8	31.5%	2.18:1	+218	18	62.4%	1:1.66	-166
9	35.0%	1.86:1	+186	19	65.0%	1:1.86	-186
10	38.4%	1.60:1	+160	20	67.5%	1:2.08	-208

Odds

Tables 32 and 33 have columns entitled Odds. The odds reflect the fair price you should get for risking 1 unit. 3 to 1 (also written as 3-1 or 3:1) means that the fair price is to win $3 for every $1 risked.

To convert from percentages to odds when the percentage is 50% or less, do the following:

1. The percentage is X%.
2. Take 100% - X% and call it Y%.
3. Y% / X% to 1 is the odds.

Example 1

1. The percentage is 20%.
2. 100% - 20% is 80%.
3. 80% / 20% is 4. 4 to 1 is the odds (also written as 4:1 or 4-1).

To convert from percentages to odds when the percentage is greater than 50%, do the following:

1. The percentage is X%.
2. Take 100% - X% and call it Z%.
3. 1 to X% / Z% is the odds.

Table 33
Odds of Completing a Draw on the River

Turn: 46 unknown cards

Outs	*Pct*	*Odds*	*SB Odds*	*Outs*	*Pct*	*Odds*	*SB Odds*
1	2.2%	45:1	+4500	11	23.9%	3.18:1	+318
2	4.3%	22:1	+2200	12	26.1%	2.83:1	+283
3	6.5%	14.33:1	+1433	13	28.3%	2.54:1	+254
4	8.7%	10.50:1	+1050	14	30.4%	2.29:1	+229
5	10.9%	8.20:1	+820	15	32.6%	2.07:1	+207
6	13.0%	6.67:1	+667	16	34.8%	1.88:1	+188
7	15.2%	5.57:1	+557	17	37.0%	1.71:1	+171
8	17.4%	4.75:1	+475	18	39.1%	1.56:1	+156
9	19.6%	4.11:1	+411	19	41.3%	1.42:1	+142
10	21.7%	3.60:1	+360	20	43.5%	1.30:1	+130

Example 2

1. The percentage is 90%.
2. 100% - 90% is 10%.
3. 90% / 10% = 9. 1 to 9 is the odds (also written as 1:9 or 1-9).

To convert from odds to percentages, do the following in all cases:
1. The number to the left is X; the number to the right is Y.
2. Calculate Y / (X+Y).

Example 3

1. 4:1 odds.
2. 1 / (4+1) = 1/5 = 20%.

Example 4

1. 1:7 odds.
2. 7 / (1+7) = 7/8 = 87.5%.

Sportsbook Odds

Sportsbooks use a slightly different way to reflect their odds. If an event is an underdog (has less than 50% chance of occurring), then they multiply the odds by 100. For example an event with a 25% chance of occurring is an event with 3:1 odds against. The sportsbook lists this as +300. If the event is greater than 50%, then the sportsbook views it from the underdog side and then puts a minus sign in front of the number. For example an event with a 80% chance of occurring is an event with 1:4 odds for. The sportsbook lists this as -400.

Tricky Odds: X for Y

Some casinos express odds with "for" instead of "to." In the "for" method the casino counts the original bet as part of the payoff. For example crap tables show a hard eight paying 10 for 1. If you bet $1, you will have $10 if you win. Your original wager of $1 is part of that $10. 10 for 1 is the same as 9 to 1, as your win is $9.

More Tables

Table 34 lists the odds of different starting hands. Table 35 lists the odds of getting certain flops to go with various starting hands.

Table 34
Probability of Types of Starting Hands

Type of Hand	*Computation*	*Prob*	*Odds*
Pair	52/52 x 3/51	5.9%	16-1
At least one A	1-(48/52 x 47/51)	14.9%	5.7-1
Both cards are T or higher	20/52 x 19/51	14.3%	5.98-1
Suited Cards	52/52 x 12/51	23.5%	3.25-1

Table 35
Given a Specific Starting Hand, the Probability of Getting Certain Flops

Start Hand	*Flop*	*Computation*	*Probability*	*Odds*
Pair	At least a set	1-[48/50 x 47/49 x 46/48]	11.8%	7.51-1
Suited	3 cards that suit	11/50x10/49x9/48	0.8%	117.8-1
Suited	2 cards that suit	11/50x10/49x39/48x3	10.94%	8.14-1
Suited	1 card that suit	11/50x39/49x38/48x3	41.59%	1.40-1
Suited	0 cards that suit	39/50x38/49x37/48	46.63%	1.14-1

APPENDIX D GLOSSARY

Advertising Play: A play that usually has negative expectation for the particular hand, and is meant to make other players incorrectly adjust their play in future hands.

Aggressive Player: A player who bets and raises often. An aggressive player can be good or bad, tight or loose.

All-In: A player goes all-in by putting all her chips in. In No-Limit Hold'em this is usually a strong, aggressive play because bet sizes can be very large. In Limit Hold'em it happens only when the player is almost out of money, because betting occurs in specified increments.

Backdoor Flush: Same as a runner-runner flush. Making a flush with two cards of the same suit in a hand by hitting one card of that suit on the Flop, another on the Turn and the last one on the River.

Bet: v. To put chips into the pot when no one else has yet. n. The chips a player puts into the pot after no one else has put in any.

Big Bet: In Limit Hold'em the bet size of the last two rounds (Turn and River) is a big bet. Example: In a $20-$40 game a big bet is $40 (twice the small bet).

Big Blind: An involuntary small bet put up by the player two seats to the left of the button. The term is used to refer to both the player and the chips.

Blank: A card that does not appear to help any player.

Bluff: To bet or raise without the best hand in an attempt to make players with better hands fold so that the bluffer can take the pot uncontested.

Board: The community cards (Flop, Turn and River).

Bottom Pair: A split pair using one card from the hand and the lowest card on the board.

Busted draw: A draw that did not get completed by the Turn or River.

Button: The player with the dealer button who acts last in every round (except for the pre-Flop round where the blinds act last). Also refers to the physical object that looks like a white hockey puck embellished with the word "Dealer." The button is rotated to the left after every hand.

Call: To put in chips to match someone else's bet or raise.

Check: To pass on betting.

Check Change: When a player gives the dealer cash for chips, the dealer may call out "check change" to have the floor person to verify the transaction.

Check-Raise: To check initially but raise after someone else has bet.

Cold-Call: To call after another player has raised. The cold-caller puts in at least 2 bets to call.

Collection: The rake or time charged by the casino.

Connectors: Cards (especially pocket cards) of consecutive ranks. Example: KQ, 98.

Counterfeited: A hand is counterfeited when a card on the board replaces a hole card in a made hand, allowing other players to make the same hand or a better hand. Also when a card gives the board such a strong hand that the player plays the board.

Cutoff: The player to the right of the button.

Dominate: One hand dominates another hand if both hands contains one identical card and the other card is a higher card. Examples: AT dominates KT, AK dominates KT.

Double Inside Straight Draw: A hand-board combination that can make two different inside straights. Example: A hand of J9 with a board of K-T-7, where a Q and a 8 both make an inside straight. Unlike an inside straight, this hand has 8 outs.

Double Belly Buster: The same as a double inside straight. Coined by Doyle Brunson in his book *Super System*.

Draw: v. To wait for a card that is needed to improve a hand. n. A hand that needs another card to come to improve it.

Draw Dead: To play with a second-best hand that has no outs.

Draw Thin: To play with a second-best hand that has few outs.

Early Position: A player in early position is one of the first players to act after the blinds.

Expected Value (EV): A mathematical term describing the average result over the realm of all outcomes.

Fifth Street: Same as the River. The round when the last community card is dealt. This term is more popular in Seven-Card Stud.

Flop: The three cards that are dealt first on the board. Follows the pre-Flop round and precedes the Turn. Can also be used as a verb; Example: "I flopped a straight."

Fourth Street: Same as the Turn. The round when the second-to-last community card is dealt. The term is more popular in Seven-Card Stud.

Free Card: After a round where no one has bet, the next card is considered a Free Card because no one had to put in any bets to see it.

Gutshot Straight Draw: An inside straight draw. A gutshot (noun) is the card that makes the inside straight draw.

Heads-Up: A heads-up game is a game with two players. A hand with more players in it can become heads-up after everyone folds except two players.

Infinite Odds: The odds that a player gets by getting a free card.

Inside Straight Draw: A straight draw that can only be filled by a card inside the straight. Only one rank of card will fill an inside straight; so it has only 4 outs.

Kicker: The highest unpaired card in a player's hand. When players have matching hands, such as the same two pair, the winner is determined by who has the highest kicker.

Late Position: A player in late position is among the last to act. In a full game the cutoff and the button are in late position. In a shorthanded game (five or fewer players) only the button is in late position.

Limp (also Limp In): To call instead of raising or folding in the pre-Flop round.

Loose: A loose player plays a lot of hands with bad cards and stays in hands too long.

Loss leader: A play, like an advertising play, that is expected to have negative EV for the hand in question, but may increase EV in future hands.

Made Hand: A hand that already has value, such as top pair or trips.

Main Pot: After a player goes all-in, the main pot is the part of the pot that the all-in player can win. The all-in player cannot win the side pot.

Maniac: A super-aggressive and loose player who constantly bluffs and semi-bluffs.

Married (or Get Married): To continue to play a strong starting hand after it clearly is no longer the best hand.

Middle Position: A player in middle position acts after the early-position players and before the late-position players. In a full game the middle-position player is after the first two or three players and before the last two or three players. In a five-handed game the middle-position player is between the under-the-gun player and the button.

Middle Pair: A split pair using one card from the hand and a middle card on the board.

Muck: v. To fold. n. The discarded cards.

Multiple-Player Pot: A pot that is contested by at least three players.

Nuts (also **Nut Hand)**: The best hand possible given the board.

Nut Draw: A draw to the best hand possible.

Offsuit: Two cards which are not of the same suit, particularly hole cards.

Open-Ended Straight Draw: A straight draw with four consecutive cards that can be completed at either end. An open-ended straight draw has 8 outs.

Open-Raise: To raise in the pre-Flop round when all other players before have already folded.

Outs: The cards that improve a hand to the best hand. An open-ended straight draw has 8 outs.

Overcard: A hole card that is higher than any card on the board.

Overpair: A pocket pair that is higher than any card on the board.

Passive Player: A player who bets or raises rarely.

Piece of the Flop: When the Flop improves the hand to a pair or a draw, the hand has a piece of the Flop.

Play Back: To show aggression against an aggressor. To play back against a bet is to raise, and against a raise is to reraise.

Play the Board: To play the five cards on the board as the hand, not using any of the hole cards.

Pre-Flop: The first round when the starting hands are dealt and the first betting round.

Ragged (also **Rough)**: A board that does not appear to help any player.

Rainbow: A Flop or board with cards of different suits. Rainbow also means there are no possible flush draws at the moment.

Raise: After a player has bet, another player can put in 2 bets which other players must meet to go to the next round.

Rake: The chips the dealer takes from the pot as the poker room's fee.

Represent: To imply a certain hand by betting.

Reraise: A raise after someone else has raised.

Ring Game: Same as a side game. Typically a full game (seven to ten players) at the table, where players are free to leave and cash out their chips at any time. If there is an empty seat, other players can come in. The term is used to distinguish such games from tournament games.

River: In Hold'em the fourth betting round and the fifth (last) card dealt on the board.

Rope-a-Dope: To slowplay; to check or call the opponent's bet when a player thinks he has the best hand but thinks the opponent will fold if he raises.

Runner-Runner: A hand that gets made by catching perfect Turn and River cards.

Runner-Runner Flush: Same as a backdoor flush. Making a flush with two cards of the same suit in a hand by hitting one card of that suit on the Flop, another on the Turn and the last one on the River.

Run Over: To take advantage of another player by betting aggressively.

Second-Best Hand: A hand that is not currently the best hand.

Semi-Bluff: To bet or raise with a hand that is probably not the current best hand but which has a chance to improve to the best hand.

Set: Three-of-a-kind made of a pocket pair and one card on the board. All sets are three-of-a-kinds; but not all three-of-a-kinds are sets.

Sharp Player: A good player who can adapt to the environment and to the other players.

Shorthanded: A table that has six or fewer players is shorthanded.

Showdown: n. After the betting is done on the River, the players reveal their cards in a showdown to see who has the best hand. Also used as a verb. Example: I dreaded having to show down such bad cards.

Side Game: Same as ring game. Typically a full game (seven to ten players) at the table, where players are free to leave and cash out their chips at any time. If there is an empty seat, other players can come in. The term is used to distinguish such games from tournament games.

Side Pot: A pot created by the remaining players after one player goes all-in.

Slowplay: To hide the true strength of a hand by checking or calling with the intention of betting or raising at a later point in the hand or of drawing a bet from other players.

Small Bet: In Limit Hold'em the bet size of the first two rounds (pre-Flop and Flop) is a small bet. Example: In a $20-$40 game a small bet is $20 (half the big bet).

Small Blind: An involuntary bet of one half of a small bet put up by the player immediately to the left of the button. The term is used to refer to both the player and the chips.

Split Pair: A pair made with one card from the hand and one on the board.

Steal: v. To bluff successfully. n. A successful bluff.

Steamer: A player who is on tilt.

Stuck: Describes a player who is having a losing session. Different people have different points at which they consider themselves stuck.

Suited: When both hole cards are of the same suit. For example ATs refers to an ace and a ten that are of the same suit, and should be read as "ace-ten suited."

Sunk Cost: Chips you have already put into the pot are a sunk cost. They are no longer your chips; rather, they are part of the pot.

Table Captain: A player in a time game who makes sure the time is paid by all the players and the time pot is paid by the correct player. It is an unofficial and unrecognized title. Also can be used sarcastically to describe a nosy player who tries to control the game.

Take a Card Off: To call in order to see the next card without a good hand, hoping the card helps.

Tell: Any unconscious habit or behavior that gives other players information about a hand.

Three-Bet: To reraise a raiser.

Tight: A tight player plays selectively and folds many hands.

Tilt (also On Tilt): Playing in a manner worse than normal due to being frustrated or upset. Players on tilt are normally loose and/or aggressive.

Time: In higher limit games casinos often collect the rake by requiring each player to pay a fixed amount each half-hour. The amount paid by each player is called their time. For example, the dealer may say "Sir, please pay your time."

Time Game: A game where the rake is paid like a rental fee rather than on every hand. Typically collected once per dealer, which is every 30 or 20 minutes.

Time Pot: In casinos where they take time, sometimes they take the time from the pot on a specific hand. It may be the first hand when a new dealer sits in the box, or at another specified time. Sometimes the dealer takes the time from the pot regardless of the size of the pot; and sometimes the pot needs to exceed a certain size before they take the time.

Top Pair: A split pair using one card from the hand and the highest card on the board.

Trips: Three-of-a-kind.

Turn: In Hold'em, the third betting round and the fourth card dealt on the board.

Underpair: A pocket pair lower than any card on the board.

Under the Gun: n. The first player to act after the blinds are posted is under the gun.

Value Bet: To bet when the edge may seem small, but still positive.

Weak Player: A player who is afraid to bet while having the best of it, and who is too willing to fold in the face of strength.

INDEX

A

B

C

D

E

F

G

H

I

J

K

L

M

N

O

P

R

S

T

U

V

W

Y

Z